Junior
Worldmark
Encyclopedia of

Foods and Recipes of the World

Junior
Worldmark
Encyclopedia of

Foods and Recipes of the World

Karen L. Hanson, Editor

Detroit • New York • San Diego • San Francisco
Boston • New Haven, Conn. • Waterville, Maine
London • Munich

VOLUME 4

Spain to Zimbabwe • Cumulative Index

JUNIOR WORLDMARK ENCYCLOPEDIA OF FOODS AND RECIPES OF THE WORLD

Karen Hanson, *Editor*

Susan Bevan Gall, *Consulting Editor*

Timothy L. Gall, *Managing Editor*

Barbara Walker Dickinson, Janet Fenn, Rebecca Nelson Ferguson, Patricia Hale, Tara Hohne, Jennifer Jackson, Dianne K. Daeg de Mott, Rosalie Wieder, *Contributors*

Bram Lambrecht, *Graphics and Layout*

Jennifer Wallace, *Editorial Assistant*

U•X•L Staff

Allison McNeill, *U•X•L Senior Editor*

Carol DeKane Nagel, *U•X•L Managing Editor*

Thomas L. Romig, *U•X•L Publisher*

Evi Seoud, *Assistant Manager, Composition Purchasing and Electronic Prepress*

Rita Wimberley, *Senior Buyer*

Michelle DiMercurio, *Cover Designer*

Front cover images © PhotoDisc 1995; back cover—Mother warming milk, India *(EPD Photos/Himanee Gupta);* Orange Salad, Brazil *(EPD Photos);* Saudi boy welcomes visitors, Saudi Arabia *(EPD Photos/Brown W. Cannon III).*

0-7876-5423-X (set)

0-7876-5424-8 (v1)

0-7876-5425-6 (v2)

0-7876-5426-4 (v3)

0-7876-5427-2 (v4)

Library of Congress Cataloging-in-Publication Data

Junior Worldmark encyclopedia of foods and recipes of the world / Karen Hanson, editor.

   p. cm.

Includes bibliographical references and index.

Summary: Profiles the food, recipes, and culture of sixty countries.

   ISBN 0-7876-5423-X (set)

1. Food--Encyclopedias, Juvenile. 2. Cookery, International--Encyclopedias, Juvenile. [1. Food--Encyclopedias. 2. Cookery, International--Encyclopedias.] I. Title: Food and recipes of the world. II. Hanson, Karen, 1977-

   TX349 .J86 2001

   641.3 ' 003 -- dc21

                             2001035563

10 9 8 7 6 5 4 3 2 1

Contents

READER'S GUIDE vii

MEASUREMENTS AND CONVERSIONS xi

GETTING STARTED WIH COOKING xii

GLOSSARY xv

SPAIN 1

SWEDEN 11

TANZANIA 23

THAILAND 35

TURKEY 45

UKRAINE 57

UNITED KINGDOM 65

UNITED STATES: AFRICAN AMERICANS 77

UNITED STATES: AMISH AND PENNSYLVANIA DUTCH 87

UNITED STATES: GREAT LAKES REGION 95

UNITED STATES: JEWISH AMERICANS 105

UNITED STATES: LATINO AMERICANS 115

UNITED STATES: MIDWEST REGION 123

UNITED STATES: NATIVE AMERICANS 131

UNITED STATES: NORTHEAST REGION 139

UNITED STATES: SOUTHERN REGION 149

UNITED STATES: WESTERN REGION 159

VIETNAM 169

ZIMBABWE 181

INDEX 189

Reader's Guide

Junior Worldmark Encyclopedia of Foods and Recipes of the World presents a comprehensive look into the dietary lifestyles of many of the world's people. Published in four volumes, entries are arranged alphabetically from Algeria to Zimbabwe. Several countries—notably Australia, Brazil, Canada, and the United States—feature entries for specific ethnic groups or regions with distinctive food and recipe customs.

Junior Worldmark Encyclopedia of Foods and Recipes of the World features more than 700 recipes in 70 entries representing 57 countries. In selecting the countries, culture groups, and regions to include, librarian advisors were consulted. In response to suggestions from these advisors, the editors compiled the list of entries to be developed. The editors sought, with help from the advisors, to balance the contents to cover the major food customs of the world. Countries were selected from Africa (Algeria, Cameroon, Cote d'Ivoire, Ethiopia, Ghana, Kenya, Liberia, Morocco, Mozambique, Nigeria, South Africa, Tanzania, Zimbabwe); Asia (China, India, Indonesia, Japan, Korea, the Philippines, Thailand, Vietnam); the Caribbean (Cuba, Haiti, Jamaica); Europe (Czech Republic, France, Germany, Greece, Hungary, Ireland, Italy, Kazakhstan, Poland, Russia, Slovenia, Spain, Sweden, Turkey, Ukraine, United Kingdom); Central America (Guatemala);

the Middle East (Egypt, Iran, Iraq, Israel, Lebanon, Pakistan, Saudi Arabia); North America (Canada, Mexico, and the United States); Oceania (Australia, Islands of the Pacific); and South America (Argentina, Brazil, Chile, Peru).

For the United States entry, the advisors suggested preparing an innovative combination of five regional entries (including Great Lakes, Midwest, Northeast, Southern, and Western) and five ethnic/culture group entries (African American, Amish and Pennsylvania Dutch, Jewish American, Latino American, and Native American). Researchers interested in other major American ethnic and cultural groups, such as Chinese American, German American, and Lebanese American, are directed to the entries for the home countries of origin (such as China, Germany, and Lebanon).

Recipes were selected to reflect traditional national dishes as well as modern lifestyles. Persons familiar with the cuisines of the countries were consulted to ensure authenticity. The editors acknowledge the invaluable advice of these individuals, without whose help this encyclopedia would not be as authoritative: Thelma Barer-Stein; Stefanie Bruno; staff of Corky and Lenny's delicatessen, Beachwood, Ohio; Terry Hong; Marcia Hope; Solange Lamamy; staff of Middle East Restaurant, Cleveland, Ohio;

staff of Pearl of the Orient, Shaker Heights, Ohio, John Ranahan, Christine Ritsma, and Nawal Slaoui.

Profile Features

This new addition to the *Junior Worldmark* series follows the trademark format of the *Junior Worldmark* design by organizing each entry according to a standard set of headings.

This format has been designed to allow students to compare two or more nations in a variety of ways. Also helpful to students are the translations of hundreds of foreign-language terms (which can be found in italics throughout the text) to English. Pronunciations are provided for many unfamiliar words.

Every profile contains two maps: the first displaying the nation and its location in the world, and the second presenting the nation's major cities and neighboring countries. Each entry begins with a recipe table of contents guiding the student to specific page numbers.

Most entries feature approximately ten recipes, including appetizers, main dishes, side dishes, beverages, desserts, and snacks. Recipes were selected to balance authenticity and ease of preparation. Wherever possible the recipes use easy-to-find ingredients and familiar cooking techniques. Recipes are presented with the list of ingredients first, followed by the directions in a numbered procedure list. The editors tested the recipes for most of the more than 700 dishes included in the work, and photographed steps in the procedure for many of them.

A complete glossary of cooking terms used in the entries, from allspice to zest, is included at the front of each volume.

The body of each country's profile is arranged in seven numbered headings as follows:

1 GEOGRAPHIC SETTING AND ENVIRONMENT. Location, fertile/non-fertile areas, climate (temperature and rainfall), total area, and topography (including major rivers, bodies of water, deserts, and mountains), are discussed. Various plants (including crops) and animals may also be mentioned.

2 HISTORY AND FOOD. The influences of early cultures, outside influences (such as explorers and colonists), and the origins of staple foods and preparation techniques are discussed. Historical dietary influences between various ethnic or religious groups may also be discussed.

3 FOODS OF THE (COUNTRY OR CULTURE GROUP). Foods and beverages that comprise the staples of the country's daily diet, including national dishes, are presented. Identifies foods by social class and ethnic group, where applicable. May also discuss differences between rural and urban mealtime practices.

4 FOOD FOR RELIGIOUS AND HOLIDAY CELEBRATIONS. Discusses dietary guidelines, restrictions, and customs for national secular and religious holidays, both in food and food preparation. Origins of holiday traditions may also be discussed. Traditional holiday menus for many holidays are presented.

5 MEALTIME CUSTOMS. Customs related to consumption of food at home, at restaurants, and from street vendors; entertainment of guests for a meal; number and typical times of meals; and typical school lunches and favorite snacks are discussed.

6 POLITICS, ECONOMICS, AND NUTRITION. Statistics from international organizations, including the United Nations and the World Bank. Discussion of health status of the population, with a focus on nutrition of the nation's children. Food laws and current dietary issues are discussed, where applicable.

7 FURTHER STUDY. An alphabetical list of books and web sites. Web sites were selected based on authority of hosting agency and accessibility and appropriateness for student researchers. Each web site lists when the site was last accessed. A few entries include listings of feature films notable for the role food and/or dining played in the story.

Volume 4 contains a cumulative index that provides easy access to the recipes by title and menu category (appetizers, beverages, bread, soup, main dish, side dish, snacks, vegetables, cookies and sweets, and desserts).

Acknowledgments

Special acknowledgement goes to the many contributors who created *Junior Worldmark Encyclopedia of Foods and Recipes of the World.*

Sources

Due to the broad scope of this encyclopedia, many sources were consulted in compiling the descriptions and recipes presented in these volumes. Of great importance were cookbooks, as well as books dedicated to the foods of a specific nation or culture group. Travel guides, where food specialties are often described for a country, were instrumental in the initial research for each entry. Cooking and lifestyle magazines, newspaper articles, and interviews with subject-matter experts and restaurateurs were also utilized. Publications of the World Bank and United Nations provided up-to-date statistics on the overall health and nutritional status of the world's children.

Advisors

The following persons served as advisors to the editors and contributors of this work. The advisors were consulted in the early planning stages, and their input was invaluable in shaping the content and structure of this encyclopedia. Their insights, opinions, and suggestions led to many enhancements and improvements in the presentation of the material.

Elaine Fort Weischedel, Franklin Public Library, Franklin, Massachusetts

Linda Wadleigh, Media Specialist, Oconee County Middle School, Watkinsville, Georgia

Mary Mueller, Librarian, Rolla Junior High School, Rolla, Missouri

Susan A. Swain, Cuyahoga County Public Library, Ohio

Comments and Suggestions

We welcome your comments on the *Junior Worldmark Encyclopedia of Foods and Recipes of the World*. Please write to: Editors, *Junior Worldmark Encyclopedia of Foods and Recipes of the World,* U•X•L, 27500 Drake Road, Farmington Hills, Michigan 48331-3535; call toll-free: 1-800-877-4253; or send e-mail via www.galegroup.com.

Measurements and Conversions

In *Junior Worldmark Encyclopedia of Foods and Recipes of the World*, measurements are provided in standard U.S. measurements. The tables and conversions below are provided to help the user understand measurements typically used in cooking; and to convert quantities and cooking temperatures to metric, use these equivalents.

Note: The system used in the United Kingdom, referred to as UK or British, is not described here and is not referred to in this work, but educated readers may encounter this system in their research. The British cup is 10 ounces, while the U.S. is 8 ounces; the British teaspoon and tablespoon are also slightly larger than those in the United States.

U.S. measurement equivalents

Pinch is less than a teaspoon.

Dash is a few drops or one or two shakes of a shaker.

3 teaspoons = 1 Tablespoon

2 Tablespoons = 1 liquid ounce

4 Tablespoons = ¼ cup

8 Tablespoons = ½ cup

16 Tablespoons = 1 cup

2 cups = 1 pint

2 pints = 1 quart

4 cups = 1 quart

4 quarts = 1 gallon

Liquid measurement conversions from U.S. to metric

1 teaspoon = 5 milliliters

1 Tablespoon = 15 milliliters

1 U.S. cup = about ¼ liter (0.237 liters)

1 U.S. pint = about ½ liter (0.473 liters)

1 U.S. quart = about 1 liter (1.101 liters)

Solid measurement conversions from U.S. to metric

1 U.S. ounce = 30 grams

1 U.S. pound = 454 grams

Butter: 7 Tablespoons = about 100 grams

Flour: 11 Tablespoons = about 100 grams

Sugar: 11 Tablespoons = about 100 grams

Oven temperatures

Fahrenheit equals Centigrade (Celsius)

250°F = 121°C

300°F = 150°C

325°F = 164°C

350°F = 177°C

375°F = 191°C

400°F = 205°C

425°F = 219°C

450°F = 232°C

500°F = 260°C

Getting Started with Cooking

Cooking is easier and the results are better if you take some time to learn about techniques, ingredients, and basic equipment.

TECHNIQUES

There are three important rules to follow when using any recipe:

First, be clean. Always start with very clean hands and very clean utensils. Keep your hair tied back or wear a bandana.

Second, keep your food safe. Don't leave foods that can spoil out longer than absolutely necessary. Use the refrigerator, or pack your food with ice in a cooler if it will be cooked or eaten away from home.

Third, keep yourself safe. Always have an adult help when using the stove. Never try to do something else while food is cooking. Keep burners and the oven turned off when not in use.

In addition to these rules, here are some helpful tips.

Read through the recipe before starting to cook.

Get out all the utensils you will need for the recipe.

Assemble all the ingredients.

Wash up as you go to keep the cooking area tidy and to prevent foods and ingredients from drying and sticking to the utensils.

If food burns in the pan, fill the pan with cold water. Add a Tablespoon of baking soda and heat gently. This will help to loosen the stuck-on food.

If you follow these three rules and helpful tips—and use common sense and ask for advice when you don't understand something—cooking will be a fun activity to enjoy alone or with friends.

The basic techniques used in the recipes in *Junior Worldmark Encyclopedia of Foods and Recipes of the World* are described briefly below.

Baking. To cook in the oven in dry heat. Cakes and breads are baked. Casseroles are also baked. When meat is prepared in the oven, cooks may use the term "roasting" instead of baking.

Basting. To keep foods moist while cooking. Basting is done by spooning or brushing liquids, such as juices from the cooking pan, a marinade, or melted butter, over the food that is being cooked.

Beating. To mix ingredients together using a brisk stirring motion. Beating is often done using an electric mixer.

Boiling. To heat a liquid until bubbles appear on its surface. Many recipes ask that you bring the liquid to a boil and then lower the heat to simmer. Simmering is when the surface of the liquid is just moving slightly, with just a few bubbles now and then around the edges of the liquid.

Chopping and cutting. To prepare food for cooking by making the pieces smaller. To chop, cut the food in half, then quarters, and continue cutting until the cutting board is covered with smaller pieces of the food. Arrange them in a single layer, and hold the top of the chopping knife blade with both hands. Bring the knife straight up and down through the food. Turn the cutting board to cut in different directions. To dice, cut the food first into slices, and then cut a grid pattern to make small cubes of the food to be cooked. To slice, set the food on a cutting board and press the knife straight down to remove a thin section.

Dusting with flour. Sprinkle a light coating of flour over a surface. A sifter or sieve may be used, or flour may be sprinkled using just your fingers.

Folding. To stir very gently to mix together a light liquid and a heavier liquid. Folding is done with a rubber spatula, using a motion that cuts through and turns over the two liquids.

Greasing or buttering a baking dish or cookie sheet. To smear the surfaces with butter or shortening (or sometimes to spray with nonstick cooking spray) to prevent the food from sticking during cooking.

Kneading. Working with dough to prepare it to rise. First dust the surface (countertop or cutting board) with flour. Press the dough out into a flattened ball. Fold the ball in half, press down, turn the dough ball one-quarter turn, and fold and press

again. Repeat these steps, usually for 5 to 10 minutes.

Separating eggs. To divide an egg into two parts, the white and the yolk. This is done by cracking the egg over a bowl, and then carefully allowing the white to drip into the bowl. The yolk is transferred back and forth between the two shell halves as the whites drip down. There must be no yolk, not even a speck, in the white if the whites are to be used in a recipe. The yolk keeps the whites from beating well.

Turning out. To remove from the pan or bowl.

INGREDIENTS

A trip to the grocery store can be overwhelming if you don't have a good shopping list. Cooking foods from other countries and cultures may require that you shop for unfamiliar ingredients, so a list is even more important.

Sources for ingredients

Most of the ingredients used in the recipes in *Junior Worldmark Encyclopedia of Foods and Recipes of the World* are available in large supermarkets. If you have trouble finding an ingredient, you will need to be creative in investigating the possibilities in your area. The editors are not recommending or endorsing any specific markets or mail order sources, but offer these ideas to help you locate the items you may need.

Ethnic grocery stores

Consult the "Grocers" section of the yellow pages of your area's telephone book. If the stores are listed by ethnic group, try looking under the country name or the the region (such as Africa, the Middle East, or Asia) to find a store that might carry what you need.

Ethnic restaurants

Ethnic restaurants may serve the dish you want to prepare, and the staff there will probably be willing to help you find the ingredients you need. They may even be willing to sell you a small order of the hard-to-find item.

Local library

Some libraries have departments with books in other languages. The reference librarians working there are usually familiar with the ethnic neighborhoods in your city or area, since they are often interacting with the residents there.

Regional or city magazine

Advertisements or festival listings in your area's magazine may lead you to sources of specialty food items.

Internet and mail order

If you have time to wait for ingredients to be shipped to you, the Internet may lead you to a grocery or specialty market that will sell you what you need and ship it to you.

BASIC EQUIPMENT

The recipes in *Junior Worldmark Encyclopedia of Foods and Recipes of the World* typically require that you have these basic items:

Baking pans. Many recipes require specific baking pans, such as an 8-inch square baking pan, round cake pan, 9-inch by 13-inch baking pan, or cookie sheet. Make sure you have the pan called for in the recipe before beginning.

Knives. Knives for cutting must be sharp to do the job properly. It is a good idea to get an adult's help with cutting and chopping.

Measuring cups. Measuring cups for dry ingredients are the kind that nest inside each other in a stack. To measure liquids, cooks use a clear glass or plastic measuring cup with lines drawn on the side to indicate the measurements.

Measuring spoons. Measuring spoons are used to measure both liquids and dry ingredients. It is important to use spoons made for measuring ingredients, and not teaspoons and tablespoons used for eating and serving food.

Saucepans and pots. These round pans are taller, and are generally used for cooking dishes that have more liquid, and for boiling or steaming vegetables.

Skillets and frying pans. These pans are shallow, round pans with long handles. They are used to cook things on top of a burner, especially things that are cooked first on one side, and then turned to cook on the other side.

Work surface. A very clean countertop or cutting board must be available to prepare most dishes.

Glossary

A

Allspice: A spice derived from the round, dried berry-like fruit of a West Indian allspice tree. The mildly pungent taste resembles cinnamon, nutmeg, and cloves.

Anise seed: A licorice-flavored seed of the Mediterranean anise herb. It is used as an ingredient in various foods, particularly cookies, cakes, and candies.

Arugula: An aromatic salad green with a peppery taste. It is popularly used in Italian cuisine.

B

Baguette: A long and narrow loaf of French bread that is often used for sandwiches or as an accompaniment to a variety of dishes.

Baking soda: A fine, white powder compound often used as an ingredient in such recipes as breads and cakes to help them rise and increase in volume.

Basil: An aromatic herb cultivated for its leaves. It is eaten fresh or dried and is most frequently used in tomato sauces or served with mozzarella cheese. The sweet basil variety is most common.

Baste: To moisten food periodically with liquid while cooking, such as broth or melted butter. Basting helps add flavor to food and prevents it from drying out.

Bay leaf: A pungent, spicy leaf used in a variety of cuisines, including meats, vegetables, and soups. It is most often used in combination with other herbs, such as thyme and parsley.

Blini: A Russian pancake made of buckwheat flour and yeast. It is commonly served with caviar and sour cream.

Bouillon: A clear, thin broth made by simmering meat, typically beef or chicken, or vegetables in water with seasonings.

Braise: To cook meat or vegetables by browning in fat, then simmering in a small quantity of liquid in a covered container.

Bratwurst: A small pork sausage popular with German cuisine.

Brisket: A cut of meat, usually beef, from the breast of an animal. It typically needs longer to cook to become tender than other meats.

Broil: To cook by direct exposure to heat, such as over a fire or under a grill.

C

Canapé: A cracker or a small, thin piece of bread or toast spread with cheese, meat, or relish and served as an appetizer.

Caraway seed: The pungent seed from the caraway herb used as a flavoring and seasoning in various foods, including desserts, breads, and liquors.

Cassava: A tropical, tuberous plant widely used in African, Latin American, and Asian cuisines. It is most commonly used to make starch-based foods such as bread, tapioca, and pastes. It is also known as manioc or yucca (in Spanish, *yuca*).

Charcoal brazier: A metal pan for holding burning coals or charcoal over which food is grilled.

Cheesecloth: A coarse or fine woven cotton cloth that is often used for straining liquids, mulling spices, and lining molds.

Chili: A spicy pepper of varying size and color. It is most frequently used to add a fiery flavor to foods.

Cilantro: A lively, pungent herb widely used in Asian, Caribbean, and Latin American cuisines as a seasoning or garnish. It is also known as coriander.

Citron: A large, lemon-like fruit with a thick aromatic rind, which is commonly candied and used in desserts such as fruitcakes.

Clove: A fragrant spice made from the dried, woody flower bud of an evergreen tree native to tropical climates. In Indonesia, where cloves are grown, cigarettes are made from the crushed buds. Cloves also describe a single bud of garlic, shallot, or other bulb root vegetable.

Colander: A simple piece of kitchen equipment that resembles a metal bowl with holes in it. It is used to drain foods, such as pasta or vegetables, that have been cooked in boiling water (or other liquid).

Coriander: See cilantro.

Cream of tartar: A fine, white powder that is added to candy and frosting mixtures for a creamier consistency, or added to egg whites before being beaten to improve stability and volume.

Cumin: An herb cultivated for its aromatic, nut-flavored seeds. It is often used to make curries or chili powders.

Currant: A raisin-like colored berry that is commonly used in jams and jellies, syrups, desserts, and beverages.

D

Daikon: A large, Asian radish with a sweet flavor. It is often used in raw salads, stir-fry, or shredded for a garnish.

Dashi: A clear soup stock, usually with a fish or vegetable base. It is frequently used in Japanese cooking.

Double boiler: Two pots formed to fit together, with one sitting part of the way inside the other, with a single lid fitting on both pans. The lower pot is used to hold simmering water, which gently heats the mixture in the upper pot. Foods such as custards, chocolate, and various sauces are commonly cooked this way.

F

Fermentation: A process by which a food goes through a chemical change caused by enzymes produced from bacteria, microorganisms, or yeasts. It alters the appearance and/or flavor of foods and beverages such as beer, wine, cheese, and yogurt.

G

Garlic: A pungent, onion-like bulb consisting of sections called cloves. The cloves are often minced or crushed and used to add sharp flavor to dishes.

Garnish: To enhance in appearance and/or flavor by adding decorative touches, such as herbs sprinkled on top of soup.

Gingerroot: A gnarled and bumpy root with a peppery sweet flavor and a spicy aroma. Asian and Indian cuisines typically use freshly ground or grated ginger as a seasoning, while Americans and Europeans tend to use ground ginger in recipes, particularly in baked goods.

J

Jalapeno: A very hot pepper typically used to add pungent flavor. It is often used as a garnish or added to sauces.

Julienne: Foods that have been cut into thin strips, such as potatoes.

K

Kale: Although a member of the cabbage family, the large leaves do not form a head. Its mild cabbage flavor is suitable in a variety of salads.

Knead: To mix or shape by squeezing, pressing, or rolling mixture with hands. Bread is typically prepared this way before baking.

L

Leek: As part of the onion family, it has a mild and more subtle flavor than the garlic or onion. It is commonly used in salads and soups.

Lemongrass: Long, thin, grayish-green leaves that have a sour lemon flavor and smell. Popular in Asian (particularly Thai) cuisine, it is commonly used to flavor tea, soups, and other dishes.

M

Mace: The outer membrane of the nutmeg seed. It is typically sold ground and is used to flavor a variety of dishes.

Manioc: See cassava.

Marinate: To soak a food, such as meat or vegetables, in a seasoned liquid for added flavor or to tenderize.

Marzipan: A sweet mixture of almond paste, sugar, and egg whites, often molded into various shapes.

Matzo meal: Ground unleavened (flat), brittle bread often used to thicken soups or for breading foods to be fried. It is widely popular in Jewish cuisine.

Mince: To cut or chop into very small pieces, typically used to prepare foods with strong flavors, such as garlic and onion.

Mint: A pungent herb that adds a refreshing and sweet flavor to a variety of dishes, either dried and ground or fresh. Peppermint and spearmint are the most common of over thirty varieties.

Miso: A thick, fermented paste made of cooked soybeans, salt, and rice or barley. A basic flavoring of Japanese cuisine, it is frequently used in making soups and sauces.

Molasses: A thick syrup produced in refining raw sugar or sugar beets. It ranges from light to dark brown in color and is often used as a pancake or waffle topping or a flavoring, such as in gingerbread.

N

Napa: A round head of cabbage with thin, crisp, and mild-flavored leaves. It is often eaten raw or sautéed. Also known as Chinese cabbage.

O

Okra: Green pods that are often used to thicken liquids and to add flavor. It is commonly used throughout the southern United States in such popular dishes as gumbo, a thick stew.

Olive oil: Oil derived from the pressing of olives. Varieties are ranked on acidity. Extra virgin olive oil is the least acidic and is typically the most expensive of the varieties.

Oregano: A strong, pungent herb commonly used in tomato-based dishes, such as pizza.

P

Parchment paper: A heavy, grease- and moisture-resistant paper used to line baking pans, wrap foods, and make disposable pastry bags.

Parsley: A slightly peppery, fresh-flavored herb that is most commonly used as a flavoring or garnish to a wide variety of dishes. There are over thirty varieties of parsley.

Pâté: A seasoned meat paste made from finely minced meat, liver, or poultry.

Peking sauce: A thick, sweet and spicy reddish-brown sauce commonly used in Chinese cuisine. It is made of soybeans, peppers, garlic, and a variety of spices. Also known as hoisin sauce.

Persimmon: Edible only when fully ripe, the fruit resembles a plum in appearance. It has a creamy texture with a sweet flavor and is often eaten whole or used in such foods as puddings and various baked goods.

Pimiento: A sweet pepper that is often finely diced and used to stuff green olives.

Pinto bean: A type of mottled kidney bean that is commonly grown in the southwest United States and in Spanish-speaking countries, including Mexico. It is often used to make refried beans.

Pistachio nut: Commonly grown in California, the Mediterranean, and the Middle East, the mild-flavored green nut is enclosed in a hard, tan shell. They are either eaten directly out of the shell or are used to flavor a variety of dishes.

Plantain: A tropical fruit widely eaten in African, Caribbean, and South American cuisines. Plantains may be prepared by frying, boiling, steaming, or baking. Although closely resembling a banana, it turns black when ripe and may be eaten at any stage of ripeness.

Prosciutto: A seasoned, salt-cured, and air-dried ham. Eaten either cooked or raw, it is often thinly sliced and eaten with a variety of foods such as melons, figs, vegetables, or pasta.

R

Ramekin: A small individual baking dish typically made of porcelain or earthenware.

Ramen: A Japanese dish of noodles in a broth, often garnished with pieces of meat and vegetables. An instant-style of this noodle dish is sold in individual servings in supermarkets.

S

Saffron: A golden-colored spice used to add flavor or color to a wide variety of dishes. It is very expensive, so it is typically used sparingly.

Sage: A native Mediterranean pungent herb with grayish-green leaves. Its slightly bitter and light mint taste is commonly used in dishes containing pork, cheese, and beans, and in poultry and game stuffings.

Sake: A Japanese wine typically served warm in porcelain cups. The sweet, low-level alcohol sake is derived from fermented rice and does not require aging.

Saltimbocca: Finely sliced veal sprinkled with sage and topped with a thin slice of prosciutto. It is sautéed in butter, then braised in white wine.

Sashimi: A Japanese dish consisting of very thin bite-size slices of fresh raw fish, traditionally served with soy sauce, wasabi, gingerroot, or daikon radish.

Sauerkraut: Shredded cabbage fermented with salt and spices. It was first eaten by the Chinese, but quickly became a European (particularly German) favorite. It is popular in casseroles, as a side dish, and in sandwiches.

Sauté: To lightly fry in an open, shallow pan. Onions are frequently sautéed.

Scallion: As part of the onion family, it closely resembles a young onion before the development of the white bulb, although its flavor is slightly milder. It is often chopped and used in salads and soups.

Shallot: A member of the onion family that closely resembles cloves of garlic, covered in a thin, paper-like skin. It has a mild onion flavor and is used in a variety of dishes for flavoring.

Shortening, vegetable: A solid fat made from vegetable oils such as soybean or cottonseed oils. It is flavorless and is used in baking and cooking.

Sieve: A typically round device used to strain liquid or particles of food through small holes in the sieve. It is also known as a strainer.

Simmer: To gently cook food in a liquid at a temperature low enough to create only small bubbles that break at the liquid's surface. Simmering is more gentle than boiling the liquid.

Skewer: A long, thin, pointed rod made of metal or wood used to hold meat and/or vegetables in place while cooking. They are most commonly used to make shish kebabs.

Soybean: A generally bland-flavored bean widely recognized for its nutritive value. It is often cooked or dried to be used in salads, soups, or casseroles, as well as in such products as soy sauce, soybean oil, and tofu.

Star anise: A pungent and slightly bitter tasting seed that is often ground and used to flavor teas in Asian cuisines. In Western cultures it is more often added to liquors and baked goods (such as pastries).

Steam: A method of cooking in which food (often vegetables) is placed on a rack or in a special basket over boiling or simmering water in a covered pan. Steaming helps to retain the flavor, shape and texture, and vitamins and minerals of food better than boiling.

Stir-fry: A dish prepared by quickly frying small pieces of food in a large pan over very high heat while constantly and briskly stirring the ingredients until cooked. Stir-fry, which is often prepared in a special dish called a wok, is most associated with Asian cuisines.

Stock: The strained liquid that is the result of cooking vegetables, meat, or fish and other seasoning ingredients in water. Most soups begin with stock before other ingredients are added.

Sushi: Fish and vegetables prepared in bite-sized portions with rice. Fish is usually raw, but may be cooked. (Shrimp is typically cooked for sushi.)

T

Tamarind: A brown fruit that is about five inches long and shaped like a large, flat green bean. Inside the brittle shell, the fruit contains large seeds surrounded by juicy, acidic pulp. The pulp, sweetened, is used to make juices and syrups.

Tapas: Small portions of food, either hot or cold, most commonly served to accompany a drink in Spanish and Latin American bars and restaurants.

Tarragon: An aromatic herb known for its anise-like (licorice) flavor. It is widely used in classic French dishes including chicken, fish, vegetables, and sauces such as béarnaise.

Tempura: Batter-dipped, deep-fried pieces of fish or vegetables, originally a Japanese specialty. It is most often accompanied by soy sauce.

Thyme: A pungent herb whose flavor is often described as a combination of mint and lemon. It is most commonly associated with French cooking. Thyme is used to flavor a variety of dishes, including meats, vegetables, fish, poultry, soups, and sauces.

Tofu: Ground, cooked soybeans that are pressed into blocks resembling cheese. Its bland and slightly nutty flavor is popular in Asia, particularly Japan, but is increasing in popularity throughout the United States due to its nutritive value. It may be used in soups, stir-fry, and casseroles, or eaten alone.

V

Vinegar: Clear liquid made by bacterial activity that converts fermented liquids such as wine, beer, or cider into a weak solution of acetic acid, giving it a very sour taste. It can also be derived from a variety of fermented foods such as apples, rice, and barley and is most popular in Asian cuisines in sauces and marinades.

Vinegar, rice: Vinegar derived from fermented rice that is often used in sweet-and-sour dishes, as a salad dressing, or as a table condiment. It is generally milder than other types of vinegar.

W

Water bath: A small baking pan or casserole dish placed in a larger roasting pan or cake pan to which water has been added. The small pan sits in a "bath" of water in the oven while baking. The water tempers the oven's heat, preventing the contents of the small pan from cooking too quickly.

Whisk: A kitchen utensil consisting of several looped wires, typically made of stainless steel, that are joined together at a handle. It is used to whip ingredients, such as eggs, creams, and sauces.

Wok: A large, round metal pan used for stir-fry, braising, and deep-frying, most often for Asian dishes. Most woks are made of steel or sheet iron and have two large handles on each side. It is used directly on the burner, similar to a saucepan.

Worcestershire sauce: A thin, dark sauce used to season meats, soups, and vegetable juices, most often as a condiment. Garlic, soy sauce, vinegar, molasses, and tamarind are just a few ingredients that may be included.

Y

Yucca: See cassava.

Z

Zest: The thin outer layer of the rind of a citrus fruit, particularly of an orange, grapefruit, lemon, or lime. The zest is the colorful layer of the rind, while the pith is the white portion. Most commonly used for its acidic, aromatic oils to season foods, zest can also be candied or used in pastries or desserts.

Junior Worldmark Encyclopedia of Foods and Recipes of the World

Spain

Recipes

Gazpacho (Cold Tomato Soup) 3
Tortilla Española (Spanish Omelet) 3
Flan (Custard) 4
Mazapanes (Marzipan or Almond Candies) 6
Chocolate a la Española (Spanish Hot Chocolate) 7
Churros 7
Tapas 8
    Crema de Cabrales (Spread) 8
    Tartaletas de Champiñón (Mushroom Tartlets) 8
    Aceitunas Aliñadas (Marinated Olives) 9

1 GEOGRAPHIC SETTING AND ENVIRONMENT

With Portugal, Spain makes up the Iberian Peninsula, or Iberia. Iberia is separated from the rest of Europe by the Pyrenees Mountains, which rise to a height of 11,168 feet (3,404 meters). The peninsula is bordered by the waters of the Mediterranean Sea on the east, the Strait of Gibraltar on the south, the Atlantic Ocean on the west, and the Bay of Biscay on the northwest. Spain's miles of coastline (more than any other European country) provide it with bountiful seafood and fish. Spain is also a close neighbor to Africa. Morocco lies only a short distance—eight miles (thirteen kilometers)—across the Strait of Gibraltar from the southern tip of Spain.

Rich soils in interior valleys yield a variety of cultivated vegetables, while the country's arid (dry) climate provides excellent growing conditions for grapes and olives. The high plateaus and mountainsides of the interior are grazing grounds for sheep and cattle.

2 HISTORY AND FOOD

As a gateway between Europe and Africa, and the Mediterranean Sea and the Atlantic Ocean, Spain has been much fought over throughout history. The Greeks settled its coastal areas as early as the eighth century B.C., while Celts occupied interior regions. By the second century B.C., Spain was under Roman domination. In the early eighth century A.D., the Moors (Arabs from northern Africa) crossed Gibraltar and entered Spain, occupying it for the next 700 years before Christian kingdoms drove them out.

This long history of invasion is still evident in Spain's cuisine. Olives, olive oil, and wine tie it closely to Greek and Roman (Italian) culture. Meat and fish pies show the Celtic heritage. The Moorish influence

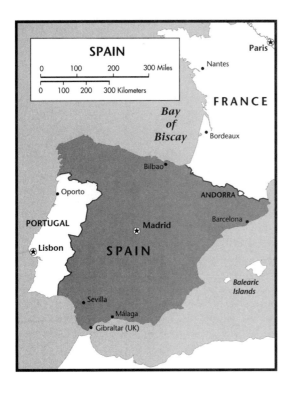

SPAIN

0 100 200 300 Miles

0 100 200 300 Kilometers

Paris

Nantes

FRANCE

Bay of Biscay

Bordeaux

Bilbao

Oporto

ANDORRA

PORTUGAL

Madrid

Barcelona

Lisbon

SPAIN

Balearic Islands

Sevilla

Málaga

Gibraltar (UK)

as well as meats and poultry. *Jamón serrano*, a cured ham, and *chorizo*, a seasoned sausage, are popular. Seafood and fish are popular in coastal areas. Other popular foods are cheeses, eggs, beans, rice, nuts (especially almonds), and bread (a crusty white bread, baked fresh daily, is common). Olive oil and garlic are common ingredients. Spain is also known for its wines, including the *rioja*, made in the northern province; sherry, a fortified wine that may be dry or sweet; and sangria, wine mixed with fruit and soda water.

The best-known Spanish dish, a stew called *paella* (pie-AY-ah), originated in Valencia, an eastern province on the Mediterranean Sea. Rice, a main ingredient, is grown in Valencia's tidal flatlands. Though there are numerous variations, paella is usually made of a variety of shellfish (such as shrimp, clams, crab, and lobster), chorizo (sausage), vegetables (tomatoes, peas, and asparagus), chicken and/or rabbit, and long-grained rice. Broth, onion, garlic, wine, pimiento (sweet red pepper), and saffron add flavor to the stew.

Every region has its own distinct cuisine and specialties. Gazpacho, a cold tomato soup, comes from Andalucía in southern Spain. Traditionally, a special bowl called a *dornillo,* was used to pound the ingredients by hand, but modern Spanish cooks use a blender. Andalusians also enjoy *freidurías* (fish, such as sole or anchovies, fried in batter). Cataluña (Catalonia), in northeastern Spain, is known for its inventive dishes combining seafood, meat, poultry, and local fruits. In the northern Basque country *(país Vasco),* fish is important to the diet, with cod, eel, and squid featured prominently.

is seen in the use of honey, almonds, citrus fruits, and spices, such as cumin and saffron (a yellow spice).

A leader in exploration and colonization, powerful Spain was among the first nations in Europe to discover the treasures of the New World. Beginning in the late 1400s, explorers returned from voyages across the Atlantic Ocean carrying such exotic new foods as tomatoes, potatoes, sweet potatoes, beans, corn, peppers, chocolate, and vanilla—all native to the Americas. These foods were slowly joined with the Spanish diet.

3 FOODS OF THE SPANIARDS

Spain's culinary traditions rely on an abundance of locally grown vegetables and fruits

The signature dish of Asturias, in northwestern Spain, is *fabada,* a bean stew. In the interior regions, such as Castilla, meats play a starring role. *Tortilla española,* a potato omelet, is served throughout the country. It can be prepared quickly and makes a hearty but simple dinner. Spain's best-known dessert is flan, a rich custard.

EPD Photos

A wedge of Tortilla Española, ready to be served.

Gazpacho (Cold Tomato Soup)

Ingredients

1½ pounds (6 large) fresh tomatoes in season, or 28-ounce can of whole tomatoes (with liquid)

1 medium green pepper, washed and cut into pieces

1 small white onion, peeled and cut into pieces

1 large cucumber, peeled and cut into pieces

4 Tablespoons red wine vinegar

¼ teaspoon tarragon

1 teaspoon sugar

3 cloves garlic, peeled

½ cup cold water (if using fresh tomatoes)

Optional garnish: crouton, diced cucumber, diced avocado

Procedure

1. Place ingredients in a blender or food processor and blend until almost smooth.

2. Transfer to a large bowl, cover with plastic wrap, and chill at least 2 hours or overnight.

3. Serve in small bowls. May be topped with croutons, diced cucumber, and diced avocado. Served with bread, gazpacho makes an excellent summer meal or first course.

Serves 6.

Tortilla Española (Spanish Omelet)

Ingredients

⅓ cup olive oil

4 large potatoes, peeled and cut into ⅛-inch slices

Salt

1 large onion, peeled and thinly sliced

4 eggs

Procedure

1. Heat 3 Tablespoons of olive oil in a nonstick skillet; add potato slices and onions.

2. Cook slowly, occasionally turning potatoes until they are tender but not brown. Remove from heat and set aside.

EPD Photos

Tortilla Española in preparation. Potatoes and onions are cooked until tender (left); the potato-onion mixture is combined with beaten eggs and returned to the skillet (center); the half-cooked tortilla is slid back into the frying pan, uncooked side down.

3. In a medium mixing bowl, beat the eggs and add potato-onion mixture; add a sprinkle of salt.

4. Return skillet to the stove, add the rest of the olive oil and turn heat to medium-high.

5. Wait 1 minute for the oil to become hot. (Be careful not to let it splatter.)

6. Pour potato and egg mixture into the skillet, spreading it evenly with a spatula. Lower heat to medium.

7. Cook until the bottom is light brown (lift the edge of the omelet with a spatula.)

8. Carefully place a large dinner plate on top of the pan, and turn it upside down (so that the omelet falls onto the plate).

9. Slide the omelet (the uncooked side will be down) back into the skillet. Cook until the other side is brown.

10. To serve, cut into wedges.

Serves 4.

Flan (Custard)

Ingredients

1¼ cups sugar

3½ cups milk

6 eggs

2 egg yolks

¼ teaspoon lemon rind, grated

Procedure

1. Preheat oven to 325°F.

2. In a saucepan, heat ½ cup of the sugar over low heat, stirring frequently until the sugar melts completely and turns amber (golden).

3. Pour it into a 1½ quart (6-cup) ring mold, tilting the mold in all directions to evenly coat the bottom and sides. Set aside.

4. Break the 6 eggs into a mixing bowl.

5. Separate the remaining 2 eggs. To separate the yolk from the white, break the egg over a small bowl or cup and allow the whites to drip out of the shell halves, then transfer the yolk back and forth between the 2 halves until all of the egg's whites have dripped into the bowl.

6. Place the egg yolks into a separate bowl. and keep yolks. (The whites may be discarded or used for another purpose). Add the 2 egg yolks to the other 6 eggs.

7. Beat eggs until blended. Add the rest of the sugar and the grated lemon rind; beat again. Set aside.

8. Measure the milk into a saucepan and warm it over medium heat, but do not allow it to boil.

9. Gradually stir the heated milk into the beaten eggs and sugar.

10. Pour the mixture into the ring mold. Place mold in a larger pan with about one-inch of hot water in it. Transfer to oven.

11. Bake for 1 hour. Flan is done when a knife inserted into the custard comes out clean.

12. Remove from oven and allow to cool. When cool, chill in refrigerator.

13. To serve, run a knife around the sides of the mold (to loosen the custard).

14. Put a large plate on top of the mold and carefully turn the mold onto the plate; the custard should gently slide out. Lift off the mold.

Serves 6 to 8.

4 FOOD FOR RELIGIOUS AND HOLIDAY CELEBRATIONS

To bring good luck in the year ahead, Spaniards traditionally eat twelve grapes, one with each chime of the clock at midnight on New Year's Eve. On February 3, St. Blaise's Day (*Día de San Blas*) is celebrated by baking small loaves of bread, called *panecillos del santo,* which are blessed at Mass in the Roman Catholic church. According to tradition, all the children in the household are to eat a bit of this bread to protect them from choking in the year ahead.

The Christmas season officially begins on December 24, called *Nochebuena* (the "good night"). It is marked by a special family dinner. A typical menu includes onion and almond soup; baked fish (cod or porgy); roasted meat (such as turkey); and red cabbage and apples (or another vegetable dish). Dessert may include flan and a variety of fruits, cheeses, and sweets—especially *turrón* (almond and honey candies) and *mazapanes* (or marzipan, a glazed concoction of almonds and sugar) which are sometimes shaped like coiled snakes to signify the end of one year and the beginning of the next. After this festive dinner, it is tradition to attend church. Christmas ends with the festivities of Three Kings Day, or *Día de los Tres Reyes.*

On January 5, parades are held to welcome the arrival of Baltasar, Gaspar, and Melchior who arrive that night to bring gifts to children. (Baltasar, Gaspar, and Melchior were the "Three Wise Men" who, according to the Christmas story, brought gifts to the baby Jesus in Bethlehem.) The next day, January 6, the traditional *Roscón de Reyes* (a sweet bread) is baked and enjoyed. A small surprise, such as a coin, is baked into the cake and the person who finds it in his piece is believed to enjoy good luck in the year ahead.

Mazapanes
(Marzipan or Almond Candies)

Ingredients for candy

½ pound almonds

1 cup sugar

4 Tablespoons water

Powdered sugar

Procedure

1. In a food processor or blender, grind the nuts on high speed to form a paste.

2. Add the sugar and beat again.

3. Gradually add water and continue beating to form shapeable dough.

4. Dust a clean, flat surface (such as the counter) with powdered sugar.

5. If the dough cracks and is too dry to work with, lemon juice may be added, drop by drop, until the dough is easier to work with.

6. Pinch off pieces of the dough. Working on the surface dusted with powdered sugar, roll the pieces of dough to make short pencils, about 4 inches long.

7. Join the ends to make rings. Place on a cookie sheet.

8. Leave uncovered in a dry place overnight to harden.

Makes about 50 candies.

Ingredients for glaze

½ cup powdered sugar

1 egg white

1 teaspoon lemon juice

Procedure

1. To separate the egg yolk from the white, break the egg over a bowl and allow the whites to drip out of the shell halves, then transfer the yolk back and forth between the two halves until all of the egg's white has dripped into the bowl. Discard the egg yolk.

2. Using a mixer, beat the powdered sugar with the egg white until mixture is creamy and thick.

3. Add the lemon juice; beat 5 minutes.

4. Dip the top of each marzipan candy into the glaze and return the candy to the cookie sheet.

5. When the glaze hardens, the marzipan candies are ready to eat.

5 MEALTIME CUSTOMS

Daily meals in Spain begin with a light breakfast (*desayuno*) at about 8 a.m. Next comes a three-course lunch (*comida*), the main meal of the day. Families gather to eat it in the mid-afternoon (about 2 p.m.). At about 10 p.m. supper (*cena*), a lighter meal, is served. In addition, *bollos* (small rolls) may be eaten in the late morning; the *merienda*, a snack of tea or *Chocolate a la España* (Spanish-style hot chocolate) and pastries may be enjoyed in the early evening (about 5 p.m.); and *tapas*, traditional Spanish appetizers, are consumed around 8 p.m., before supper.

Though American fast-food restaurants have opened in Spain's cities, traditional "food-to-go" includes *churros*, sugary fritters sold at street stands; and *bocadillos*, sandwiches typically made of a cured ham (*jamón serrano)* or other meat and cheese. *Bocadillos* may be found in the school-child's lunch box, as might a wedge of a cold *Tortilla Española* (Spanish omelet), fresh fruit, and cheese.

The tradition of tapas, now enjoyed in many U.S. restaurants, originated with the practice of bartenders covering a glass of wine or beer with a small plate of free appetizers (*tapa* means "cover"). The great variety of tapas enjoyed today are testimony to their popularity. They may be as simple as a slice of fresh bread with tuna, as extravagant as *caracoles a la madrileña* (snails, Madrid style), or as comforting as an *empanadilla*, a mini meat pie. Invariably they are accompanied by lively conversation, a hallmark of Spanish daily life.

Chocolate a la Española (Spanish Hot Chocolate)

Ingredients

½ pound sweet baker's chocolate

4 cups milk (2% okay)

2 teaspoons cornstarch

Procedure

1. Chop sweet chocolate into small pieces. Place in a small saucepan.

2. Add milk to chocolate in saucepan, and heat over low heat, stirring constantly with a wire whisk, until the mixture just begins to boil

3. Remove from heat. Dissolve cornstarch in a little cold water in a cup.

4. Add cornstarch solution to chocolate mixture. Return to low heat, and, stirring constantly, cook until the hot chocolate thickens. Serve hot.

Serves 6.

Churros

Ingredients

2 cups water

1 Tablespoon vegetable oil

¼ teaspoon salt

2 cups flour

Vegetable oil (for frying)

¼ cup sugar

¼ teaspoon cinnamon (optional)

Procedure

1. In a medium saucepan, combine water, 1 Tablespoon oil, and salt. Bring to a boil.

2. Add the flour and immediately turn heat to low; stir constantly until a ball of dough forms. Remove from heat and allow to cool.

3. When dough can be handled, place it in a pastry bag or cake decorator with a fluted tip; press the dough into 4-inch strips that are about 3/8 of an inch in diameter.

4. In a skillet, heat vegetable oil (about ½-inch deep) until very hot.

5. Reduce heat to medium and fry the churros until they begin to turn golden brown, about 2 minutes, on each side (turn them once while frying).

6. Cook only a few at a time, to keep an eye on them.

7. As churros are done frying, remove them from the pan and place on paper towels to drain.

8. Roll warm churros in sugar (mixed with cinnamon, if desired). Serve.

Makes about 30 fritters.

Tapa: Crema de Cabrales (Blue Cheese, Apple, and Walnut Spread)

Ingredients

¼ pound blue cheese (the Spanish variety is cabrales, but gorgonzola or roquefort may be used)

2 teaspoons raisins

1 Tablespoon white grape juice or cider

1 Tablespoon cream

2 Tablespoons apple, finely chopped (about half a peeled apple)

2 Tablespoons walnuts, finely chopped

⅛ teaspoon dried thyme

Procedure

1. Remove blue cheese from refrigerator and allow it to come to room temperature (let it sit on the counter for an hour or more).

2. Soak the raisins in the fruit juice for 20 minutes.

3. Using a spoon, remove the raisins from the juice and set aside.

4. When the cheese has reached room temperature, place it in a small mixing bowl.

5. Add the cream and fruit juice.

6. Using a fork or wooden spoon, combine ingredients until smooth.

7. Stir in raisins, apple, walnuts, and thyme.

8. Serve with crackers.

EPD Photos

To use toast triangles instead of tartlet shells when preparing Tartaletas de Champiñón, trim crusts from slices of white bread before toasting. Cut each piece of toast crosswise, from corner to corner, to make four triangles.

Tapa: Tartaletas de Champiñón (Mushroom Tartlets)

Ingredients

5 Tablespoons mayonnaise

1 clove garlic, crushed

½ teaspoon dried parsley flakes

1 teaspoon lemon juice

¼ pound (8 to 10) mushrooms, washed, drained, stems removed, and finely chopped

20 miniature tartlet shells or toast triangles (tartlets are available at supermarkets)

Salt and pepper

Procedure

1. In a medium bowl, mix together the mayonnaise, garlic, parsley, and lemon juice.

2. Stir in the mushrooms, cover with plastic wrap, and refrigerate mixture for 1 hour.

3. Fill the tartlet shells with the mushroom mixture and serve immediately. (If using toast triangles instead, proceed to steps 4 and 5.)

4. To prepare toast triangles, remove crusts from 5 pieces of good quality bread thin-sliced bread. Toast them in a toaster; cut each piece into four triangles by cutting an X across each slice of bread.

5. Then, using a slotted spoon, put a spoonful of the mushroom mixture onto each triangle and serve immediately.

Makes 20 tartlets.

Tapa: Aceitunas Aliñadas (Marinated Olives)

Ingredients

Large empty jar, with a lid

14-ounce can pitted black olives, with their liquid

2 cloves garlic, peeled and minced

1 teaspoon paprika

2 Tablespoons red wine vinegar

Slice of lemon or ½ teaspoon lemon juice

Procedure

1. Combine all ingredients (including the liquid from the olives) in the jar.

2. Refrigerate several days and up to a few weeks.

3. The longer the olives marinate, the more flavorful they become.

4. To serve, use a fork or slotted spoon to remove the olives from the marinade and place them in a small bowl.

6 POLITICS, ECONOMICS, AND NUTRITION

The Spanish economy is strong. Spain was one of the countries that joined the European Monetary Union in 1999, and the country adopted the European currency, the euro. Nearly all Spanish children receive adequate nutrition.

In the late 1990s, concerns about mad cow disease, which was affecting cattle in the United Kingdom, caused all Europeans to be more cautious about eating beef. The market for Spanish sheep and hogs strengthened slightly, as Spanish cooks decided to cook more lamb, mutton, and pork.

7 FURTHER STUDY

Books

Casas, Penelope. *The Foods and Wines of Spain.* New York: Alfred A. Knopf, 1982. (A complete cookbook of Spain's traditional foods. Most recipes are quite involved, but many are preceded by the author's notes on the dish and its origins.)

Goodwin, Bob, and Candi Perez. *A Taste of Spain.* New York: Thomson Learning, 1995.

Mendel, Janet. *Cooking in Spain.* London, Eng.: Garnet Publications Ltd., 1997. (Recipes and background information on Spain's cuisine)

Sterling, Richard, and Allison Jones. *Lonely Planet World Food: Spain.* Victoria, Australia: Lonely Planet Publications, 2000.

Web Sites

Spanish Gourmet. [Online] Available http://www.spanish-gourmet.com/ (accessed July 19, 2001).

Tienda. [Online] Available http://www.tienda.com (accessed August 17, 2001). (Tienda is a Virginia-based company selling food products from Spain; its web site also offers recipes).

Sweden

Recipes

Rose Hip Soup... 12
Creamy Dipping Sauce................................. 13
Glazed Carrots 13
Jansson's Frestelse ("Jansson's Temptation").............. 14
Köttbulla (Swedish Meatballs) 14
Klimp (Dumplings).. 15
Blandad Fruktsoppa (Swedish Fruit Soup).................. 15
Pepparkakor (Ginger Cookies) 16
Lussekatter (St. Lucia Saffron Buns) 17
Julgröt (Swedish Christmas Porridge) 18
Svart Vinbärsglögg (Black Currant Glögg) 18
Plättar (Swedish Pancakes) 19
Artsoppa (Pea Soup) 20
Rågbröd (Swedish Rye Bread)...................... 20
Hasselbackspotatis (Roasted Potatoes)................ 21
Smörgås med ost och päron (Cheese-Pear Sandwich) . 22

1 GEOGRAPHIC SETTING AND ENVIRONMENT

Sweden is the fourth-largest country in Europe. It is the largest Scandinavian country (the other countries in Scandinavia are Denmark, Finland, and Norway). About 15 percent of Sweden's total area lies north of the Arctic Circle. Because of the effect of warm ocean winds, Sweden has higher temperatures than its northerly latitude would suggest. Sweden's relatively slow population growth and strong conservation policies have preserved the country's extensive forests. However, air and water pollution are both serious problems. Airborne sulfur pollutants have made more than 16,000 lakes so acidic that fish can no longer breed in them.

2 HISTORY AND FOOD

Sweden's climate and location are largely responsible for the development of its cuisine. Early inhabitants stocked food supplies to prepare for the start of the country's long, cold winters by preserving meat, fish, fruits, and vegetables.

The Vikings, who inhabited all of Scandinavia more than one thousand years ago, were some of the first to develop a method for preserving foods. In preparation for long voyages, foods were salted, dehydrated, and cured. Though modern-day technology (such as the refrigerator and freezer) has eliminated the need for such preserving methods, Swedes continue to salt, dehydrate, and cure many of their foods, particularly fish.

During the Viking era, A.D. 800 to 1050, these ruthless crusaders embarked on raids all across Europe, invading lands possibly as far south as the Mediterranean Sea. The British Isles and France were in close proximity to Scandinavia, and therefore endured continuous Viking invasions. Over time, various foods such as tea from England, French sauces and soups, and honey cakes from Germany were brought back to Scandinavian territory and incorporated into the diet. Swedes still find soups a great way to use leftover food.

Historically, Swedish cuisine has not been as popular as other European fare. (Even modern-day restaurants in Sweden tend to serve more foreign dishes than their own.) It has, however, been influential. The Russian nation is said to have been established by Scandinavian traders and warriors (called Varangians), and Sweden may be responsible for introducing fruit soups, smoked meats, cream sauces, and herring to early Russians.

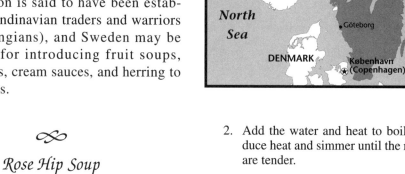

Rose Hip Soup

Ingredients

1½ to 2 cups dried rose hips (fruit of a rose plant; available at health food stores)

1½ quarts (6 cups) water

¼ to ½ cup sugar

1 Tablespoon potato starch (cornstarch may be substituted)

Procedure

1. Rinse the rose hips and put them in a large kettle. Crush them lightly against the pan, using a wooden spoon.

2. Add the water and heat to boiling. Reduce heat and simmer until the rose hips are tender.

3. Transfer to a blender or food processor and purée. (There should be about 5 cups of liquid; if there is less, add water.)

4. Pour the puréed rose hips back into the saucepan and add the sugar.

5. Stir and cook over medium heat. Dissolve the potato or cornstarch in a small amount of cold water and stir into the soup slowly.

6. Remove from heat when it begins to boil.

7. Chill before serving. Serve cold with ice cream or whipped cream.

8. Top with slivered almonds or corn flakes.

Serves 5 to 6.

Creamy Dipping Sauce

This tastes delicious with all fish, and vegetables such as boiled artichokes and broccoli, served as separate dishes.

Ingredients
¾ cup butter

4 egg yolks

1½ cups cream

Lemon juice, to taste

Procedure

1. Melt the butter in top of a double boiler. Have water underneath simmering, not boiling.

2. Separate the egg yolks from the egg whites one at a time and discard the egg whites.

3. Beat the yolks with the cream until stiff. Add the cream and eggs and beat constantly.

4. Continue until the sauce is foamy and slightly thick.

5. Remove from the stove and add the lemon juice, to taste.

Glazed Carrots

Ingredients
12 small carrots

Water

Salt

2 Tablespoons butter

2 teaspoons sugar

Procedure

1. Rinse the carrots and boil them in salted water until tender.

2. Drain and peel while the carrots are still hot.

3. Melt the butter and sugar in a saucepan and add carrots, leaving them until they are well covered with glaze. This goes best with roasted meat.

Serves 4.

3 FOODS OF THE SWEDES

Traditional Swedish home cooking (called *husmanskost*) is simple in comparison with other European cuisines, but it is anything but ordinary. *Husmanskost*, once referring to tasteless porridge and other gruel, has come to represent savory stews, roasts, and various seafood.

The ultimate in *husmanskost* is the Swedish smörgåsbord (SMUR-gawss-boord), which is a number of small hot and cold dishes served buffet-style. The literal meaning of the word is "bread and butter table." The term has become world famous, representing a collection of various foods, presented all at once. The traditional Swedish smörgåsbord commonly includes herring (fish); smoked eel; roast beef; jellied fish; boiled potatoes; *lingonsylt* (LING-onn-seelt; lingonberry jam); *Janssons frestelse* (YAHN-sons FREH-stehl-seh; "Jansson's temptation"), a layered potato dish containing onions and cream, topped with anchovies (fish); and *köttbulla* (CHURT-boolar; Swedish meatballs), which have also won worldwide acclaim. It is easy to see why the literal meaning of smörgåsbord, "bread and butter table," does the feast little justice.

Surrounded by water on almost all sides, it is no surprise that Swedes love seafood, especially salmon, which is typically smoked, marinated, or cured with dill and salt. (No other country seems to surpass Sweden in the number of ways fish is prepared.) Herring, another popular catch, is prepared in just as many ways, and is often eaten alongside breads, cheese, and eggs for breakfast. Crayfish and eel are also enjoyed.

The method of pickling and preserving food is one way Swedish cuisine sets itself apart from other countries. Fresh, home-grown ingredients, rich and creamy sauces (a French trait), and seasonal fresh fruits, such as the country's native lingonberries, also contribute to Sweden's growing culinary reputation around the world. Aside from international differences, Swedish cuisine also has regional distinctions. *Pitepalt* (pork-filled potato dumplings) are popular in the far north, *pytt i panna* (a fried dish made from diced potatoes and meat or ham, served with eggs) is favored in the southern region, while the east coast's most important food is *strömming*, a small, silvery Baltic herring. In any of the three locations, no meal is complete without the accompaniment of Swedish rye bread.

Jansson's Frestelse ("Jansson's Temptation")

Ingredients

2 medium onions, sliced

3 Tablespoons butter or margarine, divided

4 to 5 medium potatoes

2 cans (2 ounces each) anchovy fillets (optional)

1½ cups whipping cream

Procedure

1. Preheat oven to 400°F.

2. Sauté the onions in 1 Tablespoon butter or margarine until soft.

3. Peel potatoes and slice lengthwise thinly.

4. Butter a baking dish and layer the potatoes, onions, and anchovies, finishing with another layer of potatoes. Spread remaining butter on top.

5. Bake the dish, adding half of the cream after 10 minutes. Add the remainder of the cream after another 10 minutes.

6. After 30 minutes reduce the heat to 300°F and bake for another 30 minutes.

7. Casserole is ready when potatoes are soft. Serve immediately.

Serves at least 10 as an appetizer. To reheat, add a little more cream if dry.

Köttbulla (Swedish Meatballs)

Ingredients

1½ pounds ground beef

½ pound ground lean pork

2 cups water

2 eggs

½ cup breadcrumbs

1 teaspoon pepper

2 Tablespoons salt

2 Tablespoons onion, chopped

Butter, for frying

Procedure

1. Combine ground beef and ground pork in a large mixing bowl.

2. Melt butter in a saucepan, add chopped onion, and cook until onion is golden (do not burn).

3. Add cooked onions and all the other in-gredients to the ground meat and mix thoroughly by hand until smooth.

4. Shape the mixture into balls with a spoon dipped in hot water or using your hands.

5. Place the balls in the remaining butter in the same saucepan used to prepare the onions, and brown evenly.

Serves 6.

Klimp (Dumplings)

Ingredients

2 Tablespoons butter or margarine

5 Tablespoons flour

1¾ cups milk

2 egg yolks

Salt and pepper

Parsley, finely chopped, for garnish

Procedure

1. Melt butter in a saucepan. Add the flour and stir well.

2. Add the milk and bring to a boil while stirring. Continue to boil for a few min-utes, then remove the saucepan from the burner.

3. Beat in egg yolks and simmer for 2 to 3 minutes.

4. Season with salt and pepper.

5. Place dough into a bowl that has been rinsed in water. Allow the dough to cool.

6. Tip the bowl to slide the dough onto a plate. Form the dough into little balls, using a spoon dipped in water.

7. Sprinkle with parsley to garnish.

Makes 4 servings.

Blandad Fruktsoppa (Swedish Fruit Soup)

Ingredients

1 package (11-ounce) mixed dried fruits (1¾ cups)

½ cup golden seedless raisins

Cinnamon sticks, 3 to 4 inches long

4 cups water

1 medium orange cut in ¼-inch slices

2¼ cups unsweetened pineapple juice

½ cup currant jelly

¼ cup sugar

2 Tablespoons quick-cooking tapioca

¼ teaspoon salt

Procedure

1. Combine mixed dried fruits, raisins, cin-namon, and water in a large pot.

2. Bring to a boil, then simmer uncovered until fruits are tender, about 30 minutes.

3. Add the remaining ingredients. Bring to a boil again and cover, cooking over low heat 15 more minutes, stirring occasion-ally.

4. Serve warm or chilled.

Makes 8 to 10 servings.

4 FOOD FOR RELIGIOUS AND HOLIDAY CELEBRATIONS

Lutheranism is Sweden's state religion, with approximately ninety percent of Swedes belonging to the Church of Sweden. The Christian holiday of Christmas (*Jul*) is uniquely celebrated in Sweden. Lasting for an entire month, Christmas commences on December 13, Saint Lucia Day, named for Lucia of Sicily who was murdered for her Christian faith. (According to legend, Lucia brought food to Sweden during a famine, centuries after her death.) The eldest daughter of each household, dressed in a white gown, a red sash, and a halo of brightly lit candles (modern-day halos feature battery-operated candles with light bulbs) adorning her head, plays the role of Lucia each year. Before dawn, she wakens her parents and serves them hot coffee and saffron buns.

The largest feast of the year takes place on Christmas Eve, when either a juicy ham, or *lutfisk* (sometimes spelled *lutefisk,* dried fish cured with a lye mixture) with creamy dipping sauce, is served as the main dish. *Julgröt*, porridge similar to rice pudding, is also traditionally served. A lucky almond, often hidden in one of the porridges, is believed to grant good fortune to the person who finds it.

After a full month of feasting on ginger cookies, cardamom (a type of spice) breads, and egg coffee, *Tjugondag Knut* (Saint Knut's Day), January 13, ends the Christmas season.

The Swedes feast on traditional foods that are unique to the Easter season. Halibut or salmon are the typical entrées of choice on Good Friday, with the main meal on Easter Sunday being lamb and hard-boiled eggs, often decorated with food coloring and designs. Shrove Tuesday, the last day before Lent, is traditionally observed by eating *semlor*, a cream- and almond-filled bun floating in a bowl of warm milk.

The Feast of Valborg (also known as Walpurgis Night, April 30) and the summer solstice (Midsummer Day) are two of the most important secular holidays in Sweden. Both days celebrate the blessings of the sun. With every day that follows Walpurgis Night, the sun shines brighter and longer until the summer solstice arrives, when potatoes and fresh strawberries with whipped cream are commonly eaten.

Pepparkakor (Ginger Cookies)

Ingredients

1 cup butter
1½ cups sugar, sifted
1 Tablespoon corn syrup
1 large egg
1 teaspoon baking soda
2 teaspoons cinnamon
2 teaspoons ginger
1 teaspoon cloves
2½ cups flour, sifted

Procedure

1. Preheat oven to 350°F.
2. Mix together the butter, sugar, and syrup until smooth and creamy.
3. Add the egg and beat well.
4. Stir in the baking soda, cinnamon, ginger, and cloves.

A Typical Christmas Eve Menu

Baked lutfisk with cream sauce
Swedish meatballs
Boiled potatoes
Green peas
Rice pudding
Egg coffee
An assortment of Christmas cookies

---

5. Slowly add the flour to make a stiff dough. Add enough flour to make dough easy to handle without sticking to fingers or cookie press.

6. Using the bar design of a cookie press, press out several long strips of dough on ungreased cookie sheets.

7. If no cookie press is available, shape dough into rectangles with your hands.

8. Bake for 7 minutes until cookies are medium brown.

9. Remove them from the oven and let rest for 1 minute before cutting them into 2-inch pieces.

10. Remove cookies from cookie sheets when cool. Store in an airtight container.

Makes 7 to 8 dozen.

EPD Photos

Form the dough for Lussekatter into S-shapes (like figure eights) and arrange the buns on a cookie sheet. Place a raisin in the center of each coil before baking.

Lussekatter
(St. Lucia Saffron Buns)

Ingredients

2 packages active dry yeast

½ cup warm water

⅔ cup lukewarm milk

½ cup sugar

½ cup margarine, softened

2 eggs

½ teaspoon cardamom, ground

1 teaspoon salt

½ teaspoon powdered saffron

5 to 5½ cups flour

½ cup raisins

Margarine, softened

1 egg, slightly beaten

1 Tablespoon water

2 Tablespoons sugar

Procedure

1. Dissolve the yeast in warm water.

2. Stir in the milk, ½ cup sugar, ½ cup margarine, 2 eggs, cardamom, salt, saffron, and 3 cups of the flour. Beat until smooth.

3. Stir in enough of remaining flour to make dough easy to handle.

4. Turn dough onto lightly floured surface; knead until smooth (about 8 minutes).

5. Place in a greased bowl, cover, and let rise until doubled (about 1 hour).

6. Punch down on dough; divide into 24 parts.

7. Preheat oven to 350°F.

8. Shape each piece into rope, and form an S-shape, tucking the ends into a coil.

9. Place a raisin in the center of each end coil. Place rolls on greased cookie sheet.

10. Brush the tops lightly with margarine and let rise until doubled (about 30 minutes).

11. Mix 1 egg and 1 Tablespoon water and brush the buns lightly. Sprinkle with 2 Tablespoons of sugar.

12. Bake for 15–20 minutes.

Makes 24 buns.

Julgröt
(Swedish Christmas Porridge)

Ingredients

1 cup rice

4 cups water

½ cup butter

½ pint light cream

1 teaspoon salt

1 Tablespoon sugar

Procedure

1. Rinse the rice in a sieve or colander. Measure the water into a saucepan and heat it to boiling.

2. Add the rice and simmer on low heat until soft, about 1 hour.

3. Measure the cream into a bowl, and whip it, using an electric mixer, until soft peaks form.

4. When the rice is soft, remove from heat and cool slightly (about 10 minutes). Add cold butter and whipped cream; mix well.

5. Return pan to low heat and heat the porridge thoroughly, being careful not to let it boil.

6. Add the salt and sugar and mix well. Serve with cold milk.

Serves 6.

Svart Vinbärsglögg
(Black Currant Glögg)

Ingredients

¾ cup apple juice

1½ cups black currant fruit syrup (may substitute other berry syrup if black currant is not available)

1½ cups water

1 teaspoon cardamom seeds

1 cinnamon stick

4 whole cloves

½ cup blanched sweet almonds and ½ cup raisins, as accompaniments

Procedure

1. Stir the ingredients together in a large saucepan and bring to a boil.

2. Remove from heat and let stand in a cool place overnight.

3. Strain the spices and reheat the glögg.

4. Serve in mugs together with almonds and raisins.

Makes about 1 quart, serving 4 to 6.

5 MEALTIME CUSTOMS

The Swedish smörgåsbord, perhaps Sweden's best known culinary tradition, has specific customs to follow. Despite the meal's pick-and-choose display, dishes should be eaten in a specific order. It is most appropriate to begin with herring and other fish, followed by cold meats, salads, and egg dishes. Next, hot dishes such as Swedish meatballs and cooked vegetables should be selected. Fruit salad or *ostkaka* (cheesecake) may be eaten last. A clean plate should be used with each new trip to the food table, but diners take only small portions, since wasted food is considered impolite. Scandinavian Airlines (SAS) began offering a small smörgåsbord at the gate before boarding the aircraft in the late 1990s, including sandwiches, yogurt, fruit, candy, and juice, and continued this tradition into the early twenty-first century.

Guests in a Swedish home should observe certain customs. In many households, wearing shoes beyond the front door is discouraged. Hosts will often walk around in socks (and will expect their guests to do the same). A small gift of appreciation given to the host is often appropriate, particularly if a visit is unexpected. In addition, guests should not be surprised to see pancakes for dinner, and coffee only offered black. When a popular alcoholic beverage, *aquavit,* is served, everyone at the table makes eye contact and takes the first sip simultaneously.

EPD Photos

Plättar, Swedish pancakes, are traditionally baked in batches of seven on a special griddle with indentations for each small pancake.

Plättar (Swedish Pancakes)

Ingredients

3 eggs

1¼ cups milk

¾ cup flour, sifted

1 Tablespoon sugar

½ teaspoon salt

Lingonberry sauce (raspberry sauce may be substituted)

Procedure

1. Beat the 3 eggs until thick.

2. Stir in the milk, flour, sugar, and salt, mixing until smooth.

3. Drop a small amount of batter (about 1 Tablespoon for a 3-inch pancake) onto a moderately hot, buttered griddle.

4. Spread the batter evenly to make thin cakes.

5. Turn the cakes over when the underside is lightly browned.

6. Keep finished pancakes on towel-covered baking sheet in a warm oven.

7. Before serving, spoon melted butter over the pancakes and sprinkle them with sugar.

8. Serve with lingonberry sauce for dessert after pea soup on Thursdays.

Makes about 42 pancakes.

Children find sandwiches tasty and easy to prepare; however, schools provide free lunches, typically consisting of meatballs, gravy, potatoes, pickles, and milk.

Authentic Swedish cuisine can be found in abundance throughout the country. *Frukost* (breakfast) is likely to be fairly large, serving coffee, juice, or tea, followed by *bröd* (breads), *ost* (cheese), *ägg* (eggs), and *strömming* (herring). *Äta* (lunch), normally served between noon and 1 P.M., may be an open-face meat sandwich, *kaldolmar* (stuffed cabbage), or even a hamburger from one of the many local fast food restaurants. *Middag* (dinner) immediately follows the end of the workday and consists of a variety of hot and cold dishes. Formerly, Swedish Catholics observed the tradition of not eating meat on Fridays, so the traditional Thursday night supper was hearty *artsoppa* (pea soup with ham) and *plättar* (pancakes). Although many have given up the meatless Friday tradition, artsoppa and plättar are still commonly served on Thursdays in Swedish homes and restaurants.

Artsoppa (Pea Soup)

Ingredients

2 cups split peas
8 cups cold water
Ham bone, scraps of baked ham
1 medium onion, chopped
1 carrot, grated
1 teaspoon salt
⅛ teaspoon pepper
1 teaspoon ginger (optional)
1 teaspoon marjoram (optional)
Croutons (optional)

Procedure

1. Rinse the peas and discard any that are shriveled or discolored.

2. In a large saucepan or soup kettle, place the peas, water, ham bone and scraps, onion, carrot, and seasonings.

3. Simmer on low heat for 2 to 3 hours, covered, stirring occasionally. Remove the ham bone and discard it.

4. Serve, with croutons floating in each bowl, if desired.

Serves 6.

Rågbröd (Swedish Rye Bread)

Ingredients

1 cup milk
1 cup water
2½ Tablespoons shortening
½ cup molasses
½ cup sugar
1 teaspoon salt
½ teaspoon anise, ground
2 packages active dry yeast
1 Tablespoon sugar
¼ cup warm water
2 cups rye flour
4 to 5 cups white flour

Procedure

1. Scald (heat just to boiling) the milk in a saucepan. Remove from heat, and add the water, shortening, molasses, ½ cup sugar, salt, and anise. Cool to lukewarm.

2. Dissolve the yeast and 1 Tablespoon sugar in the ¼ cup of warm water.

3. When the milk mixture is lukewarm, add the yeast mixture and rye flour and mix until smooth.

4. Add the white flour, one cup at a time, until the dough is easy to handle. Knead the dough for 8 minutes.

5. Clean the mixing bowl, and butter it thoroughly. Place the dough into the greased bowl, turning the dough to coat it with butter on all sides.

6. Cover the bowl with plastic wrap, and allow it to sit in a warm place until the dough is about doubled in size. (About 1 hour.)

7. Divide dough into 3 balls. Cover the balls with plastic wrap and let them "rest" for 15 minutes.

8. Form the balls into loaves and place them in well-greased tins. Cover the pans with plastic wrap, and let the dough rise until double in size. (30 minutes to 1 hour.)

9. Preheat oven to 375°F.

10. Bake for 35 to 40 minutes.

11. After removing loaves from the oven, brush with melted butter. Remove from pans and allow to cool on wire racks.

EPD Photos

When baked, Hasselbackspotatis have a fan-like appearance. This is made by cutting thin slices about three-fourths of the way through the potato.

Hasselbackspotatis (Roasted Potatoes)

Ingredients

8 medium potatoes

4 Tablespoons butter, melted and divided

Salt

3 Tablespoons breadcrumbs

Procedure

1. Preheat oven to 425°F.

2. Peel the potatoes and slice down through each at ⅛-inch intervals, but do not slice completely through.

3. Pat potatoes dry with a paper towel.

4. Generously butter a baking dish and place the potatoes in it, cut side up.

5. Baste the potatoes with 2 Tablespoons of the melted butter and sprinkle them with salt. Bake for 30 minutes.

6. Baste the potatoes with the remaining butter and sprinkle with breadcrumbs.

7. Bake for another 15 minutes or until done.

Serves 8.

Smörgås med ost och päron (Cheese and Pear Sandwich)

Ingredients

1 Tablespoon butter or margarine

5 slices white bread

5 small lettuce leaves

¼ pound blue cheese

2 ripe pears

½ lemon

1 red pepper, finely sliced

Procedure

1. Butter the bread and trim off the crusts.
2. Slice the bread diagonally, making triangles.
3. Top each slice with a lettuce leaf.
4. Mash the blue cheese with a fork.
5. Slice the unpeeled pears lengthwise into slices about ¼-inch thick.
6. Rub them with the lemon half and put a slice of pear on each bread triangle.
7. Top the pears with a spoonful of mashed blue cheese.
8. Garnish with a thin slice of red pepper.

Makes 10 portions.

6 POLITICS, ECONOMICS, AND NUTRITION

Sweden has been called the model welfare state because every citizen is guaranteed medical care. In the 1990s, health care reform issues such as universal and equal access to medical services, as well as equal funding of health care were addressed. Sweden's deep concern for equal human rights has helped lead to a healthier population.

Infant mortality has been sharply reduced in recent years, and remains one of the lowest rates in the world, much in part to the country's excellent prenatal services for unborn children. In addition, children and teens receive free dental care until the age of 20. Most health problems are associated with the environment and lifestyle choices, such as smoking, excessive alcohol consumption, and overeating.

7 FURTHER STUDY

Books

Ingeborg, Helen. *How to Make a Swedish Christmas!* Sedro-Woolley, WA: The Tailor's Daughter Pinstripe Publishing, 1991.

Norberg, Inga. *Good Food from Sweden.* New York: Sweden House, Inc., 1996.

Ojakangas, Beatrice. *Scandinavian Cooking.* Tucson, AZ: HPBooks, 1983.

Thompson, Martha Wiberg, ed. *Superbly Swedish Recipes and Traditions.* Iowa City, IA: Penfield Press, 1983.

Visson, Lynn. *The Russian Heritage Cookbook.* Dana Point, CA: Ardis Publishers, 1998.

Web Sites

City Guide: Sweden. [Online] Available http://cityguide.se/inbrief/gourmet.phtml (accessed March 12, 2001).

GoSweden. [Online] Available http://www.gosweden.org (accessed March 12, 2001).

Svensk Hyllningsfest 2001. [Online] Available http://www.svenskhyllningsfest.org/ (accessed March 12, 2001).

Sweden Information Smorgasbord. [Online] Available http://www.sverigeturism.se/smorgasbord/smorgasbord/culture/lifestyle/food.html (accessed March 12, 2001).

Swedish Chef Too. [Online] Available http://www.martin-enterprises.co.uk/swedishchef.html (accessed March 12, 2001).

Swedish Kitchen. [Online] Available http://www.swedishkitchen.com (accessed March 13, 2001).

Tanzania

Recipes

Chai (Tea) 24
Coconut Bean Soup 25
Ugali 27
Chapatti (Fried Flat Bread) 27
Mango-Orange Drink... 28
Ndizi Kaanga (Fried Bananas or Plantains) 28
Wali wa Nazi (Rice in Coconut Milk)........................... 28
Supu Ya Ndizi (Plantain Soup) 30
Date Nut Bread 30
Sweet Potato Pudding... 31
Mchicha (Spinach with Coconut and Peanuts) 32
Makubi (Spinach with Tomatoes)................................ 32

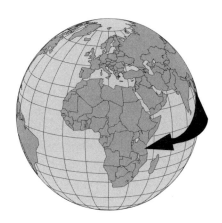

1 GEOGRAPHIC SETTING AND ENVIRONMENT

Situated in East Africa just south of the equator, Tanzania is made up of a mainland area and the islands of Zanzibar, Pembe, and Mafia. Mainland Tanzania lies between the area of the great lakes—Victoria, Tanganyika, and Malawi (Niassa)—and the Indian Ocean. It contains a total area of 945,090 square kilometers (364,901 square miles), slightly larger than twice the size of the state of California. A plateau makes up the greater part of the country. The Pare mountain range is in the northeast, and the Kipengere mountain range is in the southwest. Mt. Kilimanjaro (5,895 meters/19,340 feet) is the highest mountain in Africa. On the borders are three large lakes: Victoria, Tanganyika, and Lake Malawi.

Two-thirds of Zanzibar Island consists of low-lying coral country covered by bush and grass plains. The western side of the island is fertile, and Pemba, apart from a narrow belt of coral country in the east, is fertile and densely populated.

There are four main climatic zones: the coastal area and immediate interior, where conditions are tropical; the central plateau, which is hot and dry; the highland areas; and the high, moist lake regions.

2 HISTORY AND FOOD

The earliest known inhabitants in Tanzania's long and colorful past were primarily hunter-gatherers. In addition, Tanzania has had many of years of influence from other parts of the world. In the first five hundred years A.D., vegetables, millet, and sorghum, and fruits and fish were mostly eaten. By A.D. 800, however, Muslim Arabs established trade routes to and from the country. They introduced citrus fruits, cotton plants,

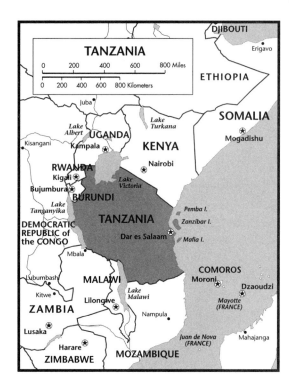

Arabs regained control in 1698. Despite nearly two hundred years of rule, the Portuguese left little behind. The introduction of cassava, a root crop that has become an important staple in the Tanzanian diet, and groundnuts (peanuts) were probably their most significant contributions.

The number of East African slaves who were bought to work Tanzania's plantations increased as the result of the discovery of clove, a key spice in the country's cuisine. After slavery was abolished in 1873, the British and Germans battled for control over Tanzania (then known as Tanganyika). At first, the British (who introduced tea and boiled vegetables) prevailed, encouraging the cultivation of crops that could be exported for profit. By 1891, the Germans took control. They established coffee and cotton plantations. The success of the plantations, however, diminished during World War I (1914–1918), when nearly 100,000 troops and civilians died as a result of fighting, influenza (flu), and famine. Tanzania became an independent nation on December 9, 1961.

and *pilau* and *biriani* (spicy rice and meat dishes), having the greatest effect on the cuisines of coastal regions and the island of Zanzibar. The inhabitants introduced coconut oil and various tools and textiles to the Arabs in return.

Portuguese explorer Vasco da Gama arrived in East Africa in 1498 and aggressively took control of the coastal regions and trade routes. Da Gama (called *afriti*, a devil, by locals), who was on his way to the Middle East and India, stopped at present-day Tanzania to rest his men, who were suffering from scurvy (a lack of vitamin C). *Chungwa* (oranges, rich in vitamin C), relatively unknown to Europeans at the time, were introduced to the ailing crewmen. The Portuguese dominated the region until the

Chai (Tea)

Ingredients

3 to 4 cups water

3 to 4 cups milk

3 to 4 teaspoons tea (plain black is best)

Cardamom, ground

Ginger, ground

Sugar

Procedure

1. Combine all the ingredients together in a large saucepan.

2. Add a few pinches of cardamom and a pinch of ginger.

3. Bring the mixture to a low boil and simmer for a few minutes.

4. Strain the tea into a teapot and serve immediately.

Coconut Bean Soup

Ingredients

1 Tablespoon oil

½ cup onions, chopped

½ cup green peppers, chopped

1 teaspoon curry powder

1 teaspoon salt

¼ teaspoon pepper

3 Tablespoons butter or margarine, softened

1 cup fresh tomato, seeded and cut into chunks

2½ cups canned kidney beans with liquid (or black-eyed peas)

2 cups coconut milk

3 cups water

½ cup cooked rice

½ cup shredded coconut

Procedure

1. In a large saucepan, heat the oil and sauté the onions until softened.

2. Add green peppers, curry powder, salt, pepper, butter or margarine, and tomato, and simmer for 2 minutes.

3. Add the kidney beans with their liquid, the coconut milk, and water.

4. Simmer gently for 10 minutes, Stir in the cooked rice and heat for about 2 minutes.

5. Ladle into bowls. Top each serving with 1 Tablespoon of shredded coconut, and serve.

Serves 8 to 10.

3 FOODS OF THE TANZANIANS

Most food that makes up Tanzanian cuisine is typical throughout all of East Africa. Meat is not widely consumed in comparison with other areas of the continent. Cattle are normally slaughtered only for very special occasions, such as a wedding or the birth of a baby. Cattle, sheep, and goats are raised primarily for their milk and the value they contribute to social status. When meat is consumed, however, *nyama choma* (grilled meat) and *ndayu* (roasted, young goat) are most popular.

The Tanzanian diet is largely based on starches such as millet, sorghum, beans, pilaf, and cornmeal. A meal that could be considered the country's national dish is *ugali*, a stiff dough made of cassava flour, cornmeal (maize), millet, or sorghum, and usually served with a sauce containing either meat, fish, beans, or cooked vegetables. It is typically eaten out of a large bowl that is shared by everyone at the table. *Wali* (rice) and various *samaki* (fish) cooked in coconut are the preferred staples for those living in coastal communities.

The introduction of various spices by the Arabs is highly evident in a popular coastal dish, *pilau*. It consists of rice spiced with curry, cinnamon, cumin, hot peppers, and cloves. *Matunda* (fruits) and *mboga* (vegetables) such as plantains, similar to the banana, *ndizi* (bananas), pawpaw (papaya),

Cory Langley

Bananas and plantains are among the staples of the daily diet in Tanzania. Here a vendor loads his bicycle with chane za ndizi (bunches of bananas) to take to the market to sell.

biringani (eggplant), *nyana* (tomatoes), beans, *muhogo* (cassava), spinach and other greens, and maize (similar to corn) are frequently eaten, many of which are grown in backyard gardens. *Ndizi Kaanga* (fried bananas or plantains) is a local dish that is very popular with Tanzanians and tourists alike. In the cities, Indian food is abundant.

Chai (tea), the most widely consumed beverage, is typically consumed throughout the day, often while socializing and visiting with friends and family. Sweet fried breads called *vitumbua* (small rice cakes) are com-monly eaten with *chai* in the mornings, or between meals as a snack. *Chapatti* (fried flat bread), also served with tea, is a popular snack among children. Street vendors commonly sell freshly ground black coffee in small porcelain cups, soft drinks, and fresh juices made of pineapple, oranges, or sugar cane. Adults enjoy a special banana beer called *mbege* made in the Kilimanjaro region (northeast Tanzania). Aside from the common serving of fresh fruits or pudding, desserts such as *mandazi* (deep-fried dough-nut-like cakes) are sold by vendors.

Ugali

Ingredients

2 to 3 cups white cornmeal (cornmeal grits, farina, or cream of wheat may be substituted)

2 cups water

Procedure

1. Heat water in a saucepan until boiling.

2. Slowly pour in cornmeal, continuously stirring and mashing the lumps.

3. Add more cornmeal until it is thicker than mashed potatoes (It may resemble Play Dough consistency.) Cook for 3 or 4 minutes and continue to stir.

4. Serve immediately with any meat or vegetable stew, or any dish with a sauce or gravy.

5. To eat the ugali, a small amount of dough is torn off, shaped into a ball with a dent in it, and then used to scoop up meat, vegetables, or sauce.

EPD Photos

Chapatti is a soft, flat bread that is best enjoyed warm. It is sometimes flavored with chopped onion or other savory additions.

Chapatti
(Fried Flat Bread)

Ingredients

2 cups flour

Warm (almost hot) water

Pinch of salt

1 onion, finely chopped

Cooking oil

Procedure

1. With very clean hands, mix the flour, salt, and chopped onion with enough hot water to make a smooth, elastic dough.

2. Coat the ball of dough with oil and roll flat on a floured surface until about ½-inch thick.

3. Cut the dough into ½-inch wide strips.

4. Roll the strips of dough into spirals and let them rest on a floured surface.

5. Roll each spiral into a round, flat pancake, about ¼-inch thick.

6. Cook over a medium to high heat griddle or frying pan.

7. Fry the first side without oil, just until the dough sets.

8. Turn over and lift one side enough to pour 1 teaspoon of cooking oil underneath.

9. Turn and press the *chapatti* gently into the oil, with the back of a spoon, so it absorbs the oil evenly and fries to a light golden color. Turn just once.

10. The *chapatti* should be soft and supple when finished.

Makes about 8 chapatti.

Mango-Orange Drink

Ingredients

3 cups water

½ cup sugar

1 Tablespoon orange peel, grated

2 cups mango, mashed

1 cup orange juice, fresh

½ cup lemon juice, fresh

Procedure

1. Heat the water with the sugar and orange peel over low heat until the sugar is dissolved.

2. Cool down to room temperature.

3. Add the mango flesh and the orange and lemon juices and mix well. Serve cold.

Makes about 2 quarts.

Ndizi Kaanga
(Fried Bananas or Plantains)

Ingredients
8 whole plantains or green bananas, peeled

Lemon juice

Brown sugar (optional)

Butter, melted

Nutmeg

Procedure

1. Melt butter in a frying pan.

2. Cut and quarter the bananas or plantains.

3. Dip the banana pieces in lemon juice and place them in the buttered frying pan.

4. Lightly brown, remove, and drain on paper towels. Sprinkle with nutmeg and brown sugar, if desired. (*Ndizi* is typically not sweetened in Tanzania.)

Serves 8 to 10.

Wali wa Nazi
(Rice in Coconut Milk)

Ingredients

2 cups rice

1 can coconut milk plus water to make 4 cups of liquid

1 teaspoon salt

Procedure

1. Measure 4 cups of liquid (coconut milk and water) into a saucepan.

2. Add 1 teaspoon salt. Heat the liquid until it boils.

3. Stir in 2 cups rice. Lower heat, cover, and simmer until all the liquid is absorbed (about 25 minutes).

4. Serve hot alone or to accompany a main dish.

Serves 8 to 10.

A Typical Christmas Dinner Menu

Pilau (rice mixed with a variety of spices)

Chicken, grilled lamb, or seafood cooked in coconut

Beans or eggplant

Fresh fruit

Rice or potato pudding

Chai (tea)

4 FOOD FOR RELIGIOUS AND HOLIDAY CELEBRATIONS

The people of Tanzania follow a variety of religions. Roughly one-third of the population is Muslim (believers in Islam) and one-third is Christian. Nearly all of the island of Zanzibar and much of the mainland coastal regions consist of Muslims; most Christians live inland. Hinduism and indigenous beliefs make up the majority of the remaining one-third who believe in a specific religion.

The warm Christmas in Tanzania is a special time for Christians. The majority of people are invited to a guest's house for dinner Christmas night. *Pilau* (rice dish containing spices), *chai*, and a chicken, red meat, or seafood dish are usually served. A traditional walk along the beach following dinner may leave some very wet—Christmas falls during East Africa's rainy season.

Ramadan is probably the holiest time of the year for Muslims. During this month-long observance, neither food nor drink may be consumed between sunrise and sunset,

often a difficult responsibility in the country's warm temperatures. *Eid al-Fitr*, the feast that ends the month of fasting, is always eagerly anticipated by Muslims of all ages. In expectation of the feast, vendors sell cassava chips and tamarind juice made from the tamarind (a flat, bean-like, acidic fruit), and some rush to the stores to purchase plantains, fish, dates, and ready-made bags of *ugali* for the long-awaited meal. To make certain the feast can take place (and that Ramadan has ended), many gather around to listen to the radio, hoping to hear that the new moon has officially arrived in the night sky. When it is announced, children often dress up (similar to Halloween in the United States) and walk from house to house for cake and lemongrass tea.

Secular (nonreligious) holidays also produce a lot of excitement. On August 8 each year, Farmers and Peasants Day is celebrated. On this day, the country pays tribute and expresses appreciation to farmers and peasants for helping to feed the country and keep agriculture thriving. Zanzibar, one of the country's islands, has its own celebration every January 12, marking the anniversary of the island's independence from Britain.

On the special day of a Tanzanian wedding, gifts are often given to the bride-to-be by her family so that she is prepared to cook and care for her new husband. A *kinu* (wooden mortar for crushing grains and vegetables), a *kibao cha* (coconut grater), a *kebao cha chapatti* (round table for preparing *chapatti*), and a *upawa* (wooden ladle) are examples of traditional gifts. On such a special occasion, *mbuzi* (roasted goat) is often prepared.

Supu Ya Ndizi
(Plantain Soup)

Ingredients

2 or 3 (1 pound) green plantains, peeled

6 cups chicken broth (3 cans of chicken broth may be used)

Salt and pepper, to taste

Procedure

1. Slice the peeled plantains and put them into a blender or food processor with 1 cup of the chicken broth.

2. Blend them together until smooth and free of lumps.

3. Pour the remaining 5 cups of chicken broth into a large saucepan. Stir in blended plantain mixture.

4. Cover and cook over medium heat, stirring occasionally, until soup is thickened (about 45 minutes). Add salt and pepper to taste.

Serves 8 to 10.

EPD Photos

Tamarind nectar (juice), made from the acidic tamarind and sold by street vendors in Tanzania, may sometimes be found, sold in cans, in large supermarkets elsewhere in the world.

Date Nut Bread

Ingredients

1 cup dates, chopped

1 cup boiling water

1 teaspoon baking soda

¾ cup sugar

5 Tablespoons butter

1 egg

½ teaspoon salt

2 cups flour

½ cup nuts, coarsely chopped

1 teaspoon vanilla extract

Procedure

1. Preheat oven to 325°F.

2. Boil the water in a saucepan and place the dates and baking soda in a bowl.

3. Pour the boiling water over the dates and baking soda, stir, and let cool.

4. In a separate bowl, cream together the sugar, butter, and egg.

5. Add the salt and flour gradually to the butter mixture.

6. Add vanilla, nuts, and the date/baking soda mixture. Stir to combine.

7. Pour batter into a buttered loaf pan and bake for about 45 minutes, or until golden and the top springs back when touched.

Serves 10 to 12.

Sweet Potato Pudding

Ingredients

6 medium-size sweet potatoes (about 2 pounds), peeled and cut into ½-inch cubes

3 cups milk

1 cup heavy cream

½ cup sugar

½ teaspoon saffron, ground

½ teaspoon cardamom, ground (optional)

Procedure

1. Bring 1 quart of water to a boil in a saucepan.

2. Drop in the sweet potatoes and cook, uncovered, for 25 to 30 minutes, or until the potatoes are tender (can be piered with a fork).

3. Drain in a colander and return potatoes to the pan.

4. Stir in the milk, cream, sugar, saffron, and cardamom.

5. Heat slowly to boiling over medium-low heat, stirring frequently with a wooden spoon.

6. Reduce the heat to low, stirring from time to time, and simmer uncovered for about 1 hour, or until the potatoes are reduced to a puree and the mixture is thick enough to hold its shape.

7. With the back of a spoon, rub the pudding through a fine sieve into a serving bowl.

8. Serve at room temperature or refrigerate for 2 hours.

9. Just before serving, sprinkle the top with additional cardamom, if desired.

Serves 6 to 8.

5 MEALTIME CUSTOMS

Guests are polite and respectful when visiting a Tanzanian home. Loose-fitted clothing is appropriate attire, since most meals are served to diners seated around a floor mat or low table. Prior to the meal, a bowl of water and a towel may be passed around to the diners to wash their hands. The bowl is passed to the next person with the right hand, as the left one is considered unclean. The right hand should also be used to dip into the *ugali*, which is commonly served in a communal bowl before the main meal.

Goat, chicken, or lamb is likely to be served, for those who can afford it. Most families eat meat only on special occasions, such as a wedding. A *wali* (rice) dish and a vegetableor *maharage* (beans), may also be served along with *chai* (tea). Greens are popular side dishes, and are often prepared with coconut and peanuts *(Mchicha)* or tomatoes and peanut butter *(Makubi)*. Fresh fruit is the most common after-dinner treat, although sweets such as honey or potato cakes may also be offered. It is acceptable to leave food on a plate at the end of a meal, as this reassures the host that the guest is satisfied.

Eating customs vary throughout the country according to ethnic group and religious beliefs. However, the typical family meal is almost always prepared by the mother and daughters, usually on a wood or charcoal fire in an open courtyard, or in a special kitchen that is often separated from the rest of the house. The midday meal is usually the largest, consisting of *ugali,* spinach, *kisamuru* (cassava leaves), and stew, though *kiamshakinywa* (breakfast) is seldom forgotten. Spiced milk tea and freshly baked bread are popular in the morning. Men and women in Muslim households (about one-third of Tanzanians) often eat separately. Taboos may also prohibit men from entering the kitchen at all.

Only a little over half of all children in Tanzania attend primary school, according to UNICEF. As an added incentive to attend school, foreign countries (such as the United States) are helping to offer free lunches to students during the day. The Tanzania School Health Program aims to ensure child health, including the maintenance of clean water and periodic physical examinations. In addition, the program promotes the growth of school gardens to assist in nutritional education. A typical Tanzanian school lunch may be porridge made of millet, groundnuts (peanuts), and sugar, cooked outside in large kettles over an open fire, often accompanied by milk.

Mchicha
(Spinach, Coconut, and Peanuts)

Tanzanians often prepare spinach as a side dish.

Ingredients

4 Tablespoons butter

2 packages (12 ounces each) frozen chopped spinach, thawed

½ cup coconut, grated

½ cup peanuts, finely chopped

Procedure

1. In a 2-quart saucepan, melt the butter and add the 2 packages of thawed spinach, grated coconut, and chopped peanuts.

2. Toss lightly until the ingredients are combined, heated through, and all the liquid is absorbed. Add salt and pepper, if desired.

3. Serve as a vegetable with any meat, poultry, or fish dish.

Serves 8.

Makubi

This dish combines spinach with tomatoes and creamy peanut butter.

Ingredients

2 packages frozen spinach, thawed (or 2 cups fresh)

1 can (16 ounces) tomatoes, chopped

Salt, to taste

½ cup smooth peanut butter

Procedure

1. Combine the 2 packages (or 2 cups fresh) spinach and can of chopped tomatoes in a saucepan and heat until bubbly. Add salt to taste.

2. Stir in peanut butter and continue cooking over low heat until heated through. Serve.

Serves 8.

6 POLITICS, ECONOMICS, AND NUTRITION

About 40 percent of the population of Tanzania is classified as undernourished by the World Bank. This means they do not receive

EPD Photos

Mchicha combines spinach with the sweetness of coconut and the crunchy texture of chopped peanuts. When chopping peanuts by hand (left), always keep your fingers on the top edge of the knife.

adequate nutrition in their diet. Of children under the age of five, about 31 percent are underweight, and nearly 43 percent are stunted (short for their age).

Tanzania is one of the world's poorest countries and undernourishment is prevalent, especially in children. The young life expectancy age of 42.3 years is mostly due to malnutrition, tropical diseases such as malaria, and very unsanitary conditions. Open sewers, uncovered garbage piles, and contaminated streams and lakes are sources of disease. Although living conditions in larger towns and cities are typically better than in rural areas, unsanitary conditions and malnourishment are widespread throughout both. Childhood deficiencies in Vitamin A (which can cause blindness) and iodine are the country's most serious malnourishments.

7 FURTHER STUDY

Books

Asch, Lisa. *Tanzania*. Lincolnwood, Illinois: NTC/ Contemporary Publishing Company, 1997.

Camerapix Publishers International. *Spectrum Guide to Tanzania*. New York: Interlink Publishing Group, Inc., 1998.

Frey, Elke and Kavid Kyungu. *Explore the World: Tanzania*. München: Nelles Verlag, 1998.

Lauré, Jason and Ettagale Blauer. *Tanzania*. Canada: Children's Press, 1994.

Tanzania, Zanzibar & Pemba. Victoria, Australia: Lonely Planet Publications, 1999.

Webb, Lois Sinaiko. *Holidays of the World Cookbook for Students.* Phoenix, AZ: The Oryx Press, 1995.

Web Sites

CultureConnect.com. [Online] Available http://cultureconnect.com/content/travel/gemma1-1.htm (accessed April 4, 2001).

Life in Africa. [Online] Available http://www.lifeinafrica.com/fun/recipes/chapati.htm/ (accessed April 3, 2001).

Recipes of Africa. [Online] Available http://www.balaams-ass.com/journal/homemake/rcpafras.htm (accessed April 3, 2001).

Sallys-Place.com. [Online] Available http://www.sallys-place.com/ (accessed April 3, 2001).

The Swahili Coast Magazine. [Online] Available http://www.swahilicoast.com/ (accessed April 5, 2001).

Unicef. [Online] Available http://www.unicef.org (accessed April 3, 2001).

Zanzibar.org. [Online] Available http://www.zanzibar.org (accessed April 5, 2001).

Thailand

Recipes

Nam Pla Prig (Dipping Sauce) 37
Thai Beef Curry 37
Chicken Satay 38
Cucumber Salad... 39
Poa Pee (Thai Egg Rolls) 39
Sang Ka Ya (Thai Coconut Custard)........................... 40
Banana with Coconut Milk 41
Ka Nom Jeen Sour Nam (Pineapple-Fish Noodles)....... 42
Pad Thai.. 42
Coconut-Chicken Soup 43

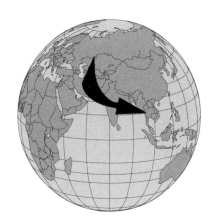

1 GEOGRAPHIC SETTING AND ENVIRONMENT

Comprising an area of 514,000 square kilometers (198,456 square miles) in Southeast Asia, Thailand (formerly known as Siam) extends almost two-thirds down the Malay Peninsula. Comparatively, the area occupied by Thailand is slightly more than twice the size of the state of Wyoming.

Thailand may be divided into five major physical regions: the central valley, fronting the Gulf of Thailand; the continental highlands of the north and northwest, containing Thailand's highest point, Doi Inthanon (2,565 meters/8,415 feet); the northeast, much of it often called the Khorat Plateau; the small southeast coastal region facing the Gulf of Thailand; and the Malay Peninsula, extending almost 960 kilometers (600 miles) from the central valley in the north to the boundary of Malaysia in the south.

Thailand has a tropical climate. In most of the country, the temperature rarely falls below 13°C (55°F) or rises above 35°C (95°F).

2 HISTORY AND FOOD

Until 1939, the country we call Thailand was known as Siam. It was the only Southeast Asian country never colonized by the West. This helped Thailand to maintain its own special cuisine (cooking style). However, that cuisine had already been influenced by Thailand's Asian neighbors.

The Thai (pronounced TIE) people migrated to their present homeland from southern China about 2,000 years ago. They brought with them the spicy cooking of their native Yunan province, as well as its dietary staple, rice. Other Chinese influences on Thai cooking included the use of noodles, dumplings, soy sauce, and other soy products. Like the Chinese, the Thais based their recipes on blending five basic flavors: salty, sweet, sour, bitter, and hot.

From nearby India came not only the Buddhist religion, but also spicy seasonings such as cumin, cardamom, and coriander, as well as curry dishes. The Malays, to the south, further shared seasonings, as well as their love of coconuts and the *satay* (a dish that is similar to shish kebabs). Since 1970, Thai cooking has become extremely popular in both North America and Britain.

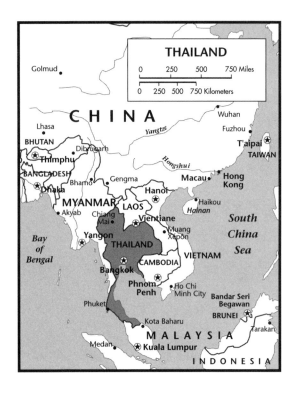

3 FOODS OF THE THAIS

Rice is the main dietary staple of Thailand. Thais eat two kinds of rice: the standard white kind and glutinous, or sticky, rice. Sticky rice rolled into a ball is the main rice eaten in northeastern Thailand. It is also used in desserts throughout the country. Rice is eaten at almost every meal and also made into flour used in noodles, dumplings, and desserts. Most main dishes use beef, chicken, pork, or seafood, but the Thais also eat vegetarian dishes.

Thai food is known for its unique combinations of seasoning. Although it is hot and spicy, Thai cooking is carefully balanced to bring out all the different flavors in a dish. Curries (dishes made with a spicy powder called curry) are a mainstay of Thai cooking. Hot chilies appear in many Thai dishes. Other common flavorings are fish sauce, dried shrimp paste, lemon grass, and the spices coriander, basil, garlic, ginger, cumin, cardamom, and cinnamon. Soup, eaten with most meals, helps balance the hot flavors of many Thai dishes as do steamed rice, mild noodle dishes, and sweet

desserts. Many dishes are served with sauces, such as Nam Pla Prig, for dipping.

Coconuts play an important role in the Thai diet. Coconut milk and shredded coconut are used in many dishes, especially desserts. Thais eat a variety of tropical fruits for dessert, including mangoes, papayas, custard apples with scaly green skins, and jackfruit, which is large and prickly and has yellow flesh.

Thai food differs somewhat from one region to another. Seafood is popular in the southern coastal areas. The Muslims in that part of the country favor curries. The spiciest food is found in the northeast.

EPD Photos

Spicy Thai dishes are often balanced with the tart flavors of such ingredients as lemon grass, ginger, lemons, and limes.

Nam Pla Prig (Dipping Sauce)

This sauce is used as a dip. It is provided on the table at every Thai meal, in the same way that salt and pepper are provided on most tables in North America.

Ingredients

2 cloves garlic

1 teaspoon crushed red pepper flakes

4 Tablespoons sugar

2 Tablespoons fresh lime or lemon juice

4 Tablespoons fish sauce (available at supermarkets and Asian food stores)

2 Tablespoons water

Procedure

1. Combine all ingredients in a small bowl.
2. Stir to dissolve sugar.
3. If sauce is too salty, add more water.
4. Serve at room temperature in individual bowls.
5. Keeps for up to 2 weeks in the refrigerator, tightly covered.

Thai Beef Curry

Ingredients

10 ounces beef flank steak with the fat trimmed off

2 cups coconut milk, unsweetened

2 Tablespoons red curry paste

1 teaspoon fish sauce

1 cup bamboo shoot strips

1 teaspoon sugar

3 Tablespoons water

20 leaves of fresh basil

¼ medium red pepper, cut into thin strips

2 Tablespoons green peas, frozen

2½ cups rice, steamed

Procedure

1. Slice the steak into pieces ¼-inch thick, 2 inches long, and about 1-inch wide.
2. Heat 1 cup of the coconut milk in a wok or frying pan and add the red curry paste.
3. Stir to dissolve and cook at high heat for 5 to 6 minutes, until the oil of the coconut milk rises to the top and the sauce thickens.
4. Add fish sauce and stir it in.
5. Add the second cup of coconut milk and the beef. Reduce heat to medium.
6. Add the bamboo shoot strips and the sugar. Return the heat to high and add 3 Tablespoons water.
7. Cook, stirring for 3 minutes until bubbling.
8. Add ¾ of the basil leaves, the red pepper strips and the green peas.
9. Stir and cook for another 30 seconds, folding all the ingredients into the sauce.
10. Remove from heat and transfer to a serving dish.
11. Top with the rest of the basil leaves and the additional red pepper strips.

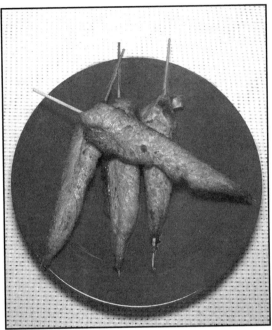

EPD Photos

Chicken satay may be served as an appetizer, snack, or main course.

12. Serve immediately, accompanied by steamed rice.

Serves 8.

Chicken Satay

Ingredients
1 pound skinless, boneless chicken breast
1 teaspoon black pepper
1 teaspoon ground cumin
1 teaspoon ground coriander
½ teaspoon turmeric
1 teaspoon chopped garlic
1 Tablespoon sugar
1 Tablespoon vegetable oil
1 Tablespoon soy sauce

1 Tablespoon lemon juice

1 teaspoon fish sauce

Small amount of oil or coconut milk

Fresh coriander leaves

Lettuce leaves

Procedure

1. Slice chicken breasts into thin slices lengthwise. Each slice should be about 4 inches by 1 inch by ¼ inch. (Optional: place chicken in freezer for 15 to 20 minutes to make it easier to slice.) Place the chicken strips in a mixing bowl.

2. Add remaining ingredients, first the solids, then the liquids, to the bowl. Toss until well mixed.

3. Let the chicken marinate (absorb the flavoring) in the refrigerator for at least 2 hours and as long as 24 hours.

4. When ready to cook the satay, stir the chicken in the sauce and remove.

5. Thread each slice onto a skewer, pushing the skewer in and out down the middle of the slice.

6. Baste (rub) the chicken with oil or coconut milk and grill on a barbecue or under the broiler.

7. Cook for about 2 minutes on each side, watching carefully and turning to keep the chicken from burning.

8. Baste once more with oil or coconut milk. The satay is done when it's golden brown and crispy along the edges. Serve with optional garnish with fresh coriander leaves.

Serves 8.

Cucumber Salad

Ingredients

1 long cucumber

½ small red onion

⅓ medium red pepper

1 Tablespoon sugar

Vinegar

½ teaspoon salt

Fresh coriander leaves

Procedure

1. Wash and dry the cucumber, and peel it if desired.

2. Cut in half lengthwise and then into quarters.

3. Slice the quarters into ¼-inch pieces and arrange on a plate.

4. Slice the red pepper and onion into thin strips. Scatter them over the cucumber.

5. In a small bowl, combine the sugar, vinegar, and salt.

6. Pour dressing over the vegetables and top with the coriander leaves.

Serves 4 to 6.

4 FOOD FOR RELIGIOUS AND HOLIDAY CELEBRATIONS

Although most Thais are Buddhists, there are no food taboos in Thailand. The Thais celebrate a number of seasonal festivals and Buddhist holidays with feasts and banquets. Some of the foods eaten at these meals have a symbolic meaning. Among these are "golden threads," a thin layer of egg or noodles wrapped around small pieces of food. It is thought that they bring good luck and wealth to the person who eats them. Like the Chinese, the Thais believe that long noodles symbolize long life. Grilled, baked, or fried chicken is a popular food for holiday banquets. While everyday meals end with fruit, sweet desserts are served on special occasions. These fall into two categories: cakes (*kanom*) and liquid desserts, such as bananas and coconut milk.

One of the most important feast days is *Songkran*, the traditional Thai New Year, celebrated in April. People throw buckets of water at each other to let everyone start fresh for the coming year. Egg rolls are traditionally eaten for Songkran, as well as other holidays. Custard is another traditional dish served on Songkran.

Poa Pee (Thai Egg Rolls)

Ingredients

3½ ounces (one-half package) rice noodles or cellophane noodles

½ pound ground pork

½ pound ground beef

1 cup carrots, peeled and shredded

1 cup bean sprouts or shredded cabbage

½ medium onion, chopped

1 Tablespoon fish sauce

¼ Tablespoon pepper

½ clove garlic, finely chopped

1 teaspoon sugar

1 package of lumpia papers (rice-paper wrappers may be substituted; both are sold in gourmet or frozen foods section of supermarket or Asian grocery store)

½ cup vegetable oil

3 black mushrooms (optional; sold in Asian grocery stores and some supermarkets and gourmet stores)

1 egg

Cory Langley

Thai fruit and vegetable vendors often sell their wares from long boats, moving from dock to dock to serve their customers.

Procedure

1. If using black mushrooms, soak them in hot water for 15 minutes. Drain well in a strainer.

2. Discard mushroom stems and shred caps.

3. Soak noodles in hot water according to package directions. When soft, drain and cut into 2-inch pieces with a sharp knife or scissors.

4. In a large bowl, beat egg well. Add black mushrooms, noodles, pork, beef, carrots, bean sprouts, onion, fish sauce, pepper, garlic, and sugar. Mix well.

5. Place 1 wrapper on a flat surface. Cover remaining wrappers with a slightly damp kitchen towel so they don't dry out.

6. Place about 1½ Tablespoons of filling just below the center of each wrapper and fold up into a roll. Press edges to seal.

7. In a large skillet or wok, heat oil over medium heat for 1 minute.

8. Carefully place 3 rolls in oil and fry slowly for about 10 minutes or until golden brown. Turn and fry the other side 10 minutes.

9. Keep fried rolls warm in oven heated to 200°F.

10. Serve hot with individual bowls of *nam pla prig* or with sweet-and-sour sauce.

Sang Ka Ya (Thai Coconut Custard)

Ingredients

4 eggs

¼ cup brown sugar

¼ cup white sugar

1 cup coconut milk

1 cup winter squash, thinly sliced with seeds and rind removed

Procedure

1. In a deep bowl, beat eggs well.

2. Add brown and white sugars and stir until dissolved.

3. Add coconut milk and squash and stir well.

4. Pour mixture into a 9- by 9-inch baking pan or a 9- or 10-inch pie pan.

5. Place ½ cup water into a steamer or Dutch oven large enough to hold the custard pan.

6. Bring water to a boil over high heat, and place pan with custard inside.

7. Cover and steam over high heat for 30 minutes.

8. Serve at room temperature.

Serves 12.

Banana with Coconut Milk

Ingredients

12 half-ripe bananas

4 cups fresh or canned coconut milk

¼ cup sugar

⅛ teaspoon salt

Procedure

1. Peel the bananas and cut in quarters. Place in a steamer over boiling water. Steam for 20 minutes; set aside.

2. In a large pot heat the coconut milk, sugar, and salt on high heat. As soon as it boils, add the bananas.

3. Reduce heat and simmer for 1 hour.

4. Serve hot.

Serves 8 to 12.

5 MEALTIME CUSTOMS

Thais are famous for their love of snacks. There are food stalls near every public place due to the Thai habit of snacking all day. These stalls sell hundreds of different snacks. Among the most popular are fish cakes, egg rolls, fried rice, and noodles served with a choice of seasonings.

Holiday Menu

Poa Pee (egg roll)
Spicy beef salad with lemongrass sauce
Spicy mint noodles
Chicken with basil
Sang Ka Ya (custard)

Thais eat three meals daily, plus many snacks. Dinner is the main meal. Breakfast often consists of fried rice, boiled eggs, and foods left over from the previous day's dinner. Lunch is usually a single-dish meal based on either rice or noodles. The main meal, eaten at dinnertime, consists of several different dishes chosen to balance different flavors and cooking methods. Soups are served with most main meals and are sipped throughout the meal. A typical dinner is steamed rice, a curry dish, a vegetable dish, a cold salad, and soup. Rice is the only food placed on each person's plate. All the other dishes are brought to the table in serving bowls, and people help themselves. Fresh fruit is served at the end.

Unlike their Asian neighbors, Thais do not use chopsticks unless they are eating noodles. Most of the time they use a fork and a flat-bottomed spoon. The fork is used only to push food onto the spoon, not to bring it to one's mouth. Food is already cut into bite-sized pieces, so a knife is not needed.

Thais like their food to please the eye as well as the taste buds. They carve fresh fruits and vegetables into fancy shapes and serve prepared foods in pretty containers.

Ka Nom Jeen Sour Nam (Pineapple Fish Noodles)

Ingredients

3 Tablespoons vegetable oil

2 pounds fish fillets, cut into bite-size pieces

1 clove garlic, finely chopped

1 teaspoon fresh ginger, finely chopped

1 can (20-ounces) crushed pineapple, drained thoroughly

1 cup coconut milk

2 teaspoons fish sauce

⅛ teaspoon pepper

1 teaspoon sugar

⅛ teaspoon cayenne pepper

Fresh mint and coriander for topping (optional)

Procedure

1. In a large skillet or wok, heat oil over high heat for 1 minute.

2. Add fish, garlic, and ginger.

3. Cook, stirring constantly, for 3 minutes or until fish becomes white.

4. Add pineapple, coconut milk, fish sauce, pepper, sugar, and cayenne pepper and stir well.

5. Cook, stirring constantly, for 2 minutes or until fish flakes easily.

6. Serve over hot rice noodles, topped with fresh mint and coriander.

Pad Thai

This is Thailand's most famous noodle dish.

Ingredients

12 ounces of Pad Thai noodles

8 cups cold water

¼ cup olive oil

1 Tablespoon garlic, chopped

16 medium shrimp, shelled and deveined (with the veins taken out)

2 ounces firm brown tofu, cut into ¼-inch cubes

2 eggs, beaten

¼ cup crushed unsalted peanuts

3 Tablespoons fish sauce

2½ Tablespoons rice vinegar

1 Tablespoon sugar or 1½ Tablespoons honey

2 teaspoons paprika

½ teaspoon crushed red pepper or cayenne pepper

3 ounces fresh bean sprouts

¼ cup leeks, cut into 1½ to 2-inch-long shreds

Procedure

1. In a large bowl, soak noodles in cold water 45 minutes.

2. Drain in a colander (special bowl with holes for draining) and set aside.

3. Heat olive oil in a large skillet over high heat.

4. Add garlic and sauté until lightly browned, about 1 minute.

5. Add shrimp and tofu and sauté 1 minute.

6. Add eggs and stir 30 seconds.

7. Add noodles, peanuts, fish sauce, vinegar, sugar, paprika, and red pepper and stir constantly for 3 minutes.

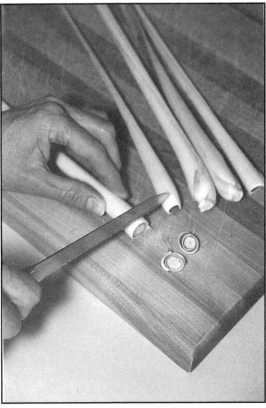

EPD Photos

Lemon grass may sometimes be found in supermarkets. Although it looks leafy, the stalk is tough and must be pounded with a rolling pin or mallet to release its flavor. The lemon grass may be pounded either before or after slicing.

8. Remove from heat and transfer to a platter. Sprinkle with bean sprouts and leeks and serve.

Serves 8 to 10.

Coconut-Chicken Soup

Ingredients

14 ounces skinless, boneless chicken breast

1 stick lemon grass

1 inch ginger root

1 Tablespoon lime juice

2 fresh hot chilies

2 cups unsweetened coconut milk

1 cup water

2 Tablespoons lemon juice

1 Tablespoon fish sauce

¼ teaspoon sugar

Fresh coriander leaves

Procedure

1. Slice chicken into thin strips.

2. Smash the lemon grass once with a rolling pin. Cut it into 1-inch slices.

3. Cut the ginger into thin slices and cut the chilies in half.

4. Heat coconut milk and water in a saucepan for 2 to 3 minutes over medium heat. (Do not let it boil.)

5. Add the lemon grass, ginger, and chilies, and cook for another 2 minutes, stirring continuously and not letting the liquid boil.

6. Add chicken strips and cook for 5 minutes, stirring over medium heat, until the chicken is cooked. Lower heat if mixture starts to boil.

7. Add lemon juice, lime juice, fish sauce, and sugar.

8. Stir and continue cooking for another minute or two.

9. Pour soup into a serving pot and serve immediately, topped with fresh coriander leaves.

Serves 6 to 8.

6 POLITICS, ECONOMICS, AND NUTRITION

About 24 percent of the population of Thailand is classified as undernourished by the

World Bank. This means they do not receive adequate nutrition in their diet. Almost all of the population (94 percent) has adequate access to sanitation. Of children under the age of five, about one-quarter are underweight, and nearly 22 percent are stunted (short for their age).

Despite malnourishment, Thailand is the world's largest rice exporter, accounting for over 22 percent of all agricultural exports by value in 1997. It also provides about 95 percent of the world's cassava (tapioca) exports. The government, however, has initiated large-scale irrigation projects, introduced higher-yielding varieties of rice, and encouraged mountain villagers to grow coffee, apples, strawberries, and other crops in an effort to increase exports and compete in the global market.

7 FURTHER STUDY

Books

Bremzen, Anya von, and John Welchman. *Terrific Pacific Cookbook.* New York: Workman Publishing, 1995.

Davidson, Alan. *The Oxford Companion to Food.* Oxford: Oxford University Press, 1999.

Halvorsen, Francine. *Eating Around the World in Your Neighborhood.* John Wiley & Sons: New York, 1998.

Harrison, Supenn, and Judy Monroe. *Cooking the Thai Way.* Minneapolis: Lerner Publications, 1986.

Rutherford, Scott, ed. *Insight Guide Thailand.* Singapore: APA Publications, 1998.

Sananikone, Keo. *Keo's Thai Cuisine.* Berkeley: Ten Speed Press, 1986.

Webb, Lois Sinaiko. *Holidays of the World Cookbook for Students.* Phoenix: Oryx Press, 1995.

Young, Wandee, and Byron Ayanoglu. *Simply Thai Cooking.* Toronto: Robert Rose, 1996.

Web Sites

Asia Foods. [Online] Available http://www.asiafoods.com (accessed February 7, 2001).

Bangkok Cuisine. [Online] Available http://bangkokcuisine.com/original/bangkok/recipes.htm (accessed July 19, 2001).

Epicurious. [Online] Available http://epicurious.com (accessed February 7, 2001).

SOAR (online recipe archive). [Online] Available http://soar.Berkeley.edu (accessed February 7, 2001).

Mail-order and online sources for specialty ingredients:

The Oriental Pantry
423 Great Road (2A)
Acton, MA 01720
(978) 264-4576
[Online] Available http://www.orientalpantry.com (accessed February 7, 2001).

Turkey

Recipes

Kaymakli Kuru Kayisi (Cream-Stuffed Apricots) 46
Pasta with Yogurt-Mint Sauce 47
Muhallabi (Rice Pudding with Cinnamon) 48
Naneli Limonata (Lemonade with Mint) 49
Halva 50
Köfte (Turkish Meatballs) 50
Simit (Sesame Rings) 51
Locum (Turkish Candy) 52
Bulgur Pilavi (Cracked Wheat Pilaf) 53
Lokma (Golden Fritters) 53
Lahmacun (Turkish Pizza) 55

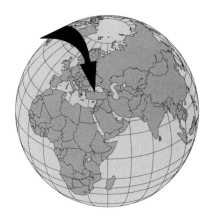

1 GEOGRAPHIC AND ENVIRONMENTAL SETTING

The Republic of Turkey consists of Asia Minor, the small area of eastern Turkey in Europe, and a few offshore islands in the Aegean Sea. It has a total area of 780,580 square kilometers (301,384 square miles), which is slightly larger than the state of Texas.

Turkey's landscape is made up of low, rolling hills, the fertile river valleys that open to the Aegean Sea, the warm plains along the Mediterranean Sea, the narrow coastal region along the Black Sea, and the rugged mountain ranges that surround and intersect the high, desert-like Anatolian plateau.

Most of Turkey lies within an earthquake zone, and recurrent tremors are recorded.

2 HISTORY AND FOOD

Turkish cuisine is often regarded as one of the greatest in the world. Its culinary traditions have successfully survived over 1,300 years for several reasons, including its favorable location and Mediterranean climate. The country's position between the Far East and the Mediterranean Sea helped the Turks gain complete control of major trade routes, and an ideal environment allowed plants and animals to flourish. Such advantages helped to develop and sustain a lasting and influential cuisine.

The Turkish people are descendents of nomadic tribes from Mongolia and western Asia who moved westward and became herdsmen around A.D. 600. Early influence from the Chinese and Persians included noodles and *manti*, cheese- or meat-stuffed dumplings (similar to the Italian ravioli),

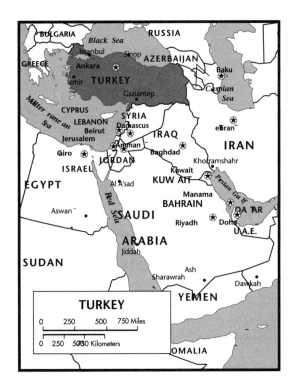

1200, they encountered chickpeas and figs, as well as Greek olive oil and an abundance of seafood.

A heavily influential Turkish cuisine was well established by the mid-1400s, the beginning of the (Turkish) Ottoman Empire's six hundred-year reign. Yogurt salads, fish in olive oil, and stuffed and wrapped vegetables became Turkish staples. The empire, eventually spanning from Austria to northern Africa, used its land and water routes to import exotic ingredients from all over the world. By the end of the 1500s, the Ottoman court housed over 1,400 live-in cooks and passed laws regulating the freshness of food. Since the fall of the empire in World War I (1914–1918) and the establishment of the Turkish Republic, foreign dishes such as French hollandaise sauce and Western fast food chains have made their way into the modern Turkish diet.

often covered in a yogurt sauce. *Manti* has often been credited with first introducing *dolma* (stuffed foods) into the Turkish cuisine. The milk and various dairy products that became staple foods for the herdsmen were nearly unused by the Chinese. This difference helped the Turks to establish their own unique diet.

By A.D. 1000, the Turks were moving westward towards richer soil where they grew crops such as wheat and barley. Thin sheets of dough called *yufka* along with crushed grains were used to create sweet pastries. The Persians introduced rice, various nuts, and meat and fruit stews. In return, the Turks taught them how to cook bulgur wheat. As the Turks moved further westward into Anatolia (present-day Turkey) by

Kaymakli Kuru Kayisi (Cream-Stuffed Apricots)

Ingredients

1 pound dried apricots

2½ cups sugar

3 cups water

1 teaspoon lemon juice

1 pound marscapone (sweet cheese); cream cheese softened with a little sour cream, heavy cream, or even milk may be substituted. Add 1 Tablespoon of the cooking syrup if using cream cheese.

¾ cup pistachio nuts, chopped

EPD Photos

Kaymakli Kuru Kayisi (Cream-Stuffed Apricots) are made with apricots and pistachios, both of which are grown in Turkey. Each July there is an apricot festival in the central region of the country.

Procedure

1. Soak the apricots in cold water overnight and drain.

2. Heat the sugar and water together over medium heat for 10 minutes, then add apricots.

3. Cook the apricots until they are tender and syrup is formed.

4. Add the lemon juice and remove from heat. With a slotted spoon, transfer apricots to a plate to cool.

5. With a spoon, open the apricots halfway and fill the inside with cream or sweet cheese.

6. Arrange the apricots (slit side up) on a platter, pouring over them as much syrup as they can absorb. Garnish with grated nuts.

Serves 18 to 20.

Pasta with Yogurt-Mint Sauce

Ingredients

1 pound penne or rigatoni pasta

3 cups yogurt, room temperature

2 to 3 teaspoons garlic, crushed

2 teaspoons fresh mint leaves, minced, or 1 teaspoon dried mint, crushed

Salt

Procedure

1. Cook pasta according to directions and drain.

2. Mix the yogurt, crushed garlic, salt, and mint leaves together in a bowl and beat with a wooden spoon until the mixture is very creamy.

3. Pour the warm sauce over the prepared pasta and toss.

Makes 4 servings.

Muhallabi
(Rice Pudding with Cinnamon)

Ingredients

1 cup long-grain rice

1 cup sugar

10 cups whole milk

1 teaspoon vanilla extract

Cinnamon

Procedure

1. In a large saucepan, mix the rice, sugar, milk, and vanilla extract together.

2. Bring to a boil on medium to high heat, stirring occasionally.

3. Immediately reduce heat.

4. Continue boiling for 1½ to 2 hours, or until a pudding consistency is reached.

5. If not boiled long enough, the rice gains remain too hard.

6. Put in individual cups or shallow serving dishes, cover the top, and chill before serving. To serve, sprinkle with cinnamon.

Cory Langley

A colorful Turkish fruit vendor poses with his melons.

7. If desired, orange zest, cinnamon, cloves, or rose water can be used instead of, or in addition to, vanilla.

Serves 12.

3 FOODS OF THE TURKS

Turkey is one of only seven countries in the world that can produce enough food to feed its people. This advantage gives the Turks access to fresh, locally grown ingredients that help to create some of the freshest dishes available. Contrary to common belief, Turkish cuisine is generally not spicy (though this varies throughout the seven regions). Seasonings and sauces, although frequently used, are simple and light and do not overpower the food's natural taste. The most popular seasonings include dill, mint, parsley, cinnamon, garlic, cumin, and *sumac* (lemon-flavored red berries of the sumac tree). Yogurt is often used to complement both meat and vegetables dishes.

Rice, wheat, and vegetables are the foundation for Turkish cuisine. *Dolma*, rice- and meat-stuffed vegetables, is frequently prepared throughout the country, most often with peppers, grape leaves, or tomatoes. The eggplant is the country's most beloved vegetable, with zucchini a popular second and then beans, artichokes, cabbage, particularly when prepared in olive oil. *Pilav* (pilaf), Turkish rice, is a common filling for *dolma*, as well as a common side dish. Various grains are used to make *pide* (flat bread), *simit* (sesame rings), and *börek*, a flaky, layered pastry filled with meat or cheese that is often eaten for breakfast.

Turkish meat usually means lamb, the main ingredient to the country's most popular national dish, *kebap* (skewered grilled meat). The *kebap* resembles the familiar shish-kebab (onions, tomatoes, and peppers threaded on a skewer between pieces of meat and grilled) commonly eaten in the United States. Patties of seasoned minced meat called *köfte* are also popular. Most cattle are raised for their milk rather than for beef, and pork is prohibited in the Islamic religion (which nearly all Turks practice). Poultry and seafood, however, are second in popularity for meat-based meals.

Naneli Limonata (Lemonade with Mint)

Ingredients
1½ cups, plus 2 Tablespoons sugar

6 cups water

2 teaspoons lemon rind

1 cup (6 to 8) fresh mint leaves

6 lemons

Procedure

1. In a large bowl, dissolve the 1½ cups sugar in the water, stirring well.

2. Using a wooden spoon, rub the lemon rind and mint leaves with the 2 Tablespoons sugar in a small bowl until the sugar absorbs the flavors. (Alternatively, pound the lemon rind, mint leaves, and sugar with a mortar and pestle.)

3. Stir in the sugar-water solution, mixing well. Strain this mixture through a sieve.

4. Squeeze the lemons to extract their juice.

5. Combine the lemon juice with the strained sugar solution, mixing well. Cover and chill.

6. Serve over ice (if desired), garnished with mint leaves.

Serves 8.

Turkish sweets are most frequently eaten with coffee or as a snack, rather than an after-dinner dessert. The most common dessert is a bowl of seasonal fresh fruit, such as strawberries or apricots. *Baklava*, widely known throughout the Western world, and other nutty pastries consisting of a sweet, flaky pastry made with honey and nuts; *Halva* (a sesame paste), *dondurma* (ice cream), and *muhallebi* (milk-based desserts, such as pudding) are all popular. Some adults prefer tea, strong Turkish coffee, or *raki*, the clear liquorice-flavored national beverage, in place of dessert. Children enjoy *ayran*, a refreshing yogurt drink, or *meyva suyu* (fruit juice).

Halva

Ingredients

1 cup farina (Cream of Wheat)

⅓ cup pine nuts

½ cup (1 stick) butter

2 cups water

1 cup sugar

½ teaspoon cinnamon, ground

Sesame seeds

Procedure

1. Mix the water, sugar, and cinnamon together in a saucepan and boil for 3 minutes. Remove from heat and let cool.

2. Using about ⅓ of the stick of butter, brown the pine nuts.

3. Add the remaining butter and farina and stir until the farina is a light brown color.

4. Very carefully add the cinnamon syrup to the farina mixture.

5. Stir until most of the water is absorbed and forms a sticky mixture.

6. Remove from the heat and leave uncovered for 1 hour, until it dries to a crumbly consistency.

7. Shape in individual molds or spoon into dishes.

8. Serve at room temperature topped with ground cinnamon and sesame seeds.

Köfte
(Turkish Meatballs)

Ingredients

1 pound minced lamb (or beef)

2 slices stale bread, crusts removed, briefly soaked in water

1 onion, grated

1 Tablespoon dried mint

1 Tablespoon fresh parsley, chopped

1 clove garlic, crushed

1 egg

Salt and black pepper

Flour

Vegetable oil for frying

Procedure

1. Squeeze out the excess water from the soaked bread.

2. Combine all the ingredients in a bowl and mix well.

3. Make walnut-shaped balls and keep them covered until they are to be eaten.

4. Place flour in a shallow dish, and roll the meatballs lightly in flour to coat.

5. Heat oil in a shallow frying pan. Carefully add meatballs and fry in hot oil for 6 to 8 minutes, turning frequently, until browned and cooked through.

6. They may be shallow- or deep-fried.

Serves 4 to 6.

Simit
(Sesame Rings)

Ingredients

8 ounces flour

½ teaspoon salt

4 Tablespoons (½ stick) margarine, melted

1 Tablespoon olive oil

1 Tablespoon milk, plus extra

1 Tablespoon water

1 egg, beaten

Sesame seeds

Procedure

1. Preheat the oven to 400°F.

2. Place the flour and salt in a large bowl and make a hole in the middle.

3. Into this hole pour the margarine, olive oil, milk, water, and beaten egg.

4. Stirring from the outside into the middle, gradually mix all the liquids into the flour until you have a dough. It will feel a bit oily.

5. With floured hands, shape the dough into rings about the diameter of a saucer, and arrange them on a baking sheet.

6. Brush them over with milk and sprinkle the sesame seeds on top.

7. Bake them for about 30 minutes, or until they are nicely browned.

4 FOOD FOR RELIGIOUS AND HOLIDAY CELEBRATIONS

Turkey celebrates three kinds of celebrations: national religious holidays, national secular (nonreligious) holidays, and local events and festivals. National Islamic holi-

A Typical Turkish Ramazan Menu

Various cheeses
Roast lamb or *sucuk* (spicy sausage)
Bulgur Pilavi (cracked wheat pilaf)
Pide (Turkish flat bread)
Various soups
Güllâç (rose-flavored pudding)
Baklava (sweet, flaky, nutty pastry)

days are important to the Turks since 99 percent are of the Islamic faith. To celebrate religious events, special dishes for family and friends are frequently prepared.

The first significant holiday of the Muslim year, Muharrem, takes place on the tenth day of the first lunar month. On this day in history, the grandson of the Prophet Mohammed was martyred and Noah and his family were able to leave the Ark after the floodwaters receded. A thick, sweet pudding called *aure* (also called Noah's pudding) is traditionally prepared. Its ingredients (fruits, nuts, and grains) are supposedly the same ones that remained on the Ark after it was able to land.

The ninth month marks Ramazan (also known as Ramadan in Arabic countries), a month-long period of fasting in which Muslims refrain from food and drink during daylight hours. *Iftar* is the meal eaten at the end of each day that breaks the daily fasting period.

Seker Bayrami, or translated as Candy Festival or Festival of Sugar, is a three-day national festival marking the end of Ramazan (also known as *Eid al-Fitr* in Arabic countries). On this day, elaborate desserts are prepared throughout the country and children visit door to door, asking for sweets. On this special day, *lokma* (deep-fried batter in syrup) and *locum* (a popular Turkish candy, also known as Turkish Delight), are commonly distributed to neighborhood children in small tins.

Locum (Turkish Candy)

Ingredients

3 envelopes unflavored gelatin

1½ cups water

2 cups sugar

3 Tablespoons white corn syrup

¾ cup cornstarch

Juice of 1 lemon

1 cup nuts, coarsely-chopped (pistachio, almonds, or walnuts)

¾ cup powdered sugar

Procedure

1. Sprinkle gelatin into ½ cup water and set aside to soften for about 5 minutes.

2. Pour another ½ cup water into a medium-size saucepan, bringing to a boil over medium to high heat.

3. Add the sugar and corn syrup, stirring until the sugar dissolves, about 1 minute.

4. Continue cooking until mixture reaches 240°F on a candy thermometer, or until it forms a soft ball when ½ teaspoon of mixture is dropped into a cup of cold water.

5. Reduce heat to medium.

EPD Photos/Cyril Gonsorcik

Rings of sucuk (spicy sausage) hang outside the butcher shop. Sucuk may be part of a dinner menu all year round.

6. Dissolve cornstarch in remaining ½ cup water and mix well.

7. Add to sugar mixture, and stirring constantly, simmer slowly until very thick, about 3 minutes; remove from heat.

8. Add lemon juice and gelatin mixture, stirring until gelatin dissolves.

9. Add nuts and stir thoroughly.

10. Line bottom and side of 8-inch cake pan with foil and sprinkle with thick layer of powdered sugar.

11. Pour in candy. Allow to stand, undisturbed, for about 4 hours, or until firm.

12. Cut into 1-inch squares, and roll each piece in powdered sugar to coat all sides.

Makes about 60 pieces.

Bulgur Pilavi
(Cracked Wheat Pilaf)

Ingredients

4 Tablespoons butter or margarine

1 onion, finely chopped

1 cup bulgur cracked wheat (available at most supermarkets and health food stores)

3 cups water or canned beef broth

Salt, to taste

Procedure

1. Melt 2 Tablespoons butter or margarine in large skillet over medium to high heat.

2. Add onion, and stirring constantly, fry until soft, about 3 minutes.

3. Add bulgur and remaining 2 Tablespoons butter or margarine, and fry for another minute, stirring constantly to coat well.

4. Stir in water or broth, and bring to a boil.

5. Reduce heat to simmer, cover, and cook for about 25 minutes until bulgur is tender.

6. Add salt to taste, and stir well. Serve warm.

Serves 4 to 6.

Large feasts are also prepared for national secular holidays such as Independence day and Children's Day, both on April 23, New Year's Day on January 1, and Victory Day on August 30, marking independence from Greece in 1922. In addition, June's Strawberry Festival in Bartin, July's Apricot Festival in Malatya (Turkey's apricot capital), and September's Watermelon Festival in Diyarbakir draw large, local crowds who gather to honor these crops.

Lokma (Golden Fritters)

Ingredients

1½ cups sugar

2 cups water

1 teaspoon lemon juice

1 teaspoon active dry yeast

1½ cups warm water

Pinch of sugar

2 cups flour

1 Tablespoon unsalted butter, melted

Pinch of salt

Oil, for frying (preferably peanut oil)

Procedure

1. Make the syrup by simmering the 1½ cups sugar and 2 cups water for 5 minutes.

2. Stir in the lemon juice, bring to a boil, and set aside.

3. To make the dough, dissolve the yeast in the warm water with a pinch of sugar, and leave in a warm place for 10 minutes until frothy.

4. Put the flour in a large bowl, make a well in the center, and put in the butter, salt, and yeast mixture.

5. Mix into a batter and beat for 5 minutes, using an electric mixer fitted with a dough hook or a paddle. (Alternatively, knead it for about 8 minutes.)

6. Cover and let rise for 1 to 2 hours.

7. Heat the oil for deep-frying (a small square of bread should brown in 30 seconds).

8. Keeping the heat at medium, drop small balls of dough into the hot oil.

9. Drop 5 or 6 *lokma* into the oil, depending on the size of the pan, but do not crowd them.

10. They should immediately rise to the surface and puff up. Stir them to ensure an even browning.

11. They should brown in 3 or 4 minutes.

12. Drain on paper towels, then dip them briefly into the syrup mixture.

13. Serve warm or cold.

Makes 6 to 8 servings.

5 MEALTIME CUSTOMS

Turks enjoy three meals a day. *Kahvalti* (kah-vall-tuh), or breakfast, is generally a light meal consisting of fresh tomatoes, *beyaz* (salty cheese), black olives, bread with jam and honey, and an occasional soft-boiled egg. Freshly baked bread and tea are almost always present. *Sucuk* (a spicy sausage) and *pastirma* (seasoned beef) are frequently prepared in the wintertime. Those in a hurry often stop at a street cart or *büfe* (food stand) to grab a quick *börek*, a flaky, mince- or cheese-filled pastry or *simit*, a bread ring topped with sesame seeds. Muslims almost never consume pork products, making bacon absent from most menus.

Öyle yemek (oy-leh yem-eck), or lunch, is traditionally a heartier (and warmer) meal than breakfast. *Çorbalar,* or soups, are served in a variety of ways, most commonly including lentils and various vegetables and meats. Larger lunch items include baked lamb or chicken served with peppers and eggplant, and fresh grilled fish with a side of lemon. Rice and bulgar pilaf dishes are also popular. *Lahmacun* (lah-mah-jun), Turkish pizza, is popular among children. It consists of a thin crust and a layer of spicy ground lamb and tomato sauce. Tost, a grilled cheese sandwich, will please even the pickiest eater.

Akam yemek (ak-sham yem-eck), or dinner, is the largest meal of the day. *Mezeler* (or *mezze*, singular), are "appetizers" served before the main meal. Ironically, most *mezeler* dishes are large enough to comprise an entire meal by themselves. Salads, soups, pilaf-stuffed fish, and *köfte* (fried minced meatballs) can leave diners quite full. A meat dish accompanied by starchy vegetables (such as potatoes) typically follows. Seasonal fresh fruits or milky puddings are most often enjoyed for dessert.

Turks, who are extremely hospitable and enjoy company, will welcome even unexpected guests with Turkish coffee. Meals are traditionally served on a large tray, placed on a low table or on the floor. The family and guests sit on cushions on the floor around the prepared foods. To avoid accidentally insulting the host, it is best to not refuse second or third helpings. It is also customary to remove one's shoes at the door and offer a small gift to the host for their generosity.

Restaurants, open markets, and *büfe* (food stands) offer a wide variety of on-the-go snacks, including *simit, köfte,* seeds and nuts, and seasonal fruit and fruit juice. *Patates Firin* (baked potato carts) can be found for *kumpir* (potatoes) topped with lentils, butter, cheese, pickles, and mayonnaise.

Lahmacun (Turkish Pizza)

Ingredients

Pitas

1 pound ground beef

1 pound white onion

1 or 2 tomatoes (or 2 Tablespoons tomato puree)

Salt and black pepper, to taste

Procedure

1. Preheat oven to 400°F.
2. Peel and quarter onions with the tomatoes in a food processor or blender and process (blend) until smooth.
3. Add the salt, black pepper, and meat, and ground for 30 seconds more.
4. With a spoon, spread the mixture over the pitas. Place them in the oven and bake for 20 to 30 minutes.
5. Make certain meat is fully cooked (not pink inside). Serve hot.

Makes 6 to 8 pizzas, serving 12 to 16.

6 POLITICS, ECONOMICS, AND NUTRITION

About 2 percent of the population of Turkey are classified as undernourished by the World Bank. This means they do not receive adequate nutrition in their diet. Of children under the age of five, about 10 percent are underweight, and over one-fifth are stunted (short for their age).

Crops such as wheat, barley, sugar beets, grapes, maize (corn), sunflower seeds, hazelnuts, and oranges are grown on 90% of Turkey's arable land. Crops are sensitive, however, to variations in rainfall and output is often unpredictable. Some years enough is produced for export, while at other times limited rainfall may only produce enough grain to feed the Turkish population. Despite such uncertainty, Turkey is one of the few countries in the world that produces enough food to feed its people. In addition, the adoption of modern machinery has allowed more land to be used for cultivation, helping to increase food production.

7 FURTHER STUDY

Books

Ayliffe, Rosie, Marc Dubin, and John Gawthrop. *Turkey: The Rough Guide, 3rd edition*. London: Rough Guides Ltd., 1997.

Facaros, Dana and Michael Pauls. *Cadogan Guides: Turkey*. Guilford, CT: The Globe Pequot Press, 2000.

Let's Go Publications. *Let's Go Turkey*. New York: St. Martin's Press, 2001.

Peck, Adam and Manja Sachet. *Turkey Guide*. Cold Spring Harbor, NY: Open Road Publishing, 1999.

Robertson, Carol and David. *Turkish Cooking: A Culinary Journey through Turkey*. Berkeley, CA: Frog, Ltd., 1996.

Salaman, R. *The Cooking of Greece and Turkey*. Cambridge, England: Martin Books, 1991.

Web Sites

Beltur. [Online] Available http://www.beltur.com.tr/ing/yemek.htm (accessed March 8, 2001).

Cankan Real Estate Agency. [Online] Available http://www.cankan.com/izmir/200tcuisine.htm/ (accessed March 8, 2001).

Cypriot-Turkish Cuisine. [Online] Available http://www.cypnet.com/.ncyprus/cypcuisine/ (accessed March 26, 2001).

GlobalGourmet.com. [Online] Available http://www.globalgourmet.com/destinations/turkey/ (accessed March 21, 2001).

Istanbul Homepages. [Online] Available http://www.guideistanbul.net/ (accessed March 8, 2001).

Mersina. [Online] Available http://www.mersina.com/food_and_drink/turkish_delights/turkish.htm (accessed March 8, 2001).

Ministry of Tourism, Republic of Turkey. [Online] Available http://www.turizm.gov.ru/cu2.html (accessed March 22, 2001).

Sallysplace.com. [Online] Available http://www.sallys-place.com/ (accessed March 2, 2001).

Story of Turkish Food. [Online] Available http://www.public.asu.edu/~okenes/tr_ye_01.htm (accessed March 2, 2001).

Toto Hostel and Guest House. [Online] Available http://www.totohostel.com/foods-entertainment.htm/ (accessed March 8, 2001).

Turkish Cuisine. [Online] Available http://www.fspronet.com/sheilah/turkish.html (accessed March 21, 2001).

Turkish Cultural Foundation. [Online] Available http://www.turkishculture.org/culinary_arts/food.html (accessed March 21, 2001).

Ukraine

Recipes

Potato Varenyky (Potato Dumplings)........................... 58
Cabbage Borshch.. 59
Holubtsi (Stuffed Cabbage Rolls) 60
Kartoplia Solimkoi (Deep-Fried Straw Potatoes) 60
Nachynka (Cornbread Stuffing)................................... 61
Kotlety Po-Kyivskomy (Chicken Kiev).......................... 61
Kutya (Sweet Porridge) 63
Makiwnyk (Glazed Poppy Seed Cake)......................... 63

1 GEOGRAPHIC SETTING AND ENVIRONMENT

Ukraine is the second largest country in Europe. It is located between Poland and Russia. It is slightly smaller than the state of Texas. Much of the southeastern part of the country borders the Black Sea.

Most of Ukraine's land is made up of fertile plains, or steppes, and plateaus. Mountains are found only in the west and extreme south in the Crimean Peninsula. This area's climate is subtropical. Winters vary from cool along the Black Sea to cold farther inland. The temperature inland ranges from 66°F in July, to 21°F in January. Northern and western Ukraine average 27 inches of rainfall a year. This temperate climate is ideal for growing crops. In fact, more than 57 percent of the Ukraine's fertile soil is suitable for growing such crops as sugar beets, wheat, and potatoes.

2 HISTORY AND FOOD

The earliest known farmers in the Ukraine were the Trypillians (4500–2000 B.C.). The territory of the Ukraine had rich soil and a favorable climate perfect for cultivating crops. The Trypillians grew barley, millet, rye, and wheat. They also herded sheep, pigs, and cattle. Wheat was plentiful, and soon trading routes were established along Ukraine's Black Sea coast to market the grain. The Ukraine territory became the crossing road connecting Arabia, Europe, and Asia.

Life depended on the activities of cultivating soil for crops. In pre-Christian times, holidays were celebrated during times of transition from one type of agricultural activity to another. These seasonal festivities were later incorporated into Christian holidays, such as Christmas and Easter.

UKRAINE

0   500   1000 Miles

0   500   1000 Kilometers

Potato Varenyky (Potato Dumplings)

Ingredients

2 cups flour

1 egg

1 teaspoon salt

3½ cups instant mashed potatoes, prepared

¾ cup cheddar or processed cheese, shredded

Salt and pepper, to taste

Procedure

1. To make filling: prepare instant potatoes according to package directions.

2. In a mixing bowl, add cheese and mix well. Set aside.

3. In a large mixing bowl, combine flour, egg, and salt.

4. Mix in a little water at a time until dough is stiff.

5. Roll out dough on floured surface, about ¼-inch thick.

6. Using the rim of a glass or cookie cutter, cut out circles of dough.

7. Fill each circle of dough with about 1 Tablespoon of the potato-cheese mixture. Fold over and seal edges.

8. To cook, bring a large pot of water to a boil and drop in the *varenyky* one at a time. They are done when they float to the top.

Serves 4 to 6.

Over time, Ukraine fell under the power of many different countries, including Poland, Austria, and Russia. Despite being under Russian domination for almost 200 years, (gaining independence only in 1991), Ukrainians proudly kept their native traditions, customs, and cuisine.

Kovbasa (sausage) and sauerkraut have Polish origins. *Varnyky* (dumplings) and *holubtsi* (stuffed cabbage) were originally imported from Turkey. Strudels, breaded meats, and desserts, such as cheesecake and tarts, were carried over from Austro-Hungarian times. Although Ukrainian dishes have origins from different countries, how they are prepared are uniquely Ukrainian.

3 FOODS OF THE UKRAINIANS

In the southern part of the Ukraine, plains called steppes have what is considered some of the most fertile soil in the world. Abundant rain and a mild climate made the Ukraine famous for its *chornozem,* or

AP Photo/Richard Drew

A visiting politician is greeted with the traditional Ukrainian welcome of bread, representing hospitality, and salt, representing friendship. The specially decorated loaf of bread and the salt are offered by young women dressed in folk costume.

"black earth." For centuries, the Ukraine was called "the breadbasket of Europe."

Ukrainian cuisine stems from peasant dishes based on the plentiful grains and staple vegetables grown in the country. Staple crops include sugar beets, potatoes, grapes, cabbages, and mushrooms. These are often key ingredients in soups and salads. The most popular dish is *borshch*, a hearty soup made in a variety of ways, depending on the person who is cooking it. Mushroom, bean, and pea soups, and thick millet (a type of grain) chowders are also common. Other vegetable dishes include *holubtsi* (stuffed cabbage) and *kartoplia solimkoi* ("straw

potatoes"). *Kotlety Po-Kyivskomy* (Chicken Kiev), a chicken breast stuffed with a buttery filling, is a well-known dish outside Ukraine.

Cabbage Borshch

Ingredients

3 cans beef broth (approximately 6 cups)

1 pound cabbage, shredded

1 beet, peeled and grated

1 medium onion, grated

3 medium tomatoes, diced

½ Tablespoon salt

1 teaspoon celery salt

½ teaspoon pepper (or more, to taste)

1 Tablespoons lemon juice

1 Tablespoon sugar

Procedure

1. Measure the beef broth into a large pot. add the vegetables, celery salt, and pepper.
2. Cover and cook over medium to low heat for 25 minutes.
3. Add the lemon juice and sugar. Cook an additional 5 minutes.
4. Serve with bread.

Serves 6.

Holubtsi (Stuffed Cabbage Rolls)

Ingredients

¼ pound ground beef

1 medium onion, chopped

4 Tablespoons vegetable oil

4 cups cooked rice

4 cups water

Salt and pepper, to taste

¾ cup tomato juice

1 medium cabbage, core removed

1 Tablespoon vinegar

Procedure

1. To make filling: cook rice according to package directions.
2. In a frying pan, add the oil and heat over medium heat.
3. Brown the onions and hamburger.
4. Combine rice, onion, and hamburger in a mixing bowl. Season with salt and pepper. Set aside.
5. Preheat oven to 350°F.

6. In a large pot, bring the water and vinegar to a boil.
7. Place the cabbage into the pot and simmer long enough for the cabbage leaves to become limp, about 5 to 10 minutes. Do not overcook.
8. Remove cabbage and tear off cabbage leaves from the cabbage head.
9. Remove the hard center part of the leaf.
10. Place a spoonful of the rice mixture into the center of the leaf and roll tightly.
11. Place cabbage rolls into a casserole dish and cover with the tomato juice.
12. Bake for 1 to 1½ hours.

Makes 20 to 30 cabbage rolls.

Kartoplia Solimkoi (Deep-Fried Straw Potatoes)

Ingredients

4 medium potatoes, peeled

3 cups vegetable oil

Salt, to taste

Procedure

1. Cut the potatoes into small strips, about ⅛-inch thick.
2. Drop them into a bowl of ice water, then drain.
3. Spread out onto paper towels and thoroughly dry.
4. Heat the oil in a deep frying pan over high heat. Drop small bunches of potatoes at a time into the oil and fry until golden brown.
5. Drain on paper towels and season with salt.

Serves 4 to 6.

Grains, such as wheat, rye, barley, oats, corn, and buckwheat are cultivated and made into many different types of breads. Some examples are *agnautka*, a flat whole-grained loaf that is commonly eaten at meals; *polianitsa*, a large, round white bread; and *ikrainka*, a heavy, dark wheel-shaped loaf weighing about three pounds. *Nachynka* is a baked cornmeal side dish served with meat.

Nachynka (Cornbread Stuffing)

Ingredients

1 small onion, finely chopped

3 Tablespoons butter

1 cup cornmeal

1 teaspoon salt

1 teaspoon sugar

¼ teaspoon black pepper

3½ cups heated milk

½ cup half-and-half cream

2 eggs, beaten

Procedure

1. Preheat oven to 350°F.
2. In a frying pan, heat the butter over medium heat. Add onion and cook until tender, but do not brown.
3. In a mixing bowl, combine cornmeal, salt, sugar, and pepper. Add to frying pan and mix well.
4. Pour in the heated milk gradually and stir well until mixture is smooth and free of lumps.
5. Add the eggs and mix well. Pour the mixture into a greased casserole dish.
6. Bake the *nachynka* uncovered for 1 hour, or until golden brown.

Serves 6 to 8.

Kotlety Po-Kyivskomy (Chicken Kiev)

Ingredients

8 skinless, boneless chicken breasts

8 Tablespoons butter (1 stick)

1 Tablespoon parsley, chopped fine

2 eggs

½ cup flour (approximately)

1½ cups soft bread crumbs

Vegetable oil for frying

Procedure

1. Cut the butter into eight equal parts, each about the size of your little finger. (Cut the stick of butter lengthwise into quarters, and then cut the quarters in half crosswise.)
2. Roll the butter rectangles in parsley to coat, and set them aside in a cool place.
3. Place the chicken breasts, one at a time, between two sheets of wax paper, and pound them with a rolling pin or kitchen mallet until they are thin. Carefully remove the wax paper.
4. Place one butter rectangle on each chicken breast, and roll the breast around the butter. Press the roll together to form a compact roll. Repeat until all 8 breasts have been rolled.
5. Beat the two eggs lightly in a shallow dish. On a sheet wax paper, spread some flour; spread some bread crumbs on another sheet of wax paper.
6. Dip the rolls first into the flour, then the eggs, and then the bread crumbs.
7. When four rolls are done, heat some oil in a large skillet, and carefully add the rolls. Fry, turning several times, for about 15 to 20 minutes until the chicken rolls are golden brown and cooked through. Transfer to a serving dish, cov-

er, and repeat with the remaining 4 rolls. (Keep the first batch warm in the oven set at the lowest temperature.)

Serves 8.

In Ukrainian cuisine, when the dough isn't baked, it is usually boiled, such as *kasha* (hot cereal), or fried in the form of dumplings or fritters. Freshly made dumplings called *varenyky* are a common Ukrainian staple. *Varenyky* is dough stuffed with a variety of foods, such as potatoes, meats, cheeses, sauerkraut, and even fruit, such as blueberries or cherries, for dessert. Each region, restaurant, and family has its own recipe.

The foothills of the Carpathian Mountains, located in the western Ukraine, provide pastures for grazing beef and dairy cattle. Meats, such as *kovbasa* (sausage), poultry, and pork are important to the Ukrainian diet.

Pork is considered the national meat and pork fat is often used in cooking. It is used mostly for frying, but also can be eaten smoked or with salt. Common dairy products include milk, *syrnyky* (cottage cheese fritters), *nalynsnyk* (cheese-filled crepes), and *riazhanka* (fermented, baked milk).

Desserts are often baked into sweet breads, cakes, and cookies, and made with honey and fruits, such as plums, blueberries, and cherries.

4 FOOD FOR RELIGIOUS AND HOLIDAY CELEBRATIONS

Around 85 percent of Ukrainians are Christian. Therefore, the most important holiday in the Ukrainian church is Easter, followed by Christmas. Both holidays are celebrated

Dinner Menu for Sviaty Vechir (Christmas Eve)

Kutya (a type of wheat porridge)
Borshch (hearty vegetable soup)
Baked or fried fish
Oseledsi (pickled fish)
Holubtsi (cabbage rolls)
Varenyky (dumpling) with potato, sauerkraut, and prune filling
Cooked beans
Kapusta and peas (sauerkraut and peas)
Beets with mushrooms
Stewed fruit

according to the old-style Julian calendar, resulting in Christmas Day falling on January 7. Christmas Eve is called the *Sviaty Vechir* (Holy Evening). To celebrate, a ritual meal is traditionally prepared with 12 mostly meatless dishes, which symbolize the 12 apostles who gathered at the Last Supper. In some homes, the supper table is scattered with some hay, in memory of baby Jesus in the manger, with an elaborate tablecloth. *Kolach* is a traditional bread placed in the middle of the table. The meal usually begins with a small bowl of *kutya*, a mixture of cooked wheat, honey, poppy seeds, chopped nuts, and apples. This is followed by several fish dishes, mushrooms, *holubtsi* (stuffed cabbage), *varenyky* (dumplings), fruits, cakes, such as *makiwnyk* (poppy seed cake) and bread. *Borshch* (a hearty soup) is usually included as well.

Kutya
(Sweet Porridge)

Ingredients

1 cup cream of wheat

¼ cup margarine or butter

2 cups water

¼ cup each honey, poppy seeds, and chopped nuts

Procedure

1. Bring the water to a boil in a saucepan.

2. Add the cream of wheat and chopped nuts. Stir until soft and the water is absorbed.

3. Pour the mixture into a serving dish and add the butter and honey.

4. Mix in the poppy seeds, saving a few for sprinkling over the top.

Serves 2.

Makiwnyk (Poppy Seed Cake)

Ingredients

¾ cup poppy seeds

1⅓ cup milk

2 Tablespoons cornstarch

⅓ cup oil

½ cup sugar

1 teaspoon vanilla

½ lemon or orange rind, grated

2 cups flour

1 teaspoon cinnamon

2½ teaspoons baking powder

2 Tablespoons lemon juice

1 Tablespoon sugar

Procedure

1. Soak poppy seeds in milk for 1 hour in a large bowl.

2. Preheat oven to 350°F.

3. Add cornstarch, oil, sugar, vanilla and rind to the poppy seed-milk mixture and stir.

4. In a separate mixing bowl, combine the dry ingredients.

5. Add the dry ingredients to the poppy seed mixture and mix well.

6. Pour into a greased cake pan and bake for 45 minutes.

7. Top with glaze (see recipe).

Serves 6 to 8.

Makiwnyk Glaze
(Poppy Seed Cake Glaze)

Ingredients

2 Tablespoons lemon juice

1 Tablespoon sugar

Procedure

1. Add the lemon juice and sugar to a small saucepan and heat over medium heat.

2. Stir gently until it forms a syrup.

3. Drizzle over Makiwnyk.

A Ukrainian Easter meal also has its ritual foods. In the morning, breakfast foods such as hard-boiled eggs, *kovbasa* (sausage), baked cheese, breads, butter, and relishes, are placed into a basket and taken to church to be blessed. For Easter dinner, ham or roast pork, vegetable salads, cheesecake, tortes, and other pastries are eaten.

Besides Christmas and Easter, there are special breads for almost every important

Ukrainian occasion. A bride and groom are blessed, and the dead remembered with *kolach*, a rich, intricate, braided bread, which symbolizes good fortune and eternity. For a typical wedding, seven bridesmaids grind flour from wheat grown in seven different fields to bake a *korovai*, a bread that symbolizes good luck. There are dozens of different ways of preparing and baking breads in the Ukraine.

5 MEALTIME CUSTOMS

In general, Ukrainians eat a light breakfast. It can be bread with butter served with coffee or tea, or pastries, such as a cream-filled blintz. *Kasha* (cereal), steamed buckwheat, barley, or millet with milk may also be served. Their main meal is eaten around mid-afternoon and usually consists of soup, such as *borshch* and a dish with meat or poultry. The third meal of the day takes place around 6 or 7 p.m. It is usually a time when all family members get together. Eating at a restaurant is considered a luxury, and is usually not done very often.

Ukrainians eat with a fork in their left hand and a knife in their right hand. It is considered impolite to hold your hands under the table during dinner, or to put your elbows on the table. In order not to seem wasteful, Ukrainians may eat everything on their plates. When they are visiting, Ukrainians may ask for second helpings to show appreciation for the food. Hosts often give guests a loaf of bread with salt on top, a tradition that dates back many centuries. Bread and salt were once considered necessary ingredients for health. The bread represents hospitality and the salt represents friendship.

6 POLITICS, ECONOMICS, AND NUTRITION

About one-third of Ukraine's land is used as pasture. Crops include sugar beets, potatoes, rye, and wine grapes. Before its independence, Ukraine was the most productive agricultural area in the Soviet Union. The land accounted for one-quarter of Soviet Union grain production, one-fifth of its meat and dairy, and more than one half of its sugar beet production. Farmers raise cereal crops, such as wheat and corn. Since its independence, Ukraine has suffered financially, resulting in high food prices, a shortage of medical equipment, and modern facilities, especially in rural areas. Despite having economic difficulties, most Ukrainians receive adequate nutrition. In fact, less than one percent of children under five are malnourished, and only 6 percent of children are too short for their age. Since Ukraine joined the World Bank in 1992, many different programs have been implemented to help the country's economy.

7 FURTHER STUDY

Books

Farley, Marta Pesetska. *Festive Ukrainian Cooking*. Pittsburgh, PA: University of Pittsburgh Press, 1990.

Zahny, Bohdan. *The Best of Ukrainian Cuisine.* New York, NY: Hippocrene Books, 1998.

Web Sites

Insider.com. [Online] Available http://www.sdinsider.com/community/groups/ukraine/Bread_and_Salt_Mean_.html (accessed April 22, 2001).

Ukraine—The Breadbasket and the Sugar Bowl. [Online] Available http://russia-in-us.com/Cuisine/Dadiani/ukraine.htm (accessed April 22, 2001).

United Kingdom

Recipes

Salmon Kedgeree (British-Indian Salmon)................... 66
Lemon Curd... 68
Haggis 68
Welsh Rarebit 69
Cornish Pasties 69
Toad-in-the-Hole 70
Cucumber Sandwiches.. 71
Scones 71
Tatties n' Neeps 72
Individual Mincemeat Pies... 73
Wassail 74
Sunday Lunch Cauliflower Cheese............................... 74
Tea with Milk 75

1 GEOGRAPHIC SETTING AND ENVIRONMENT

The United Kingdom (UK) is located just west of the mainland of Europe. It is made up of several islands, the largest of which is Great Britain. Great Britain is made up of Scotland in the north, England in the southeast and Wales in the southwest. Northern Ireland is the northwestern part of Ireland, a separate island nation just west of Great Britain, but it is also part of the UK. There has been violence in Northern Ireland for centuries because of religious and political conflict there. Because ocean waters surround the UK, it has a mild, rainy climate. The country's farmers produce about 60 percent of the food the UK needs. From 1980–90 the farming became more mechanized, with farmers using machinery to plant and harvest crops. The productivity of UK farms increased during that period by about 10 percent. More farmers raise livestock than crops, and some of the world's best beef and lamb is raised in the UK.

2 HISTORY AND FOOD

The United Kingdom (UK) has also been called the British Isles or Great Britain at different times in history. The UK consists of England, Wales, Scotland, and Northern Ireland. Each region has its own special cuisine. At various times the English have ruled over the entire region, including all of Ireland. The English style of cooking does not use many seasonings and is sometimes criticized for its bland taste. During the 1700s and 1800s, English explorers and colonists were trading and developing settlements in the Caribbean region, Asia, Africa, and North America. Their colonial interests around the world became known as the British Empire. The English were influenced by

the cultures of their colonies, so English cooking began to use new spices and cooking techniques acquired in such places as India.

Salmon Kedgeree (British-Indian Salmon)

Ingredients

2 eggs

1 small onion, chopped

1¾ cups water

½ teaspoon salt

8 oz.

can of salmon

¾ cup white rice

1 Tablespoon unsalted butter

2 Tablespoons chopped parsley leaves

1 Tablespoon lemon juice

Lemon wedges as garnish, if desired

Procedure

1. Prepare hardboiled eggs: Place eggs in a saucepan and cover them with cold water.

2. Put the saucepan on a burner over medium-high heat and wait until the water just begins to simmer. (Tiny bubbles will form and move slowly to the surface of the water.) Lower the heat, and simmer the eggs for 15 minutes.

3. Remove from heat and run cold water into the pan to stop the cooking. Allow the eggs to cool, and then remove the shells carefully. Cut the eggs lengthwise into quarters.

4. Cook the rice: Prepare rice according to instructions on the package to yield about 2 cups of cooked rice.

5. Next chop the onion.

6. Heat butter in a large skillet until melted and add chopped onion. Cook onion, stirring constantly with a wooden spoon, until softened. Stir rice into the onion.

7. Drain canned salmon and add to rice mixture, breaking up the salmon with the wooden spoon. Add parsley, and lemon juice. Cook together until heated through.

8. Serve, garnished with slices of egg and lemon wedges.

Serves 6 to 8.

3 FOODS OF THE BRITISH

In Scotland the national dish is *haggis*. Haggis is comprised of sheep innards boiled in a sheep stomach. In Wales leeks, a relative of the onion, are used in many dishes. Welsh *rarebit,* comprised of a cheesy sauce over

Charming inns may be found in almost every town and village in the United Kingdom. Most serve hearty food along with beer, ale, wine, and other spirits.

toast, is popular as an appetizer or a light meal. Throughout the United Kingdom, *pasties* or meat pies are popular. These combine ground meat, vegetables, and potatoes inside a pastry crust. Other favorite meals are fish and chips. Both fish and chips and curry (a dish introduced by immigrants from India) are popular take-out foods. At around 4 P.M., people in the UK traditionally took a break for tea. Traditional "high tea" included formal preparation of tea, accompanied by an array of finger foods, such as cucumber sandwiches, cheese and chutney (a type of pickle relish) sandwiches, scones, and small, delicate

teacakes. To spread on the scones, clotted cream, marmalade, or strawberry jam might be served. People's schedules in the modern UK are sometimes too busy to allow a break for traditional high tea, but most people stop their work activities for an abbreviated tea break at around 4 p.m. For the more casual tea break, tea and biscuits (nicknamed "bikkies") is the common fare. Biscuits are small, crisp cookies, and all English kitchens have a "biscuit tin." Other beverages that the English enjoy include *ribena* (blackcurrant juice) and *squash* (sweet fruity beverage similar to Kool-aid).

Clotted cream and lemon curd?

Clotted cream—the name sounds like something that's been in the refrigerator past the expiration date, but clotted cream is truly a rich treat. It is thicker than whipped cream and is sold in containers, like sour cream or margarine, in the dairy section. Lemon curd is almost like a thick pudding. English people enjoy it for breakfast, or as a filling for little tarts.

Lemon Curd

Prepared lemon curd may be purchased at many supermarkets. It is usually found near the jams and jellies.

Ingredients

2 sticks unsalted butter

½ cup fresh lemon juice, strained through a sieve

½ sugar

3 egg yolks

Procedure

1. In a double boiler (one pot set inside a larger pot that contains about 2 inches of boiling water), melt the butter with the lemon juice and sugar, stirring until all the sugar dissolves.

2. Add the egg yolks, one at a time, stirring constantly.

3. Keep stirring until the mixture is as thick as yogurt (about 15 minutes).

4. Pour the mixture through a sieve into a bowl.

5. Cover with plastic wrap, making sure the plastic wrap touches the surface of the lemon curd to prevent a skin from forming. Refrigerate until cool.

6. Serve on toast or fill purchased miniature tart shells with it.

Serves 12 to 15. Serve with tea.

Haggis

Ingredients

1 sheep's stomach

1 sheep heart

1 sheep liver

½ pound suet, fresh (kidney fat is preferred)

¾ cup oatmeal

1 teaspoon salt

½ teaspoon pepper

¼ teaspoon cayenne

½ teaspoon nutmeg

¾ cup stock

Procedure

1. Wash stomach; rub with salt and rinse.

2. Remove membranes and excess fat.

3. Soak in cold salted water.

4. Turn stomach inside out.

5. Boil the heart and liver in water, and simmer for 30 minutes.

6. Chop the heart and grate the liver.

7. Toast the oatmeal until golden brown.

8. Combine all ingredients and pack into the stomach, leaving enough room for the oatmeal to expand.

9. Press excess air out of the stomach and sew it up.

10. Simmer for three hours in a pot of water, pricking small holes in the stomach so that it doesn't explode.

Serve on a hot platter.

Welsh Rarebit

Ingredients

½ pound cheddar cheese, grated

1 Tablespoon butter

¼ cup milk (or beer)

1 teaspoon dried mustard powder

Dash of Worcestershire sauce

4 slices thick bread, toasted

Salt and pepper to taste

Tomatoes, sliced

Procedure

1. Preheat oven to 325°F.

2. Put grated cheese, butter, milk, mustard powder, Worcestershire sauce, and salt and pepper in a saucepan.

3. Heat over low heat, stirring constantly, until cheese is melted and the mixture is smooth and creamy.

4. Toast bread, cut each piece into two triangles, and arrange in a casserole.

5. Ladle cheese sauce over toast, and bake in the oven until crusty (about 15 minutes).

6. Carefully remove two triangles of toast to a plate for each person, top with a slice of tomato, and serve.

EPD Photos

Pasties—pastry filled with a mixture of beef, lamb, or chicken combined with potatoes, and vegetables—may be eaten warm or cold.

Cornish Pasties

Pastry ingredients

1 cup flour

Pinch of salt

¾ cup butter

Cold water

1 egg, broken into a small bowl and beaten

Filling ingredients

½ pound ground beef

1 medium onion, chopped

1 potato, chopped

½ teaspoon salt

½ teaspoon pepper

Procedure

1. Preheat oven to 375°F and grease a cookie sheet.

2. *Make pastry* (or purchase commercial piecrust mix or refrigerated piecrust): Combine flour and butter in a bowl, using two knives or a large fork to cut the butter into small pieces.

3. Continue mixing until all the butter has been broken up and is thoroughly mixed with flour.

4. Add cold water, one tablespoon at a time, until a soft dough is formed (2 to 4 tablespoons of water).

5. *Make filling:* In a bowl, mix the ground meat, onion, potato, salt, and pepper.

6. Stir with a wooden spoon to combine.

7. *Assemble pasties:* Dust the counter or a large wooden cutting board with flour and roll out the pastry, using a rolling pin.

8. Using a saucer as a template, cut dough into 5-inch rounds.

9. Place about ¼ cup of the meat mixture in the center of each round.

10. Pinch up the edges of the dough, almost covering the filling.

11. Using a pastry brush, brush the pastry with the beaten egg.

12. Place the pastie carefully on a greased baking sheet.

13. Repeat to make 3 more pasties.

14. Bake at 375°F for 50 to 55 minutes.

15. Pastry should be golden brown, and filling should look bubbly and hot.

Toad-in-the-Hole

No one really knows the history behind the name of this traditional light supper dish.

Ingredients

2 cups all-purpose flour

¼ teaspoon salt

2 cups milk

6 eggs

2 pounds pork sausage links

Applesauce as accompaniment

Procedure

1. Preheat oven to 350°F.

2. Prick sausages all over with a fork.

3. Place in lightly greased 13x9-inch baking dish.

4. Bake for 15 minutes at 350°F.

5. While sausages are baking, measure flour and salt into a medium bowl.

6. In another bowl, combine milk with eggs, and beat lightly with a wire whisk or fork.

7. Gradually stir milk and eggs into flour mixture, stirring to make a smooth batter.

8. Let stand for 30 minutes.

9. When the sausages have baked for about 15 minutes, turn them and return pan to oven for 15 minutes more.

10. Remove sausages to paper towels, and drain fat from pan.

11. Return sausages to pan.

12. Increase oven temperature to 425°F.

13. Stir batter and pour over baked sausages.

14. Bake the combination for 25 to 30 minutes, or until puffed and golden.

15. Serve immediately.

EPD Photos

The crusts from thin-sliced white bread are trimmed to make cucumber sandwiches to serve at teatime. The cucumber is peeled and sliced thinly.

Cucumber Sandwiches

Ingredients

1 seedless cucumber

8 slices very thin-sliced white bread

Salt, to taste

Unsalted butter, at room temperature

Procedure

1. Peel cucumber and slice crosswise very thin.

2. Spread unsalted butter on one side of each slice of bread.

3. Arrange cucumber slices in a single layer on 4 slices of bread.

4. Salt lightly.

5. Top with second slice of bread.

6. Carefully trim crusts from sandwiches and discard.

7. Cut each sandwich into triangles and arrange on a china plate.

Serve with tea. Serves 4.

Scones

Ingredients

1 cup self-raising flour

1 teaspoon baking powder

Pinch of salt

¼ cup butter

1½ Tablespoons sugar

1 egg (beaten with enough milk to make ½ cup)

Handful of currants or raisins (optional)

Procedure

1. Sift flour, baking powder, and salt together in a mixing bowl.

2. Add the butter, and rub it into the flour mixture, using very clean fingertips. Add the sugar.

3. Add enough of the egg mixture to form a soft dough (not all the liquid will be needed).

4. Add the currants or raisins (optional).

5. Preheat over to 425°F.

6. Roll out the dough on a floured surface to ¾-inch thickness.

7. Use a 1½-inch round glass or pastry cutter to cut out the dough.

8. Place the scones on a greased baking sheet and brush the tops with some of the egg mixture.

9. Bake for 10 to 15 minutes.

Serve with fresh butter and jam at teatime.

4 FOOD FOR RELIGIOUS AND HOLIDAY CELEBRATIONS

On January 25 the Scots celebrate "Burns Night" for the birth of their favorite poet, Robert Burns (1759–96). The typical "Burns Night" meal includes a haggis, *cock-a-leekie* (chicken with leeks), *tatties n' neeps* (potatoes and turnips or rutabagas), roast beef, *tipsy laird* (a cream cake made with whiskey), and Dunlop cheese (resembles a soft cheddar). The Scots drink Scotch whiskey at celebrations.

Tatties n' Neeps

EPD Photos

Four potatoes and two turnips are needed to make Tatties n' Neeps

Ingredients

4 large potatoes, peeled and cut into quarters

1 Tablespoon chopped chives

2 turnips or rutabagas, peeled and cut into large chunks

1 Tablespoon butter

Salt and pepper, to taste

Procedure

1. Peel and quarter potatoes, place in a large saucepan, and cover with water.

2. Heat the water until it boils, and cook potatoes until they are soft (about 15 minutes).

3. Drain, return potatoes to the saucepan, and mash.

4. Place the peeled and cut-up turnips or rutabagas into a saucepan, cover with water, and heat the water to boiling.

5. Cook until the vegetable is soft, about 15 minutes.

6. Drain, return to pan and mash.

7. Combine the two mashed vegetables, add the butter and chives, and stir vigorously with a wooden spoon to combine.

Serves 8 to 12.

The British also celebrate Christmas, New Year's Day, Easter, and Guy Fawke's Day (November 5). A goose or turkey, mincemeat pies, wassail (spiced warm beverage), and plum pudding are served at Christmas, and crackers filled with candy and little toys are broken open by children.

Individual Mincemeat Pies

Ingredients

1 cup flour

Pinch of salt

½ cup butter (1 stick)

1 egg yolk (separate the egg and discard the white)

2 Tablespoons water

1 can mincemeat

Several Tablespoons of milk

Several Tablespoons of powdered sugar

Procedure

1. Preheat oven to 400°F.
2. Make pastry (may use commercial piecrust instead, and skip steps 2 through 6).
3. Measure flour and salt into a bowl.
4. Add butter, and rub the flour and butter together with very clean fingertips or a large fork until crumbly.
5. Mix egg yolk with water and add to flour mixture, and combine well.
6. Wrap the dough in wax paper and refrigerate for about 30 minutes, or for up to 24 hours.
7. Dust the counter or cutting board lightly with flour, and roll out dough, using a floured rolling pin.
8. Cut into rounds about 3 inches in diameter.
9. Fit a round of dough into each cup of a 12-cup muffin pan.
10. Gather up the dough scraps and cut out a second set of rounds for the top crusts. (These can be slightly smaller).
11. Put 1 tablespoon of canned mincemeat into each cup.
12. Dampen the edges of the pastry with a little water or milk, place the second round on the top, pinching the edges together to seal.
13. Using the tip of a sharp knife, make a small hole in the pastry top of each pie.
14. Using a pastry brush, brush the pastry with milk and dust with a little powdered sugar.
15. Bake for about 25 minutes, until light golden brown. Cool before serving.

Serves 12.

5 MEALTIME CUSTOMS

The British traditionally eat four meals a day, including breakfast, lunch, tea, and dinner. The traditional English breakfast is fairly large, with eggs, sausage, mushrooms, tomatoes, and fried bread. However, many English people, with schedules too busy to allow for a cooked breakfast, eat a wheat cereal similar to shredded wheat called *Wheatabix* with milk. Orange marmalade on toast is also popular. Tea with milk and sugar is the preferred beverage.

The Scots eat oatmeal for breakfast. Lunch and dinner can be interchanged, consisting of meat-and-potato dishes and small salads. Tea is taken around 4 P.M. with sandwiches, cakes, chocolate, or fruit. The biggest meal of the week, Sunday lunch, is served in the afternoon, and features roast beef, lamb, or pork; vegetables, often in a casserole or with sauce, such as Cauliflower Cheese; potatoes, and other side dishes. In casual conversation, the British use the term "pudding" in a general way to refer to dessert, even if the dessert being served is not actually pudding.

Wassail

Ingredients

1 gallon apple cider

1 large can pineapple juice (unsweetened)

¾ cup strong tea

1 Tablespoon whole cloves

1 Tablespoon whole allspice

2 sticks cinnamon

Cheesecloth

Procedure

1. Make a mug of tea, using 2 teabags.

2. Place the spices in a square of cheesecloth, and tie securely with clean kitchen string. (If cheesecloth is not available, spices may be added directly to the mixture and strained out before serving.)

3. Pour juices and tea into a large kettle, and place over low heat. Add cheesecloth bag filled with spices.

4. Simmer for at least one hour (up to 6 hours).

Serves up to 20 people.

Sunday Lunch Cauliflower Cheese

Ingredients

1 large head cauliflower

3 Tablespoons butter

3 Tablespoons flour

1 teaspoon prepared mustard (Dijon-style preferred)

2 cups milk

1½ to 2 cups grated cheddar cheese

Procedure

1. Cook cauliflower: Cut cauliflower into bite-sized flowerets, and place in a saucepan.

2. Add 2 cups of water (or less) to cover the bottom of the pan to about 1 inch. Cover the pot, and heat until the water boils.

3. Cook for about 10 minutes, until the cauliflower is tender but not soft.

4. Remove from heat, remove cauliflower from pot, and place it in a serving dish.

5. Cover with foil and keep warm.

6. Make sauce: Melt butter in a saucepan.

7. Stir in flour gradually, stirring constantly with a wooden spoon or wire whisk.

8. Lower heat and cook for about 5 minutes until the mixture thickens slightly.

9. Stir in milk slowly, stirring constantly. Heat until the mixture just begins to boil.

10. Lower heat, add mustard, and continue stirring and simmering the mixture for about 8 minutes.

11. Remove the pot from the heat, and stir in the grated cheese gradually.

12. Pour hot sauce over warm cauliflower, and serve immediately.

Serves 6 to 10.

EPD Photos

A special spoon designed to hold loose tea may be used when brewing an individual cup of tea. Most people in the UK would brew a full pot of tea at teatime.

Tea with Milk

Ingredients

Teabags of English tea, such as English Breakfast Tea or Earl Grey Tea

½ pint whole milk

Sugar cubes

Water

Procedure

1. Fill a teakettle with water. Heat the water to boiling.

2. Run hot water from the tap into the teapot to warm it.

3. Place teabags, one for each cup desired, into the pot.

4. (If the teabags have strings attached, wind the strings around the teapot handle to keep them from falling into the pot.) Carefully pour the boiling water over the teabags in the teapot.

5. Allow to steep for three minutes.

6. To serve, pour a small amount of milk into each teacup and pour in the tea..

7. Add one or two sugar cubes (or more), if desired. Stir until sugar is completely dissolved.

8. Sip tea and nibble on *bikkies* (biscuits, the English name for cookies).

6 POLITICS, ECONOMICS, AND NUTRITION

The UK depends on its farmers to grow good crops and raise healthy livestock. There is a law requiring all bulls be licensed by the government to help keep the cattle herds healthy and to guarantee that good breeding practices are observed. In the 1980s and 1990s, British livestock farmers struggled to combat diseases such as Mad Cow Disease (BSE—bovine spongiform encephalopathy) in cattle. After the first case was discovered in 1986, beef consumption in the UK dropped dramatically. Many countries also stopped buying beef raised in the UK, as a precaution against spread of the disease. At the beginning of the twenty-first century, an outbreak of "hoof and mouth disease" posed another serious threat against the livestock of the UK. Government agencies in the UK and elsewhere sought ways to combat and control these diseases, both of which could have devastating effects on the UK economy.

The children in the UK receive adequate nutrition generally, and there are few incidents of severe malnutrition in the country.

7 FURTHER STUDY

Books

Classic British: Authentic and Delicious Regional Dishes. New York: Smithmark, 1996.

Curran, William. *The Best of Robert Burns*. Edinburgh: The Book Guild, Ltd., 1999.

Denny, Roz. *A Taste of Britain*. New York: Thomson Learning, 1994.

Macdonald of Macdonald, Lady. *Lady Macdonald's Scotland: The Best of Scottish Food and Drink*. Boston: Little, Brown, 1990.

Passmore, Marian. *Fit For Kings: A Book of Recipes*. Bruton, England: King's School, 1994.

Paterson, Jennifer and Clarissa Dickson Wright. *Cooking with the Two Fat Ladies*. New York: Clarkson Potter, 1998.

Web Sites

BBC Online—Food. [Online] Available http://www.bbc.co.uk/food/recipes/ (accessed August 7, 2001).

Epicurious Food. [Online] Available http://food.epicurious.com (accessed January 15, 2001).

A Taste of Scotland. [Online] Available http://www.taste-of-scotland.com/ (accessed August 7, 2001).

A Taste of UK. [Online] Available http://web.ukonline.co.uk/tuk/index.html (accessed August 7, 2001).

United States
African Americans

Recipes

Collard Greens 78
Hush Puppies 78
Molasses Water 79
Sweet Potato Pie 80
Red Beans and Rice 80
Potato Salad... 81
Baked Macaroni and Cheese 82
Kwanzaa Brownies 83
Fried Apples 83
Tomato, Cucumber, and Onion Salad 84
Fried Bologna.. 84

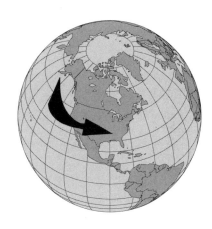

1 GEOGRAPHIC SETTING AND ENVIRONMENT

There are African Americans living in all fifty of the United States. The ten states with the largest populations of African Americans are New York, California, Texas, Florida, Georgia, Illinois, North Carolina, Louisiana, Michigan, and Maryland. Although most African Americans live in cities, it is impossible to generalize about how and where they live. African American families, like European American families, make their homes in every type of community—urban, suburban, and rural.

2 HISTORY AND FOOD

In the 1600s, African slaves were brought to the United States, along with their food and styles of cooking. They brought okra, sesame seeds, peanuts, black-eyed peas, and rice. Using these foods, they introduced new recipes to the existing American dishes.

The slaves were also given only a small portion of food each week, so they learned to make dishes with the foods they had, such as pork, cornmeal, and vegetables. Several of these dishes such as cornbread and grits, which are dried and boiled grains from corn, are still made as of the twenty-first century. African Americans also continue to use molasses as a sweetener in their dishes and in drinks, such as iced tea.

Beginning in the 1960s, interest in African American culture and heritage has grown. Many African Americans celebrate the cultural holiday Kwanzaa, don colorful dress reflecting their African heritage, and promote a unique ethnic style of cooking, sometimes called "soul food." During the 1960s and 1970s African American business people established "soul food" restaurants all over the country, where Americans of all ethnic origins could enjoy spicy barbecued meats and poultry, tasty greens, cornbread, and other home-style dishes.

Collard Greens

Ingredients

4-6 bunches collard, cleaned

5 slices of bacon

7 cups of water

1 smoked ham hock

1 large chopped onion

1 teaspoon black pepper (or more, to taste)

1 teaspoon salt

1 bunch of green onions, chopped (optional)

Hot sauce (optional)

Procedure

1. Rinse collard greens under running water to remove all grit. Lay 3 or 4 collard green leaves on top of each other, roll them up, and then cut the roll into 1-inch slices.
2. Line the bottom of a large stock pot with the bacon.
3. Cook on medium heat until the bacon is crispy. Do not drain the bacon grease.
4. Add the water to the stock pot and bring to a boil.
5. Add one-half of the chopped onion, the ham hock, and the salt and pepper.
6. Let mixture boil for about 1 hour to thoroughly cook the ham hock.
7. Add the chopped collard greens and the remaining half of the chopped onion. If there are too many greens to fit into the pot, add them in batches. As the greens wilt, add more.

8. Simmer for about 30 minutes, stirring frequently to distribute the ham flavors.
9. Serve with chopped green onions and hot sauce, if desired.

Serves 20 to 12.

Fish has always been an important staple in the African American diet. Fried catfish finds its way to the table often, served with such standard side dishes as greens, macaroni and cheese, and hush puppies. Hush puppies are derived from cornbread. It is said that hush puppies originated during the Civil War (1861–1865) when soldiers would throw fried cornbread to their dogs—to "hush the puppies."

Hush Puppies

Ingredients

2 cups corn meal

1 teaspoon baking powder

½ teaspoon baking soda

1 cup flour

1 teaspoon salt

2 eggs

1 cup buttermilk (or regular milk)

1 teaspoon pepper (or more, to taste)

Oil or fat (melted shortening or bacon grease) for frying

Procedure

1. Combine corn meal, baking powder, flour, and salt, and stir to combine. Make a well in the center.
2. Add eggs and milk to make a stiff dough.

3. Heat oil about 1-inch deep in a large skillet. (If using fat, melt about 1 cup in a large skillet.)

4. Shape dough into 1-inch balls and drop into hot oil. Fry until golden brown.

5. Drain on paper towels, and serve warm.

Serves 8 to 12.

Molasses Water

Ingredients

1 quart water

½ cup dark molasses

¼ cup lemon juice

5 sprigs fresh mint

Procedure

1. Mix water, molasses, and lemon juice together in a pitcher, stirring well to make sure molasses is thoroughly mixed in.

2. Refrigerate for at least 2 hours, or until well chilled.

3. When ready to serve, press the mint against the side of another pitcher with the back of a spoon.

4. Then add ice and pour in the molasses water.

5. Serve chilled in glasses.

Serves 4 to 6.

EPD Photos

Molasses Water combines thick, sweet molasses, shown here being poured into a measuring cup, with lemon juice and water. Molasses Water is similar to lemonade, sweetened with the distinctive molasses flavor.

3 FOODS OF THE AFRICAN AMERICANS

Sweet potatoes and yams have been a large part of African Americans' diet since African slaves brought them to the United States in the 1600s. Eating cornbread and grits (dried and boiled grains from corn) are also traditions, as well as sweetening dishes and drinks with molasses.

Other traditional African American foods and dishes include barbecued meat, sweet cornbread, fried chicken, and of course, desserts. A delicacy that has been a specialty of African Americans especially in the South is chitterlings (nicknamed "chitlins") made from pig stomach and intestines that have been boiled and then deep-fried.

The states with the largest populations of African Americans are New York, California, Texas, Florida, Georgia, Illinois, North Carolina, Louisiana, Michigan, and Maryland.

2. Boil them in their skin until easily pierced with a fork (about 20 minutes). Allow potatoes to cool slightly. Peel and mash until smooth.

3. Preheat oven to 350°F.

4. Add butter, sugar, flour, milk, eggs, and nutmeg. Mix well.

5. Add lemon extract and stir until smooth.

6. Put ingredients in pie shell and bake for 30 minutes.

Hoppin' John, a popular dish of rice and black-eyed peas, is traditionally eaten on New Year's Day to bring good luck throughout the rest of the year. Red beans and rice is another traditional dish, especially in the southern states.

Sweet Potato Pie

Ingredients

1 pie shell (9-inch), unbaked

3 medium sweet potatoes

2 eggs

½ cup milk

1½ sticks butter

1¼ cups sugar

1 Tablespoon flour

1½ Tablespoons lemon extract

2 Tablespoons nutmeg

Procedure

1. Wash and scrub sweet potatoes. Place them in a large saucepan and add water to cover them.

Red Beans and Rice

Ingredients

2 cups red kidney beans

6 cups cold water

1 large onion, chopped

1 green pepper, chopped

½ pound ham, cubed (½ pound smoked sausage, sliced, may be substituted)

2 cloves garlic, chopped

1 bay leaf

½ teaspoon salt

½ teaspoon pepper

Cooked rice (prepare rice according to package directions)

Procedure

1. Wash beans in cold water. Drain and put in covered pot with the cold water.

2. Add ham or sausage to pot. Heat to boiling.

3. Add chopped onions, garlic, green pepper, bay leaf, and salt and pepper. Lower heat. Simmer for 2 hours, stirring occasionally until beans are soft.

4. Mash some of the beans against side of the pot to make a creamy sauce.

5. Serve with cooked rice.

Serves 4 to 6.

In the early 1900s, African Americans began to eat more dairy foods, such as eggs, milk, and butter. They also planted wheat and corn and grew different kinds of fruits and vegetables. With these ingredients, they began to prepare new dishes, most of which are still eaten.

In the southern U.S. regions, African cooking became a part of everyday meals. In New Orleans, Creole cooking developed from a mix of African, French, English, and Spanish cooking. Creole dishes such as *jambalaya* and *gumbo* contained chicken or seafood and were mixed with African foods such as rice, okra, or red peppers. These dishes are still popular.

4 FOOD FOR RELIGIOUS AND HOLIDAY CELEBRATIONS

African Americans enjoy inviting family and friends over to visit during the holidays. With busy schedules like families everywhere, African Americans often plan family visits months in advance.

Many African Americans hold annual family reunions, often on July 4, Independence Day. Relatives come from all over the United States, often meeting at a different family's home each year. Large, extended families may even hold their reunions at a park where large picnic areas can accommodate the dozens of families in attendance.

Preparations begin one or two days before July 4. Barbecued meat, especially chicken and pork spareribs, is the main dish. Individual families contribute a variety of homemade pies and cakes; sweetened iced tea and lemonade are favorite beverages. Side dishes include potato salad, greens, yams, or candied sweet potatoes, and homemade butter pound cake.

Potato Salad

Ingredients

2½ pounds white potatoes

2 large celery sticks, finely chopped

1 small onion, minced

1 cup mayonnaise

½ cup sweet pickle relish

Salt and pepper, to taste

Procedure

1. Wash the potatoes and place them in a heavy saucepan with enough water to cover them. Bring to a boil over high heat.

2. Lower heat and cook potatoes until tender, about 20 minutes. Drain potatoes and allow to cool. Peel and cut potatoes into ½-inch pieces.

3. Place the chopped celery, potatoes, and onions in a large bowl.

4. Add sweet pickle relish, and gradually stir in mayonnaise until the mixture is well coated. (The whole cup of mayonnaise may not be needed.)

5. Add salt and pepper. Stir gently to combine.

6. Cover with plastic wrap and refrigerate overnight. Serve chilled.

Makes 6 servings.

For breakfast on Christmas Day, African Americans often eat grits, eggs, sausage or ham, and freshly baked biscuits with butter and syrup. For Christmas dinner a baked ham, baked chicken with cornbread stuffing, green vegetables, cornbread, candied yams, rice, and baked macaroni and cheese are staples. Apple pie and fruitcake are traditionally served for dessert.

Baked Macaroni and Cheese

Ingredients

6 cups water

1 Tablespoon salt

2 cups elbow macaroni

¼ cup, plus 2 Tablespoons butter, softened

2 eggs

2 cups evaporated milk

1 teaspoon salt

1 pound sharp cheddar cheese, grated and mixed with ½ cup grated American cheese

½ teaspoon paprika

Procedure

1. Preheat oven to 350°F.
2. Place the water and Tablespoon of salt in heavy saucepan and bring to a boil.
3. Slowly stir in the macaroni.
4. Boil for 12 minutes, stirring continuously.
5. Macaroni is done when firm, but tender.
6. Strain the macaroni and rinse with a little cold water.
7. Drain.

8. Mix the macaroni with the butter and set aside.

9. In a small bowl, beat the eggs until light yellow.

10. Add milk and teaspoon of salt.

11. In a large buttered casserole dish, put a layer of the macaroni, then add a layer of cheese.

12. Continue to do this, ending with a cheese layer on top.

13. Pour the egg mixture slowly and evenly over the top.

14. Sprinkle with paprika.

15. Bake for 30 to 40 minutes, until the top is bubbly and golden brown.

Serves 4.

Many African Americans celebrate Kwanzaa, a non-religious cultural holiday, from December 26 through January 1. During the seven days of Kwanzaa (which is derived from a Swahili word for "first fruits of the harvest"), African Americans celebrate their heritage and take pride in their African traditions. The Kwanzaa celebration was originated by Dr. Maulana Karenga, an activist and scholar, who has been involved in the development of Black Studies and African American art and student movements in the United States.

Each of the seven days of Kwanzaa represents a different principle, such as unity, purpose, and creativity. African American families celebrate this community–building holiday in their own way, with music, get-togethers, and feasting.

Kwanzaa Brownies

Ingredients for Brownies

1½ sticks butter or margarine, melted

1½ cups sugar

1½ teaspoons vanilla extract

3 eggs

¾ cup flour

½ cup cocoa

½ teaspoon baking powder

¼ teaspoon salt

⅔ cup chopped pecans (optional)

Assorted fresh fruit, sliced or cut up

Ingredients for Chocolate Cream

1 package (8 ounces) cream cheese, softened

½ cup sugar

3 Tablespoons cocoa

1 Tablespoon milk

1½ teaspoons vanilla extract

Procedure

1. Heat oven to 350°F.
2. Grease 13x9x2-inch round pizza pan.
3. Combine butter, sugar, and vanilla in large bowl.
4. Add eggs and beat with spoon.
5. Combine flour, cocoa, baking powder and salt.
6. Gradually stir into egg mixture until blended.
7. Stir in pecans (if using them).
8. Spread batter into prepared pan.
9. Bake about 20 minutes, or until top springs back when touched lightly in center.
10. Cool completely.
11. Prepare chocolate cream by beating all ingredients in a bowl until smooth.
12. Spread chocolate cream over top of brownies.
13. Refrigerate for about 30 minutes.
14. Place fruit on each slice before serving.

Makes about 2 dozen.

5 MEALTIME CUSTOMS

It is tradition for African Americans to eat a lot of food for breakfast. They may eat chicken, waffles, grits (dried and boiled grains from corn), ham, corn fritters, and bacon. Traditionally in the South, a Sunday breakfast includes fried apples, grits, and pork sausage. Salad, including leftover salad, may also be eaten as a breakfast dish.

Bologna is a popular luncheon meat for many African Americans. It is sometimes eaten at breakfast instead of bacon, and it is eaten in sandwiches for lunch.

Many African Americans enjoy inviting family and friends home for a barbecue or a fish fry. Popular snacks are roasted peanuts, pecans, and limbo cakes (deep-fried plantains, or bananas). Soft drinks, iced tea, and lemonade are popular beverages.

Fried Apples

Ingredients

6 Macintosh apples

2 Tablespoons oil

1 Tablespoon water

2 teaspoons sugar

½ teaspoon ground cinnamon

EPD Photos

Fried Apples are made from thinly sliced apples. To prepare an apple for slicing, first cut it in half, and then into quarters. Cut away the core and seeds, and then cut each quarter into thin slices.

Procedure

1. Core the apples and slice them, leaving the skin on.
2. Heat oil in heavy skillet.
3. When oil is hot, add the apples and water.
4. Cover and lower the heat.
5. Cook until the apples are soft, about 10 minutes.
6. Sprinkle them with mixture of sugar and cinnamon, and serve warm.

Serves 2 to 4.

3 Tablespoons olive oil

1 Tablespoon cider vinegar

Salt and pepper, to taste

Procedure

1. Place tomatoes, cucumber, and onions in a large salad bowl.
2. In a separate bowl, mix together the remaining ingredients to make a dressing.
3. Pour dressing over salad and serve.

Serves 4.

Tomato, Cucumber, and Onion Salad

Ingredients

2 tomatoes, sliced

1 cucumber, peeled and seeded, coarsely chopped

1 medium onion, thinly sliced

Fried Bologna

Ingredients

2 Tablespoons oil

1 pound pork bologna, sliced medium-thick

Procedure

1. Heat the oil in a heavy skillet.

2. Peel casing (thin outer skin) off bologna and make a small cut from the outside to the center of each piece so slices do not puff up too much.

3. Place bologna slices in skillet and cook, turning once, until they are lightly browned.

Many African Americans prepare their food by frying it, barbecuing, and serving dishes with gravy and sauces. It is also common to bake cakes and pies from "scratch" (not from a commercial mix). These traditions have been passed down through many generations. Contemporary African Americans, like many Americans of all ethnicities, have become more health conscious, and have added more nutritional foods, such as fruits and vegetables, to their daily diets. Many African Americans have changed to healthier, lighter cooking styles for everyday cooking, reserving the traditional dishes (many of which are higher in fat) for holidays and special occasions.

6 POLITICS, ECONOMICS, AND NUTRITION

According to estimates in 2000 there were 8.7 million African American families in the United States, about 44 percent of which were headed by single women. African American couples tend to have larger families—just over 20 percent of African American married couple families have five or more members, compared to 12 percent of white (not of Hispanic origin) married-couple families. About half of all African American married-couple families had incomes of $50,000 or more (compared to 60 percent of white married-couple families). In 1999 about 24 percent of African Americans were living in poverty, an all-time record low in the United States.

According to the U.S. Department of Agriculture (USDA) Center for Nutrition Policy and Promotion's Healthy Eating Index, most Americans eat a diet that needs improvement. Only five percent of African Americans (compared to 11 percent of whites) have a diet categorized as "good" (based on ten measures including total consumption of fat, cholesterol, and sodium), and 28 percent of African Americans (compared to 16 percent of whites) have a diet categorized as "poor."

7 FURTHER STUDY

Broussard, Antoinette. *African-American Holiday Traditions: Celebrating with Passion, Style, and Grace.* New York: Citadel Press, 2000.

Copage, Eric V. *Kwanzaa: An African-American Celebration of Culture and Cooking.* New York: William Morrow and Company, Inc., 1991.

Harris, Jessica B. *A Kwanzaa Keepsake: celebrating the holiday with new traditions and feasts.* New York: Simon & Schuster, 1995.

Harris, Jessica B. *The Welcome Table: African-American Heritage Cooking.* New York: Fireside, 1995.

Mack-Williams, Kibibi. *Food and Our History.* Vero Beach, FL: Rourke Press, Inc., 1995.

Medearis, Angela Shelf. *The African-American Kitchen: Cooking from our Heritage.* New York: Penguin Group, 1994.

Web Sites

The Chitterling Site. [Online] Available http://www.chitterlings.com (accessed August 24, 2001).

The Holiday Spot. [Online] Available http://

www.theholidayspot.com/kwanzaa/ kwanzaa_recipes.htm (accessed April 10, 2001).

Kwanzaa for Kids. [Online] Available http:// kwanzaa4kids.homestead.com/kwanzaabrown- ies~main.html (accessed April 18, 2001).

Mim's Cyber Kitchen Presents Kwanzaa. [Online] Available http://www.cyber-kitchen.com/ holidays/kwanzaa/recipes.htm (accessed August 24, 2001).

Morris, DeNita S.B. "From Fish Fry to Stir Fry: The African American Eating Experience. [Online] Available http://www.bet.com/FOOD/ 0,1821,C-9-68-188214,00.html (accessed July 23, 2001).

United States
Amish and Pennsylvania Dutch

Recipes

Pork Chops with Sauerkraut and Potatoes 89
Cream of Cabbage Soup 89
Shoofly Pie 89
Spicy Oven-Fried Chicken 91
Peachy Baked Apples 91
Sugar Cookies 92
Snow Ice Cream 93
Peanut Butter and Molasses Spread 93
Strawberry Jam 93
Old-Fashioned Spicy Lemonade 93

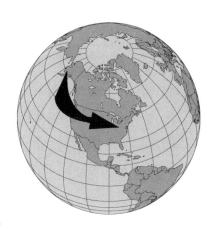

1 GEOGRAPHIC SETTING AND ENVIRONMENT

The Amish make their homes in rural areas in twenty-two U.S. states and Ontario, Canada. The states with the largest Amish populations are Ohio and Pennsylvania. The oldest Amish community (and the one most familiar to non-Amish) is made up of about 16,000 people living around Lancaster, Pennsylvania. The Amish living there are primarily Pennsylvania Dutch (people of German descent), but not all Pennsylvania Dutch are Amish.

Deutsch is the German-language word for German, so the name Pennsylvania Dutch comes from "Pennsylvania Deutsch." The food of Pennsylvania Dutch and Amish are similar, due to their common German heritage.

2 HISTORY AND FOOD

The Amish have their roots in a Swiss religious sect that was part of the Protestant Reformation in the 1500s. It was called the Anabaptist movement, and its members lived simply, rejecting material wealth. At the end of the 1600s, a small group led by Joseph Ammann broke away from the Anabaptists. They migrated to France and later were called the Amish in honor of their founder.

In the early part of the 1700s, Amish families began arriving in North America. They founded large settlements in Pennsylvania. Gradually Amish settlements spread to Ohio, Indiana, and other states.

When they came to the New World (North America), the Amish brought with them the cooking traditions of their homelands in Switzerland and the Rhine River area of Germany. This heritage can be seen in the popularity of such traditional German foods as sauerkraut, and even in the Amish name for the evening meal, "Nachtesse" ("night eating"). However, Amish cooking was also influenced by life in America. Many Amish settled in areas where wheat, rye, corn, and barley flourished. Home-baked breads, desserts, and other grain-based foods came to play an important role in the Amish diet. Products of the rural areas where they settled, including eggs and other dairy products, poultry, fresh vegetables, and apples, also became Amish staples.

The Amish have continued to live simply, without modern conveniences such as cars and electricity. They also continue to prepare the simple, hearty dishes they learned from their ancestors.

3 FOODS OF THE AMISH

The Amish generally eat foods produced in their own gardens or on their farms. As a rule, they do not eat processed, store-bought foods, such as corn flakes or potato chips. Homegrown fruits and vegetables, eaten fresh, canned, or frozen, play a very important part in the Amish diet. Vegetables often found in Amish meals include peas, corn, zucchini, beets, beans, rhubarb, and many others. Cabbage and potatoes are especially important. Sauerkraut—a type of pickled cabbage—appears at many Amish meals

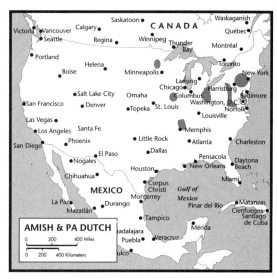

The states with the largest populations of Amish are Ohio and Pennsylvania.

and is used in everything from soups to cakes. Grain products like bread, cornmeal, and oatmeal are also staples of the Amish diet. Scrapple, a popular breakfast food, is made with fried cornmeal mush prepared with sausage and liverwurst.

Amish main meals are usually built around hearty meat dishes, such as pork chops, ham, roast beef, or meatloaf. Dairy products, especially eggs and cheese, are also important dietary staples. The Amish are known throughout the country for the quality of the cheese they produce and market. Most Amish families keep at least a few chickens so they can eat freshly laid eggs all year round. In the wintertime, hearty soups are eaten regularly.

Amish women bake a great deal, preparing breads, cookies, pies, and cakes. The best-known Amish desserts include shoofly pie, sugar cookies, and schnitz pie, which is made with dried apples.

Favorite beverages include coffee, tea, milk, and lemonade.

Pork Chops with Sauerkraut and Potatoes

Ingredients

2 medium onions, coarsely chopped

6 pork chops

Black pepper, to taste

6 small potatoes, peeled

2 cans (15-ounce each) sauerkraut, well drained

2 cans (15-ounce each) chicken broth

Optional: several whole cloves

Procedure

1. Preheat oven to 300°F.

2. In a saucepan, boil the peeled potatoes in salted water 6 to 8 minutes.

3. Set aside.

4. Grease a roasting pot and sprinkle half the onions in the bottom of the pan.

5. Place the pork chops on top; sprinkle with the pepper.

6. Arrange the potatoes around the chops.

7. Top with the sauerkraut, add the stock.

8. Drop in the whole cloves, if used.

9. Cover and bake for 2 hours.

10. Serve hot, adding some of the cooking juices to each serving.

Serves 6.

Cream of Cabbage Soup

Ingredients

½ pound bacon, chopped

2½ pounds cabbage, shredded

5 cans (16-ounce each) chicken broth

1 cup half-and-half

2 teaspoons salt

½ teaspoon pepper

Swiss cheese, grated

1 onion

Procedure

1. In a large pot, fry the bacon until crisp over medium to high heat; remove and set aside.

2. Add the cabbage and onion, reduce the heat to medium and sauté, stirring occasionally, for 10 minutes or until the cabbage is limp.

3. Add the chicken broth and simmer until the cabbage and onion are tender, about 10 to 15 minutes.

4. Stir in the half-and-half. Season with salt and pepper.

5. Serve garnished with the bacon and cheese.

Serves 8 to 10.

Shoofly Pie

Ingredients

Frozen 9-inch pie crust, unbaked

1 cup flour

⅔ cup brown sugar, packed

1 Tablespoon cold butter

¼ teaspoon salt

Molasses is the main ingredient in the filling for Shoofly Pie. The pie is topped with a sprinkling of reserved flour mixture.

1 egg

1 cup molasses

¾ cup cold water

¼ cup hot water

1 Tablespoon baking soda

Procedure

1. Preheat oven to 350°F.

2. In a mixing bowl, combine the flour, brown sugar, butter, and salt.

3. Remove ½ cup of the mixture and set aside.

4. In a small bowl, beat the egg. Add the molasses and cold water. Stir and set aside.

5. In another small bowl, mix the hot water with the baking soda and blend into the molasses mixture.

6. Add to the flour mixture and mix well Pour into the pie shell and top with the reserved crumbs.

7. Bake for 35 minutes.

8. The pie filling will appear jelly-like but will firm up as it cools.

9. Transfer to a rack to cool completely before cutting.

4 FOOD FOR RELIGIOUS AND HOLIDAY CELEBRATIONS

Instead of going to church, the Amish hold religious services in different people's homes every Sunday morning. After the service, there is a large Sunday lunch. A typical menu for this meal is homemade bread with butter, jelly or peanut butter; cheese cubes or a type of homemade cottage cheese called *schmierkase*; pickles; an apple pie called *schnitz* pie; and coffee or tea.

The Amish are known for their strong family ties. Large family reunions are important occasions that include a bountiful Amish meal, with everyone bringing something. Like church services, Amish weddings are held at home. After the ceremony, a big festive meal is served on long tables set up all over the first floor of the house.

Special rectangular doughnuts called *Fassnacht Kuche* are baked on Shrove Tuesday, a day before the beginning of Lent. Mashed potatoes are used in the batter, making the doughnuts moist and tender. They are served with black coffee.

Wedding Dinner Menu

Roast chicken

Mashed potatoes and gravy

Cole slaw

Creamed celery

Applesauce

Bread and butter

Canned peaches

Canned pears

Spiced cantaloupe

Doughnuts

Custard pies

Fruit pies

Layer cakes

Sugar cookies

Potato chips

Coffee

Spicy Oven-Fried Chicken

Ingredients

⅓ cup vegetable oil

⅓ cup butter

½ cup flour

½ cup bread crumbs

½ cup yellow cornmeal

1½ teaspoons garlic salt

1½ teaspoons paprika

1 teaspoon salt

1 teaspoon black pepper

4 pounds of chicken pieces, or about 14 pieces (legs, thighs, breast halves, wings)

Procedure

1. Preheat oven to 375°F.

2. Put the oil and butter in a shallow pan and place it in the oven until it melts. Set aside.

3. In a large paper bag, combine the flour, bread crumbs, cornmeal, and seasonings.

4. Roll the chicken pieces, 3 at a time, in the melted oil-and-butter mixture, then drop them in the sack and shake to coat.

5. Remove and place the coated chicken in the pan, skin side down.

6. Bake for 45 minutes, flip the pieces and bake 5 to 10 minutes longer, or until the top crust begins to bubble.

7. Serve hot or cold.

Serves 7 to 14.

Peachy Baked Apples

Ingredients

6 small apples, halved and cored, but not peeled

1 cup brown sugar, packed

¼ cup peach preserves

¼ teaspoon cinnamon

¼ teaspoon nutmeg

¼ cup apple juice

Procedure

1. Preheat oven to 350°F.

2. Place the apple halves cut side up in a 9x13-inch baking pan.

3. In a small mixing bowl, combine the brown sugar, preserves, cinnamon, nutmeg, juice, and butter.

4. Sprinkle over the apples and cover the pan tightly with foil.

5. Bake for 30 minutes, or until the apples are just tender.

6. Remove from oven and spoon the juice from the bottom of the pan over the apples.

7. Return to the oven and bake, uncovered, for 5 more minutes.

8. Serve warm or cold.

Serves 6.

Sugar Cookies

Ingredients

¾ cup sugar

½ cup margarine or shortening, at room temperature

1 egg

½ cup buttermilk or sour cream

1½ cups plus 3 Tablespoons flour

1 teaspoon baking powder

½ teaspoon baking soda

½ teaspoon vanilla

Raisins

Sugar

Procedure

1. Preheat oven to 375ºF.

2. Cut the margarine or shortening into chunks and place it in a mixing bowl.

3. Add the ¾ cup of sugar. Blend well.

4. Add the egg and beat the mixture again until smooth.

5. Add the buttermilk or sour cream, flour, baking powder, baking soda, and vanilla.

6. Stir with wooden spoon until creamy.

7. Grease two cookie sheets.

8. Drop the batter by teaspoonfuls onto the cookie sheets, keeping the cookies about two inches apart.

9. Gently place a raisin in the center of each cookie. Sprinkle lightly with sugar.

10. Bake for 8–10 minutes until the cookies are light brown.

11. Transfer cookies to a rack to cool.

Makes about 2 dozen cookies.

5 MEALTIME CUSTOMS

The Amish eat a hearty breakfast. For the families of Amish farmers, the day starts early, with breakfast served around 6:00 A.M. A typical Amish breakfast might include eggs, cornmeal mush, pancakes, and homemade canned fruit.

Amish schools do not have cafeterias, so all of the students take packed lunches to school. Lunches usually include sandwiches made with bologna or leftover meat from dinner, such as beef roast or meat loaf. Peanut butter and jelly, pizza, or other leftovers may also be eaten. In the winter, homemade soups are taken to school in Thermos bottles, which keep them hot. Sometimes a casserole is taken to school in a wide-mouthed Thermos bottle. Lunches also include fresh fruit and home-baked cookies, cake, or pie for dessert. One popular dessert is an Amish specialty called Whoopie Pie, a cookie sandwich with icing in the middle.

On evenings and weekends, when the whole family is home, the main meal of the day (dinner, or "Middaagesse") is eaten at midday. On these days, a light supper is eaten in the evening.

At the end of the school year, Amish children have a picnic. Their parents take casseroles, salads, cakes, candies, and puddings to school. Often a tablecloth is thrown over the bottom of a big farm wagon. The food is spread out on top and everyone eats heartily.

Popular Amish snacks include soft pretzels, peanut butter and molasses spread on bread or crackers, and ice cream made from freshly fallen snow.

Snow Ice Cream

Ingredients

2½ quarts clean snow

½ cup milk

1 teaspoon vanilla

1 cup sugar

Procedure

1. When there are several inches of freshly fallen snow on the ground, scoop up just the top layer and pile it into a one-quart saucepan.

2. Empty the contents into a mixing bowl; repeat, filling the saucepan a total of 2½ times.

3. Gently mix in the milk, vanilla, and sugar until it has been completely combined with the snow.

4. Serve immediately.

Peanut Butter and Molasses Spread

Ingredients

½ cup smooth peanut butter

¼ cup molasses

Procedure

1. Add ingredients into a mixing bowl.

2. Stir well and spread on bread or crackers.

Strawberry Jam

1 quart fresh strawberries, washed

4 cups sugar

2 teaspoons lemon juice

Procedure

1. Remove the stems and leaves from the tops of the strawberries. Cut berries into halves or quarters.

2. Place in a three-quart saucepan. Stir in two cups of sugar, mixing it well with the berries.

3. Place saucepan on stove and turn heat to medium. Heat until the mixture boils.

4. Boil gently for 5 minutes, stirring frequently.

5. Remove from heat.

6. Stir in the remaining two cups of sugar and the lemon juice.

7. Place the pan back on the stove and cook the berries over medium heat for 10 more minutes, stirring frequently.

8. Remove the pot from the stove. Leave the jam in the saucepan, covered but unrefrigerated, for 24 hours.

9. Spoon it into clean jelly jars and refrigerate until you are ready to use it.

Old-Fashioned Spicy Lemonade

Ingredients

3 Tablespoons grated lemon zest (yellow part of the lemon peel)

4 cups sugar

4 cups water

2 cinnamon sticks

¾ cup lemon juice

Lemon slices

Procedure

1. In a saucepan, combine the lemon zest, sugar, water, and cinnamon sticks.

2. Bring the mixture to a boil over medium heat.

3. Reduce heat and simmer uncovered, for 5 minutes.

4. Remove from heat and cool.

5. Strain the mixture through a fine mesh strainer or cheesecloth.

6. Add the lemon juice to the sugar syrup.

7. Transfer to a large jar or pitcher and refrigerate until ready to serve.

8. To serve the lemonade, fill a tall glass with ice. Measure ¼ cup (4 Tablespoons) of the prepared mixture into the glass, add 1 cup of cold water, and stir.

9. Garnish with lemon slices.

6 POLITICS, ECONOMICS, AND NUTRITION

Amish families generally receive adequate nutrition from their diets, although some nutritionists report that their diet may be slightly too high in sugar and carbohydrates. Because Amish rarely marry non–Amish, they have experienced a higher incidence of birth defects caused by genetics. (In simple terms, some types of birth defects are more common when the mother and father have similar genetic make-up.)

To try to minimize these birth defects, Amish families have learned more than the average American families about genetics. Also, because they have not often married outside their own cultural group, medical researchers have invited Amish people to participate in research studies involving genetics and genetically transmitted diseases, such as diabetes.

7 FURTHER STUDY

Books

Adams, Marcia. *New Recipes from Quilt Country.* New York, NY: Clarkson Potter, 1997.

Good, Phyllis, and Kate Good Pellman. *Amish Cooking for Kids.* Intercourse, PA: Good Books, 1999.

Periodicals

The Budget. P.O. Box 249, Sugarcreek, OH 44681. (330) 852-4634. Amish newspaper.

Holmes County Traveler. P.O. Box 358. Millersburg, OH 44654. (330) 674-2300. Bimonthly magazine about Holmes County, Ohio. [Online] Available http://www.gpubs.com/traveler/ (accessed July 31, 2001).

Web Sites

Amish Country Foods. [Online] Available http://www.amishfoods.com (accessed April 16, 2001).

Amish Net. [Online] Available http://amish.net/ (accessed July 31, 2001).

United States
Great Lakes Region

Recipes

Ojibwa Wild Rice..96
Fish Boil 97
Dutch Pancakes...98
German Potato Salad 98
Macaroni and Cheese.......................................99
Hummus...99
Buffalo Chicken Wings 100
Springerle (German Christmas Cookies) 101
Apple Sauerkraut...101
Potato Lefse 102
Swedish Meatballs...102
Cornish Pasty 103

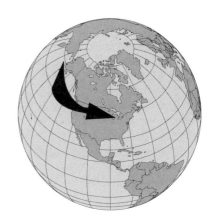

1 GEOGRAPHIC SETTING AND ENVIRONMENT

The Great Lakes region of the United States includes the states of Wisconsin, Michigan, Indiana, Ohio, Illinois, Pennsylvania, and New York. The region enjoys four distinct seasons. Although the climate is considered temperate, temperatures in the summer can exceed 100°F and can drop to –10°F in the winter. There is rich farm land, and farmers' markets offer abundant produce and fruit in the late summer and early fall across the region.

The region is also home to much manufacturing activity. Industrial pollution threatened the health of the Great Lakes, especially Lake Erie (the smallest Great Lake), until the 1960s, when a growing awareness of environmental concerns led to increased government regulation. Acid-rain, believed to be caused by air pollution gener-ated by the coal-fired utility plants in the region, is also a concern. Increased acidity in the lakes creates unhealthy conditions for fish and other living things in the ecosystem of the region.

2 HISTORY AND FOOD

Woodlands American Indian tribes, including the Iroquois, Ashinabe (made up of Ojibwa, Potowatomi, and Ottawa tribes), Huron, Fox, and Sioux, among others initially populated the Great Lakes region of North America. These American Indians gathered wild rice, berries, and maple sap, hunted deer and other game. They also fished and grew crops, such as corn, squash, and beans (known as the Three Sisters). In the early 1600s, French fur traders entered the region, and British settlers and American colonists began to move in during the 1700s. A series of conflicts including the

GREAT LAKES REGION

French and Indian War (1754–1763), the Revolutionary War (1775–1783), and the War of 1812 resulted in the British and French controlling the northern side of the Great Lakes (what is now Canada), and the United States controlling the south. The American Indians who remained were settled on reservations.

During the 1800s and 1900s, waves of immigration to the Great Lakes area came from Germany, Scandinavia, Holland, and Poland. Most were farmers who were attracted by the cheap, fertile land. The Homestead Act of 1862 offered free acreage to anyone who agreed to farm it for a certain number of years. The close-knit, family-based communities that developed retained their ethnic character for generations, cooking their traditional foods adapted to local ingredients. The population of the Great Lakes region continues to be largely German, Scandinavian, Dutch, and Polish. A number of miners originally from Cornwall,

England, also migrated to the area. The Detroit-Dearborn metropolitan area in Michigan now boasts the largest Arab American population in the United States—the city of Detroit being the prinicpal port of entry in the United States for Arab immigrants. The Arab Americans in Michigan have contributed some foods of the Middle East, such as hummus, to the "menu" of the Great Lakes region.

Ojibwa Wild Rice

Ingredients

1 cup wild rice

2½ cups water

1½ teaspoons salt

4 strips bacon cut into small pieces

6 eggs

¼ teaspoon pepper

2 Tablespoons chives, minced

⅓ cup bacon drippings

Melted butter

Procedure

1. Place the wild rice, water, and 1 teaspoon of the salt in a saucepan and bring to a boil over medium heat.

2. Reduce the heat to low and simmer, uncovered, until all the water is absorbed.

3. Meanwhile, brown the bacon in a large skillet.

4. Remove the bacon from the skillet and drain it on paper towels.

5. Save the bacon drippings from the skillet.

6. Pour the eggs into a mixing bowl and add ½ teaspoon of the salt and the pepper.

7. Pour the eggs into the skillet where the bacon was browned, and brown the eggs lightly.

8. Turn them over gently and brown on the other side.

9. When the eggs are firm, cut them into narrow strips.

10. Lightly toss the bacon, egg strips, chives, bacon drippings (plus melted butter or margarine to make ⅓ cup) with the cooked rice.

11. Serve hot.

Makes 4 servings.

Fish Boil

Ingredients

5 quarts water

¼ cup salt

12 to 24 small red potatoes

12 small white onions

4 pounds fish fillets, such as lake trout, salmon, whitefish, pike, etc.

½ pound butter or margarine, melted

6 lemons, quartered

½ cup parsley, chopped

Pepper, to taste

Procedure

1. Put water in large pot, add salt, and bring to a boil.

2. Add potatoes and onions and cook until half done, about 8 to 10 minutes.

3. Put fish steaks in a wire basket, or colander or wrap them in cheesecloth and tie into a bundle, and lower them into the pot until they are entirely covered.

4. Return to a boil and cover the pot.

5. Boil until the fish is firm but tender, about 8 to 10 minutes.

AP Photos

Wild rice is harvested in Wisconsin.

6. Remove fish and vegetables and drain both thoroughly.

7. Heap fish on a platter surrounded by the potatoes and onions.

8. Pour melted butter or margarine over all, sprinkle with chopped parsley and pepper, and serve with lemon wedges.

Serves 6 to 8.

3 FOODS OF THE GREAT LAKES REGION

The Great Lakes region was originally populated by American Indians who taught later European settlers how to hunt the local game, fish, and gather wild rice and maple syrup, as well as how to grow and eat corn and native squashes and beans. The European immigrants, mostly from Germany, Scandinavia, Holland, Poland, and Cornwall, England, each shared their traditional dishes with the rest of America. The Germans contributed frankfurters (hot dogs), hamburgers, sauerkraut, potato salad, noodles, bratwurst, liverwurst, and pretzels to the American diet. Scandinavian foods include *lefse* (potato flatbread), *limpa* (rye bread), *lutefisk* (dried cod soaked in lye), and Swedish meatballs, as well as the smorgasbord (a table laid out with several courses of small foods). The Polish introduced *kielbasa* (a type of sausage), *pierogies* (a type of stuffed pasta), Polish dill pickles, and *babka* (an egg cake). Pancakes are a Dutch contribution, along with waffles, doughnuts, cookies, and coleslaw. Miners from Cornwall brought their Cornish pasties, and small meat pies that were easily carried for lunch. Later immigrants from Arab countries settled in Detroit, Michigan, and introduced America to foods like *hummus* (puréed chickpeas), *felafel* (deep-fried bean cakes), and *tabbouleh* (bulgur wheat salad).

Dairy is a major industry in the Great Lakes region, particularly Wisconsin, known as "America's Dairyland." Dairy farmers in Wisconsin milk about 2 million cows every day, and there is one cow for every two people in the state. Not surprisingly, milk, butter, and cheese are staples in the Great Lakes diet. Pigs are also common on farms in the Great Lakes region because they take up less space and are easier to raise than beef cattle. Pork, therefore, is another common ingredient in Great Lakes cooking, especially in the form of sausage.

Dutch Pancakes

Ingredients

6 eggs

2 cups milk

½ cup flour

½ teaspoon salt

Butter or margarine

Brown sugar

Procedure

1. Measure the flour into a large bowl.
2. Beat the eggs to a froth in another mixing bowl. Add milk and salt, stirring slowly.
3. Pour the egg and milk mixture into the flour and mix well.
4. Pour a thin layer of the batter onto a hot buttered griddle or frying pan.
5. Turn over when bottom is brown and cook other side.
6. Serve hot, rolled up with butter or margarine and brown sugar.

German Potato Salad

Ingredients

5 medium potatoes

1 small onion, finely chopped

½ cup cider vinegar

2 Tablespoons vegetable oil

1 beef bouillon cube dissolved in 1 cup boiling water (you will only use part of this)

3 Tablespoons chives, finely chopped

Salt and pepper, to taste

Procedure

1. Boil potatoes in a large pot, until tender when poked with a fork, about 25 minutes.

2. While potatoes are still warm, peel and slice into ¼-inch slices.

3. Put the sliced potatoes in a large bowl, add chopped onion, cider vinegar, and oil.

4. Stir gently, making sure not to break up the potatoes.

5. Add about ⅓ cup of the dissolved beef bouillon, toss lightly, then add the chives and salt and pepper to taste.

6. Toss lightly to coat potatoes.

Serves 6 to 8.

Macaroni and Cheese

Ingredients

Vegetable oil cooking spray

Water

½ pound elbow macaroni

2 Tablespoons butter or margarine

¼ cup all-purpose flour

2 cups milk

6 ounces shredded cheddar cheese

3 ounces shredded Swiss cheese

¼ teaspoon salt

½ cup crushed croutons or cornflakes

Procedure

1. Preheat the oven to 350°F.

2. Spray a 1-quart baking dish with cooking spray.

3. Fill a large saucepan half full of water and bring to a boil.

4. Add the macaroni to the boiling water.

5. Cook until the macaroni is done, about 7 to 10 minutes.

6. Drain macaroni in a colander, then return it to the saucepan and set aside.

7. In another large saucepan, melt the butter or margarine on low heat.

8. Whisk in the flour and cook until the mixture is bubbly, about 3 minutes.

9. Do not brown.

10. Slowly add the milk to the pan and stir with a wooden spoon, turning heat up to medium.

11. Cook until mixture thickens then remove from heat.

12. Add the cheddar cheese, Swiss cheese, and salt to the pan and stir until cheese melts.

13. Add the cheese sauce to the macaroni and mix well, coating the macaroni with the sauce.

14. Place the macaroni and cheese into the baking dish and sprinkle the top with crushed croutons or cornflakes.

15. for 25 to 30 minutes.

Serves 4 to 6.

Hummus

Ingredients

2 cans chickpeas (garbanzo beans)

6 Tablespoons *tahini* (sesame seed paste, available at ethnic food shops, large supermarkets, or health food stores)

3 large cloves garlic

¼ of the liquid from 1 can of chickpeas

⅓ cup lemon juice

Salt and pepper, to taste

½ Tablespoon olive oil

Paprika

1 Tablespoon parsley, chopped

Procedure

1. Combine chickpeas, *tahini*, garlic, canned chickpea liquid, and lemon juice in a food processor or blender and pureé to a smooth paste.
2. Thin with more liquid from the canned chickpeas, if necessary.
3. Add salt and pepper to taste.
4. Place in a bowl.
5. Mix olive oil with a bit of paprika to make it red and drizzle it on top of the hummus.
6. Sprinkle with parsley.

A Great Lakes food that has become popular over all the United States is Buffalo chicken wings. There are three stories told as to how wings became famous, but perhaps the most believable is that in 1964 the Anchor Bar in Buffalo, New York, received a shipment of wings by mistake. The owner, who had been asked to supply a "meaty" appetizer for a gathering at the bar, cooked up the wings in hot sauce and served them with the house dressing, which just happened to be bleu cheese.

Buffalo Chicken Wings

Ingredients

3 to 4 pounds chicken wings

1 stick butter

3 to 4 Tablespoons hot sauce (to taste)

1 bottle bleu cheese dressing

Celery, cut up into sticks

Procedure

1. Preheat oven to 375°F.
2. Melt butter in the microwave or in a small saucepan. Stir in hot sauce.

3. Rinse chicken wings and pat dry. Arrange wings in a single layer on a cookie sheet.
4. Pour butter–hot sauce over wings. Bake for 1 hour.
5. Serve while hot with bleu cheese dressing and celery sticks.

Serves 8 to 12 as a snack.

4 FOOD FOR RELIGIOUS AND HOLIDAY CELEBRATIONS

Most people who live around the Great Lakes are Christian, with small minorities of Muslims and Jews in certain areas. German Christians brought with them many of the Christmas traditions Americans now take for granted, such as Christmas trees and Santa Claus (or Kris Kringle). They also introduced America to New Year's Eve celebrations.

Another German cultural festival that has become popular in America is Oktoberfest. The first Oktoberfest took place in 1810 in Bavaria (a region in southwest Germany) to celebrate the marriage of Crown Prince Ludwig and Therese of Saxon-Hildburghausen. Since then, it has grown into a huge fall festival that celebrates German heritage as well as the fall harvest. The largest Oktoberfest outside of Germany takes place in Cincinnati, Ohio, and many other Oktoberfests are held throughout the Great Lakes region. At all of them, sausage, bratwurst, sauerkraut, and other traditional German foods are served, along with German beer.

Norwegian Americans celebrate their cultural heritage on May 17, the day the

Norwegian constitution was signed in 1814. Among the traditional Norwegian foods served at these festivities are *lutefisk* (dried cod soaked in lye) and *lefse* (potato flat-bread).

Springerle (German Christmas Cookies)

Ingredients

3 cups flour

1 pound powdered sugar

1 teaspoon baking powder

4 eggs

1 Tablespoon lemon rind

Procedure

1. In a paper bag, shake together 1 cup of flour, the powdered sugar, baking powder, and lemon rind.

2. In a mixing bowl, beat eggs until very light and frothy.

3. Add dry ingredients from the paper bag to the beaten eggs. Beat well.

4. Work in the rest of the flour to make a soft dough.

5. Place dough onto floured surface.

6. Roll dough out to about ¼-inch thick and cut into 1½-inch by 2-inch rectangles.

7. Lay cookies out on a lightly floured cloth and let set about 2 hours to dry the tops.

8. Preheat oven to 250ºF.

9. Bake cookies on greased cookie sheet for 20 minutes or until bottoms are golden.

Makes about 3 dozen cookies.

Apple Sauerkraut

Ingredients

2 quarts prepared sauerkraut

4 strips bacon

1 onion, chopped

3 apples, peeled, cored, and quartered

½ cup chicken broth

½ cup dry white wine (or substitute white grape juice or apple juice)

2 potatoes, grated fine

1 Tablespoon white wine vinegar

2 Tablespoons brown sugar

Procedure

1. Sauté bacon in a frying pan over medium heat until crisp Remove bacon from pan and drain on paper towels.

2. Save 4 Tablespoons of the fat from the pan and pour the rest off.

3. Add onion to the pan and sauté in the remaining bacon fat until clear.

4. Rinse the sauerkraut, drain well, and stir into the onion.

5. Cover pan and simmer on low for 10 minutes.

6. Add apples, chicken broth, wine, potatoes, vinegar, and sugar.

7. Simmer gently until apples and potatoes are tender but not mushy, about 10 to 20 minutes.

8. Serve with bratwurst for an authentic German meal.

Serves 4.

Potato Lefse

Ingredients

½ cup instant mashed potatoes

1 Tablespoon butter or margarine

½ teaspoon salt

1½ cups flour

Procedure

1. Prepare instant mashed potatoes according to the directions on the box.

2. Add butter or margarine and salt, blending well.

3. Add flour, ½ cup at a time, to make a soft dough. Knead dough for about 3 minutes on a lightly floured board or countertop.

4. Divide the dough into 4 balls. Using a rolling pin, roll each ball into a very thin circle on a floured surface. (Traditional lefse is rolled with a special grooved rolling pin to give it a gridlike texture.)

5. Heat a griddle or large frying pan over high heat. Bake each lefse, turning once, until golden brown on both sides.

Serves 4.

5 MEALTIME CUSTOMS

The majority of those who live around the Great Lakes are descended from German, Scandinavian, and Dutch farmers who settled there in the 1800s. Farming life shaped the diet and mealtime schedule of the region. Hearty breakfasts and generous lunches gave the farmers the energy to finish their work. German immigrants taught America to serve meals "family-style," with all the food on the table at once, rather than bringing it out to the table in individual servings.

The Scandinavians brought their tradition of the smorgasbord to America. The smorgasbord is a large feast made up of a variety of small dishes laid out together on one table, beginning with bread and fish and moving through hot dishes, such as Swedish meatballs, all the way to dessert. Each person or family brings a dish to contribute to the smorgasbord. (The word "smorgasbord" has even been adopted into the English language to refer generally to anything offering a wide variety of items.)

Miners from Cornwall, England, had long eaten pasties (PAST-eez), small meat pies that were easy to carry for lunch. Immigrants to the Great Lakes area brought their tradition of Cornish pasties with them, and they are still a popular snack in the area.

Germans love beer and started a number of breweries around the Great Lakes. The Pabst and Schlitz breweries were both founded in Milwaukee, Wisconsin, in the 1800s by German Americans. (Milwaukee still ranks as the number-one beer-drinking city in America: While Americans on average drink 6 gallons of beer per year, Milwaukee residents average 42 gallons.) The Great Lakes region is also home to many well-known food companies, including Kellogg's, Kraft, Pillsbury, Green Giant, and Land O' Lakes.

Swedish Meatballs

Ingredients

1 pound ground beef

1 pound ground pork

4 Tablespoons bread crumbs

4 Tablespoons cream or milk

3 Tablespoons onion, finely chopped

1 egg, beaten

½ teaspoon salt

¼ teaspoon pepper

Procedure

1. Preheat the oven to 400°F.

2. Mix all the ingredients in a large bowl.

3. Shape into small meatballs and arrange on a baking sheet.

4. Bake in the oven for about 7 minutes. Wearing an oven mitt, carefully shake the baking sheet to prevent the meatballs from sticking. Bake for about 8 more minutes.

Makes about 40 meatballs.

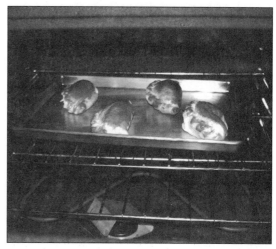

EPD Photos

Pasties may be served as a snack, carried in a lunchbox to be eaten cold, or as a light supper piping hot from the oven.

Cornish Pasty

Ingredients

Pastry for 2-crust pie (commercial pie crust mix is recommended)

12 ounces ground chuck (coarse ground as for chili is preferred)

1 medium-sized onion, finely chopped

1 turnip or 2 small carrots, finely chopped

1 large potato, finely chopped

Salt and pepper, to taste

1 egg, beaten

Procedure

1. Preheat the oven to 400°F.

2. Prepare pastry according to instruction on package.

3. Combine the ground chuck with the onion, turnip or carrots, and potato. Season with salt and pepper.

4. Roll out the pastry to ¼-inch thickness.

5. Cut it into 6-inch rounds, using a plate or saucer to measure each circle.

6. Lay the rounds on a flat surface and place an equal amount of the steak mixture in the middle of each round into the shape of a small sausage.

7. Brush the rim of each round with a little beaten egg and fold one side over, forming a half-moon shape.

8. Pinch the edges together.

9. Make two small slits on top to allow steam to escape while cooking.

10. Place the pasties on a greased baking sheet and brush the outsides with the remaining beaten egg.

11. Bake for 20 minutes at 400°F. Then reduce the heat to 350°F and bake for another 40 minutes.

Makes 4 pasties.

6 POLITICS, ECONOMICS, AND NUTRITION

A majority of people from the Great Lakes region receive adequate nutrition. The lakes surrounding the area provide a variety of fish, including walleye, perch, catfish, and bass, that are high in protein and iron. With an abundance of rich soil and farming land, the region produces many different crops, such as wheat, corn, and vegetables. Wisconsin, whose milk and cheese products are rich in calcium, is one of the top dairy-producing states in the United States.

7 FURTHER STUDY

Books

Blue, Anthony Dias. *America's Kitchen: Traditional & Contemporary Regional Cooking.* Atlanta, GA: Turner Publishing, 1995.

D'Amico, Joan, and Karen Eich Drummond. *The United States Cookbook: Fabulous Foods and Fascinating Facts from All 50 States.* New York, NY: John Wiley & Sons, 2000.

Dooley, Beth, and Lucia Watson. *Savoring the Seasons of the Northern Heartland.* The Knopf Cooks American series, no. 14. New York, NY: Knopf, 1994.

Fertig, Judith M. *Prairie Home Cooking.* Boston, MA: Harvard Common Press, 1999.

Fussell, Betty. *I Hear America Cooking: The Cooks and Recipes of American Regional Cuisine.* New York, NY: Penguin Books, 1997.

Web Sites

Allrecipes. [Online] Available at http://www.all-recipes.com (accessed April 19, 2001).

Finland & Finnish-American Web Resources. [Online] Available http://alexia.lis.uiuc.edu/~cook/food.htm (accessed April 17, 2001).

German American Corner. [Online] Available http://www.germancorner.com (accessed April 17, 2001).

Great Lakes Information Network. [Online] Available http://www.great-lakes.net (accessed April 19, 2001).

Recipe Source. [Online] Available http://www.recipesource.com (accessed April 19, 2001).

ScanSelect. [Online] Available http://www.scanselect.com (accessed April 17, 2001).

Sons of Norway. [Online] Available http://www.sofn.com (accessed April 19, 2001).

Upper Midwest. [Online] Available http://www.execpc.com/~midwest (accessed April 19, 2001).

United States
Jewish Americans

Recipes

Mother's Chicken Soup 106
Chopped Chicken Liver 107
Noodle Kugel (Noodle Casserole) 107
Potato Latkes (Potato Pancakes) 110
Charoset (Passover Dish) 110
Apple and Carrot Tsimmes 111
Matzo Balls 111
Matzo Brie 112
New York Cheesecake 113
Herring Dip 113

1 GEOGRAPHIC SETTING AND ENVIRONMENT

Although the nearly 6 million Jewish Americans live in every state of the nation, the largest populations are found in New York, California, and Florida, especially in urban areas.

2 HISTORY AND FOOD

Food has played an important role in Jewish American lives since the first Jews arrived in New Amsterdam in 1654, most from Dutch colonies in Brazil. During the Colonial period (1620–1776), Jews adapted their cooking to the foods grown regionally in their new homeland. They learned to use corn, beans, and fish, such as salmon, herring, and cod. However, they continued to observe the Jewish dietary laws, or Kashrut

(see section 4: Food For Religious and Holiday Celebrations). The second wave of Jewish immigrants (1830–1880) came mostly from Germany. Many settled in the Midwest, bringing with them their food traditions. They were known especially for their baked goods. Cincinnati, Ohio, the primary center of German Jewish culture, was also the home of Fleischmann's yeast and Crisco, a vegetable-based shortening that met Jewish dietary restrictions.

In the twentieth century, Jewish American cooking has been changed by the creation of ready-made food products, such as mixes and frozen foods. (A Jewish baker invented Sara Lee frozen cakes, which he named after his daughter.) The Orthodox Union symbol (an "O" with a "U" inside it) was devised to show that the contents of

The states with the largest populations of Jewish Americans are New York, California, and Florida.

packaged food are kosher. Foods associated with Jewish Americans, like bagels, lox (smoked salmon), cheesecake, and corned-beef sandwiches, became popular among the general public. In the late twentieth century, the trend toward lowfat and easy-to-prepare recipes has influenced Jewish American cooking.

3 FOODS OF THE JEWISH AMERICANS

Many foods that Americans have come to regard as Jewish originated in Eastern Europe, where most Jewish immigrants came from during the first half of the 1900s. (Eastern European Jews were also called Ashkenazim.) The cooking of this region was generally simple and hearty. It contained plenty of fat but was not highly spiced. Main dishes were usually meat or

poultry based. Because of the Jewish dietary restrictions (Kashruth), no pork was eaten. The restriction on serving meat and dairy products at the same meal gave rise to a set of traditional dairy dishes including blintzes, cheesecake, and noodle pudding. Both meat and vegetables were cooked until thoroughly done—vegetables were cooked until they were limp. Famous Jewish foods that came out of this tradition include chicken soup, *matzo* balls, *latkes* (potato pancakes), chopped liver, gefilte fish, *cholent* (beef and barley stew), *kneidlach* (dumplings), and *borscht* (beet soup). Certain spiced meats and fish, including corned beef, herring, and lox, are also associated with Ashkenazic Jewish cooking.

In the last decades of the twentieth century, Jewish American cooking branched out from its Ashkenazic roots. Jewish cooks adapted their recipes to make them lighter and lower in fat. The Middle Eastern food traditions popular in Israel began to influence Jewish American food as well. Foods such as *felafel* and *hummus* became more closely identified with Jewish cooking. In addition, there was a new level of interest in Sephardic Jewish traditions from Spain and North Africa, as well as other parts of the world.

Mother's Chicken Soup

Ingredients

4 boneless, skinless chicken breasts, cubed (traditional chicken soup would use whole chicken with bones, cut up)

2 stalks of celery, cut into pieces about 2 inches long

1 large onion, halved

1 medium carrot, split in half lengthwise and cut into pieces about 2 inches long

1 parsley root (looks like a baby parsnip) scrubbed and cut into 2-inch pieces (cut-up turnip or parsnip may be substituted)

Handful parsley leaves, chopped (optional)

1 teaspoon salt

Procedure

1. In a large pot, add the chicken and enough water to cover. Bring the water to a boil.

2. Add the vegetables and reduce heat to medium. Simmer for an hour, stirring occasionally.

3. When the soup is done, remove the chicken and vegetables onto a plate with a slotted spoon.

4. Throw out the celery and onions; cover and refrigerate the rest.

5. Pour the soup through a strainer or colander into a large bowl or other container.

6. Cover and refrigerate several hours or overnight.

7. Skim the fat off the top before heating and serving.

8. Serve soup with noodles, rice, or *matzo* balls. Garnish with chopped parsley leaves if desired.

Serves 6.

The chicken can be eaten hot for dinner or cut up and used in chicken salad or other recipes.

Chopped Chicken Liver

Ingredients

4 hard boiled eggs, peeled and sliced

3 to 4 Tablespoons vegetable oil

3 medium onions, diced

1 pound fresh chicken livers

Salt and pepper, to taste

Procedure

1. Heat the oil over high heat in a large skillet.

2. Sauté the onions until they start turning brown, about 5 minutes.

3. Add the chicken livers to the sautéed onions and cook, tossing the livers occasionally until cooked through and firm, about 5 minutes.

4. Combine the livers, onions, and sliced eggs in a food processor, or chop with a knife until the texture is even but not mushy.

5. Season with salt and pepper. Serve with crusty bread, matzo, or other crackers.

Serves about 4.

Noodle Kugel (Noodle Casserole)

Ingredients

12 ounces flat, wide egg noodles

½ cup (1 stick) margarine

2 apples, peeled, cored, and diced

½ cup raisins

4 eggs, beaten

Salt, to taste

Cinnamon sugar

Procedure

1. Preheat oven to 375°F.

2. Grease a 9-by-13-inch baking dish.

3. Bring a large saucepan of lightly salted water to a boil, add the noodles, and boil until al dente (done but still chewy), about 5 to 10 minutes.

4. Drain and place in a large bowl.

EPD Photos

Challah, a rich braided bread, often accompanies the Friday night Shabbat (sabbath) dinner.

5. Add the margarine, apples, and raisins and mix well.

6. Add the eggs, season with salt, and mix well.

7. Spoon the mixture into the prepared baking dish.

8. Sprinkle with cinnamon sugar.

9. Bake until the top is brown and crisp, about 35 to 45 minutes.

10. Remove from the oven and serve hot or cold, cut into squares.

Serves about 6.

4 FOOD FOR RELIGIOUS AND HOLIDAY CELEBRATIONS

Jews throughout the world have a detailed set of dietary restrictions called the laws of Kashrut. They are based on passages found in the Old Testament of the Bible. Food that follows these restrictions is called kosher food. While many Jewish Americans observe these laws (or "keep kosher"), many others do not.

Jews who keep kosher may not eat pork, pork products, or shellfish. The meat they eat ("kosher meat") must be slaughtered and packaged according to special guidelines. Meat and dairy products may not be eaten or cooked together. Foods such as vegetables, fruits, grains, and eggs are considered *parve*, meaning they can be eaten with either meat or dairy products. Jews who keep kosher also have separate sets of dishes and cooking utensils, one for meat and another for dairy products.

The Jewish religion also specifies several days of fasting throughout the year. This means Jews do not consume any food (or sometimes beverages) on these days. The most important is Yom Kippur, or the Day of Atonement, in the fall. Many Jewish Americans fast on this day. Passover is an eight-day holiday during which Jews do not eat bread, baked goods, and certain other foods. Instead of bread, Jews eat a flat (unleavened), cracker-like food called *matzo*. Crushed *matzo*, or *matzo* meal, is substituted for flour in many foods cooked during this holiday.

The most important meal of this commemoration is held on the first night of Passover, and is called the *seder*. During the meal, which includes special foods specific to this holy day, a liturgy is read that recounts the Biblical exodus of the Hebrews from Egypt. The Hebrew word *Pesach* means "passover."

Passover Seder Meal

Gefilte fish
Chicken soup with matzo balls
Roast chicken
Carrot and apple tsimmes
Chremslach (pancakes made with boiled potatoes and egg)
Green beans
Passover sponge cake
Macaroons
Tea or coffee

Jewish American Bar or Bat Mitzvah Buffet

Chopped liver on ice
Sweet and sour meatballs
Potato knishes
Kosher hot dogs with sauerkraut
Roast chicken
Vegetables
Rice
Strawberry meringue torte

Food plays an important role in many Jewish holidays. On the Jewish New Year, honey cake and apples dipped in honey are eaten for a "sweet year." During the eight-day festival of Succoth in the fall, religious Jews eat their meals in a specially built outdoor booth in their backyards called a "sukkah." Potato pancakes called *latkes* are eaten during Hanukkah, the eight–day Festival of Lights, in December. The festival of Purim, in late winter or spring, is celebrated with triangular filled pastries called *haman-taschen*.

Marking the formal entry into adulthood of boys at age thirteen (*bar mitzvah*) and girls at age twelve (*bat mitzvah*), Jewish Americans celebrate with a lavish party following a religious ceremony. The child who has attained this status, is considered ready to participate fully in the ritual days of fasting of the Jewish calendar.

Potato Latkes (Potato Pancakes)

Ingredients

1 small onion, grated

3 potatoes, grated

3 Tablespoon flour

2 eggs, beaten

¼ teaspoon salt

Pepper, to taste

½ to 1 cup vegetable oil for frying

Procedure

1. Combine the potato and onion in a large mixing bowl.

2. Stir in the flour, eggs, salt, and pepper.

3. Heat about ⅓ cup oil in a large skillet over medium to high heat until very hot.

4. Drop heaping tablespoons of the mixture into the oil and flatten with the back of the spoon.

5. Fry, flipping once or twice, until crisp and brown on both sides.

6. Drain on paper towels.

Serves 4.

EPD Photos

Oversized potato latkes, topped with a dollop of sour cream, make a filling brunch, lunch, or light supper dish.

Charoset

Charoset is a traditional Passover food that has a symbolic role in the ceremonial Seder meal.

Ingredients

2 red apples, unpeeled, cored, and finely chopped

1 cup finely chopped walnuts

2 Tablespoons honey

1 teaspoon ground cinnamon

¼ cup sweet Passover wine or water

Procedure

1. Combine all the ingredients, using only as much wine or water as needed to hold the mixture together.

2. Serve in a bowl or roll into 1-inch balls and arrange on a serving plate.

Serves 4.

Apple and Carrot Tsimmes

Ingredients

6 carrots, peeled and sliced

1 cup hot water

3 tart apples (such as Granny Smith) peeled, cored, and cut into wedges

½ cup raisins

¼ cup brown sugar or honey

Salt and pepper to taste

1 cup orange juice

2 Tablespoons potato starch

1 to 2 Tablespoons margarine

Procedure

1. Preheat oven to 350°F.

2. Place the carrots in a saucepan, add the water, and cook, covered, until tender, about 10 minutes.

3. Add the apple wedges during the last 5 minutes of cooking time.

4. Drain and pour the mixture into a lightly greased 2 ½-quart casserole dish.

5. Add the raisins, brown sugar, salt, and pepper.

6. In a small bowl mix the orange juice and potato starch until smooth.

7. Pour over the carrot-apple mixture in the casserole dish. Place small pieces of margarine on top.

8. Bake for 30 minutes or until the top is golden brown.

Serves about 6.

Matzo Balls

Matzo balls can be kept 2 days in their cooking liquid in a covered container in the refrigerator; reheat gently in cooking liquid or soup.

Ingredients

2 large eggs

2 Tablespoons vegetable oil

½ cup matzo meal

½ teaspoon salt (for boiling water)

½ teaspoon baking powder

1 to 2 Tablespoons water or chicken soup

Procedure

1. In a medium bowl, lightly beat the eggs with oil.

2. Add the matzo meal, salt, and baking powder and stir until smooth.

3. Stir in water. Let mixture stand for 20 minutes so that matzo meal absorbs liquid.

4. Once matzo ball mixture is done, bring 2 quarts of salted water to a boil.

5. With wet hands, roll about 1 teaspoon of matzo ball mixture between your palms into a ball; mixture will be very soft.

6. Set balls on a plate.

7. With a rubber spatula, carefully slide balls into boiling water.

8. Cover and simmer over low heat for about 30 minutes, or until firm.

9. Cover and keep warm until ready to serve.

Serves 2 to 4.

Matzo ball soup from a delicatessen, where the matzo balls are the size of tennis balls. Most home cooks prepare matzo balls that are smaller than this one, and serve two in each bowl of piping hot chicken broth.

Matzo Brie

Ingredients

1 Passover *matzo* (can be found in most supermarkets)

1 egg, beaten

Butter

Salt, to taste

Procedure

1. Break the matzo into medium-sized pieces.

2. Put them in a small bowl, cover with boiling water, and let them soak until soft.

3. Add the pieces of matzo to the beaten egg, stirring once or twice to coat. Season with salt.

4. Melt a pat of butter in a small or medium skillet and pour in the egg mixture.

5. Cook both sides over medium heat until the bottom is golden brown (lift and check periodically).

6. Another pat of butter can be placed underneath the matzo brie.

7. Turn off the heat when the bottom starts to brown.

8. Serve with jam, syrup, or a topping of your choice.

5 MEALTIME CUSTOMS

Most Jewish Americans observe the same mealtime customs as other Americans in the regions where they live. They generally eat three meals a day, and dinner is usually the main meal. The most special night of the week for observant (religious) Jews is Friday, when the Sabbath is welcomed. In many Jewish households, two candles are placed on the dinner table and lit at sundown as a special prayer is said. A glass of wine and a loaf of *challah* (a special type of bread) are also placed on the table and blessed. A traditional Friday dinner often consists of chicken soup, an appetizer, a chicken or beef main dish, a variety of vegetables, coffee or tea, and dessert.

In Orthodox households, family members pray before and after meals. No cooking is done on the Sabbath (Saturday). Foods eaten on Saturday must be prepared the day before. At festive gatherings, such as weddings, Orthodox men and women are seated at separate tables.

New York Cheesecake

Ingredients for crust

1¼ cups graham cracker crumbs

1 Tablespoon sugar (optional)

¼ cup (½ stick) unsalted butter or margarine, melted

Ingredients for filling

2 cups (1 pint) sour cream

1 cup plus 1 Tablespoon sugar

2½ teaspoons vanilla extract

3 packages (24 ounces) cream cheese, at room temperature

4 eggs

Procedure

1. Preheat the oven to 350°F.

2. To make the crust, in a large bowl, thoroughly blend the crumbs, sugar (if using), and melted better.

3. Spoon the mixture evenly into a 9-inch springform pan until halfway up the sides and press down firmly.

4. Refrigerate for at least 15 minutes and then bake until set, 10 minutes. Set aside to cool completely.

5. To make the filling, beat the sour cream and 1 Tablespoon of the sugar in a bowl.

6. Add 1 teaspoon of the vanilla extract and beat until well blended. Set aside.

7. In another bowl, beat the cream cheese with the remaining 1 cup sugar until light and fluffy.

8. Add the eggs, one at a time, mixing well.

9. Beat in the remaining vanilla extract.

10. Pour filling into the prepared crust.

11. Bake until the center is set and the top is golden brown, about 50 minutes. Remove from the oven.

12. Spread the prepared sour cream mixture on top and return to the oven for 5 minutes to become firm.

13. Let cool, cover, and refrigerate for 24 hours.

14. Serve chilled or at room temperature.

Serves 10 to 15.

Herring Dip

Ingredients

1 large jar herring cut up

1 green pepper, diced

1 bunch green onions, sliced

2 cups sour cream

½ cup mayonnaise

1 Tablespoon lemon juice

1 Tablespoon sugar

Procedure

1. Remove herring from jar and chop coarsely.

2. Combine all ingredients together in a mixing bowl, adding herring last.

3. Serve with bread, crackers, bread sticks, or cut-up raw vegetables.

Serves about 12.

6 POLITICS, ECONOMICS, AND NUTRITION

Jewish Americans, like Americans of every cultural and ethnic background, have become increasingly concerned about developing healthier lifestyles. Many Jewish Americans seek out ways to lower the fat and cholesterol in their diets.

For Jewish Americans who observe the Kashrut, eating in restaurants and while traveling may require advance planning.

Airlines offer kosher meals, although they must be ordered in advance. Likewise, many hotels will prepare kosher meals for guests who request them.

7 FURTHER STUDY

Books

Ashkanazi-Hankin, Gail. *Festivals of Lite Kosher Cookbook*. Gretna, LA: Pelican 1999.

Brown, Michael P. *The Jewish Gardening Cookbook: Growing Plants and Cooking for Jewish Holidays and Festivals*. Woodstock, VT: Jewish Lights, 1998.

Brownstein, Rita Milos. *Jewish Holiday Style.* New York: Simon & Schuster, 1999.

Cohen, Jayne. *The Gefilte Variations: 200 Inspired Re-creations of Classics from the Jewish Kitchen, with Menus, Stories, and Traditions for the Holidays and Year-round.* New York: Scribner, 2000.

Fiedler, Seymour. *The Beginner's Kosher Cookbook*. New York: Feldheim Publishers, 1997.

Levy, Faye. *International Jewish Cookbook*. New York: Warner Books, Inc., 1991.

Nathan, Joan. *Jewish Cooking in America.* New York: Knopf, 1998.

Zoloth, Joan. *Jewish Holiday Treats.* San Francisco: Chronicle Books, 2000.

Web Sites

The Best of Jewish Cooking. [Online] Available http://www.foodbooks.com/jewish.htm (accessed April 2001).

Judaism 101: Jewish Cooking. [Online] Available http://www.jewfaq.org/food.htm (accessed April 2001).

United States
Latino Americans

Recipes

Salsa Cruda 116
Cuban Beans and Rice 117
Fried Plantains 117
Guacamole 117
Mexican Fried Ice Cream 119
Puerto Rican Christmas Salad 120
Gazpacho 120
Cuban Avocado and Pineapple Salad 121
Chili Corn Bread 121
Tropical Fruit Salad 121

1 GEOGRAPHIC SETTING AND ENVIRONMENT

Although Latino Americans, also known as Hispanic Americans, live throughout the United States, the states with the largest populations are California, Arizona, New Mexico, Florida, and New York. Latinos may be of any race, and may trace their family history to any of the countries where Spanish is the principal language (except Spain), particularly those in Latin America. The masculine form of the word is Latino, and the feminine form is Latina.

2 HISTORY AND FOOD

Mexican Americans have lived in the United States for most of the country's history. However, other Spanish-speaking immigrants did not begin arriving in large numbers until after World War II (1939–1945). Many Puerto Ricans arrived in the 1950s. Cubans, Dominicans, Colombians,

and Costa Ricans immigrated in the 1960s. And, people from still other Latin American countries followed in succeeding years. As of 2001, the three largest Latino ethnic groups were Mexican American, Puerto Rican, and Cuban American.

Like most immigrant groups, Latino Americans have remained loyal to the food traditions of their homelands. Many shop in small ethnic markets called *bodegas* that carry specialty foods used in Latin cooking. When they cook, they follow recipes handed down to them by their parents and grandparents. Specialty food companies have thrived by supplying Latinos with traditional cooking ingredients. The most famous of these is Goya Foods, whose products can be found in grocery stores throughout the country.

The third and fourth generations of Latino families have begun to transform their cooking traditions. They vary their recipes with new ingredients and include dishes

The states with the largest populations of Latino Americans are California, Arizona, New Mexico, Florida, and New York.

Corn, beans, rice, and root vegetables are staples of the Latino diet. Some of the root vegetables commonly used in Latino cooking are sweet potatoes, yams, yucca, jicama, Jerusalem artichokes, and taro. Also popular is a pear-shaped squash called chayote. It goes by several other names, including tayote, chuchu, and xuxu. Latinos are able to enjoy many fruits native to their homelands, which are either imported or cultivated in the United States. These include plantains, guavas, mangoes, papayas, passion fruit, and prickly pears.

Turnovers are very popular in Latino cooking. These are dishes that consist of a variety of dough and filling. Two popular types of turnovers are tamales and empanadas. Nacatamales, chuchitos, humitas, and bolos are just a few of the many types of tamales eaten by Latinos in the United States.

Most Latino desserts (like flan, a type of custard) are made from dairy products. Most traditional Latino drinks contain two of the following three ingredients: milk, rum, and fruit.

from other ethnic groups in their meals. In turn, Latin American cooking has become increasingly popular among non-Latinos.

3 FOODS OF THE LATINO AMERICANS

Although Latino Americans belong to a number of different cultures, their cooking styles have certain things in common. Meat, usually pork or beef, is central to the Latino diet. It is often eaten with the spicy sauces (salsas) for which Latinos are famous. The main ingredient in salsa, as well as many other Latin dishes, is hot chili peppers. Latinos cook with fresh, dried, and ground chilies. There are many different kinds of chilies, including Habanero, Jalapeno, Malagueta, and Poblano.

Salsa Cruda

Ingredients

1 small onion or 6 green onions, chopped

2 large, ripe tomatoes

2 Tablespoons lime juice

Salt, to taste

2 serrano chilies (or other hot chilies)

Optional: a few coriander (cilantro) leaves, chopped

Procedure

1. Wearing rubber gloves for protection, chop the chilies. (Hot chilies may cause a burning sensation if they come in contact with your skin.)

2. Place the onion and chilies into a bowl.

3. Add the lime juice and a pinch of salt, tomatoes, and coriander, if using, and mix well.

4. Let the salsa set for 5 minutes to allow flavors to blend.

5. Serve with nacho chips, tacos, or grilled meat.

Cuban Beans and Rice

Ingredients

1 Tablespoon olive oil

1 cup onion, chopped

1 green bell pepper, chopped

2 cloves garlic, finely chopped

1 teaspoon salt

4 Tablespoons tomato paste

1 15-ounce can kidney or black beans (drain but save liquid)

1 cup uncooked white rice

Procedure

1. Heat oil in a large saucepan over medium heat.

2. Sauté onion, bell pepper, and garlic.

3. When the pieces of onion become clear, add salt and tomato paste.

4. Reduce heat to low and cook 2 minutes.

5. Stir in the beans and rice.

6. Pour the liquid from the beans into a large measuring cup and add enough water to make 2½ cups of liquid.

7. Add to the beans.

8. Cover and cook on low for 45 to 50 minutes, or until liquid is absorbed and rice is cooked.

Serves 4.

Fried Plantains

Plantains are a large, thick-skinned variety of banana available in specialty stores.

Ingredients

3 plantains, peeled and sliced into 1½-inch pieces

7 garlic cloves, crushed

1 Tablespoon salt

1 cup water

2 cups vegetable oil

Procedure

1. Heat the vegetable oil in frying pan and cook plantains over low heat.

2. Mix the garlic with water in a bowl.

3. When the pieces of plantain are soft, mash each one between two sheets of waxed paper. Then soak them in the water and garlic.

4. Re-fry the pieces of plantain in hot vegetable oil until they are golden brown.

Guacamole

Ingredients

1 ripe avocado, peeled, pitted, and mashed

3 to 5 teaspoons of fresh salsa (see recipe above), or bottled salsa

1 teaspoon lemon juice

½ teaspoon minced garlic (or garlic powder)

¼ teaspoon salt

1 ripe tomato, diced

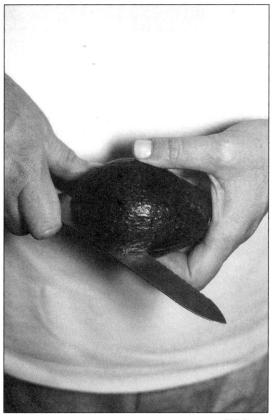

EPD Photos

To prepare an avocado for use in guacamole, first cut all the way around it carefully, so that the two halves can be gently twisted apart.

Procedure

1. Add all of the ingredients except the tomato into a bowl.
2. Use a fork to mash the avocado and the other ingredients together.
3. After dicing the tomato, stir the small pieces into the bowl with a spoon.
4. Cover the bowl with plastic wrap and put it in the refrigerator for 1 hour.
5. Serve as a dip with tortilla chips, as a sauce on top of tacos or burritos, or as topping on a baked potato.

4 FOOD FOR RELIGIOUS AND HOLIDAY CELEBRATIONS

The vast majority of Latinos are Roman Catholic and celebrate the holidays of the Christian calendar.

Making *tamales* and *pasteles* together is a popular family tradition around the Christmas holidays. Both consist of dough wrapped around meat or some other filling. The *tamale* dough is placed inside an empty cornhusk. The *pastele* dough is placed inside a wrapper made from banana leaves. Another Christmas favorite is *menudo*, a spicy stew made with hot chilies and a cow's stomach (called tripe).

A special Latino New Year's Eve tradition is to eat twelve grapes or raisins at midnight. They stand for the twelve months of the new year. Adults often welcome the new year with a drink that contains rum and tropical fruit. It is poured into a punch bowl, and a whole pineapple is put in the bowl. It is said that the people who drink this beverage will enjoy friendship throughout the coming year. On New Year's Eve, Latinos of Colombian descent enjoy a dessert called *bunuelos*. These are balls of dough made from flour, sugar, eggs, and butter and deep fried.

On Good Friday, three days before Easter, a soup called potaje do vigile is served in many Latino homes. It is made with garbanzo beans, fish, and spinach. It also contains egg yolks, garlic, almonds, and seasoning.

Mexican Fried Ice Cream

Ingredients

½ cup vegetable oil

2 flour tortillas

½ teaspoon cinnamon

2 Tablespoons sugar

¼ cup cornflake crumbs

2 large scoops vanilla ice cream

Whipped cream in a can

2 maraschino cherries with stems

Optional toppings: honey, chocolate syrup, strawberries

Procedure

1. Fry each tortilla, one at a time, in hot oil over medium to high heat until crispy.

2. This should take about one minute on each side.

3. Combine the cinnamon and sugar in a small bowl.

4. Sprinkle half of the cinnamon mixture over both sides of the fried tortillas, coating evenly. (Not all of the sugar mixture will stick to the tortillas.)

5. Combine the other half of the cinnamon mixture with the corn flake crumbs in another small bowl.

6. Pour the corn flake mixture into a wide shallow bowl or plate.

7. Place a large scoop of ice cream in the corn flake crumbs and roll the ice cream around until the entire surface is evenly and completely coated with corn flake crumbs. (You should not be able to see any ice cream.)

EPD Photos

Using two forks, gently roll the scoop of ice cream around in the corn flake crumbs until the entire surface is covered with a crunch coating.

8. Place the ice cream scoop on the center of the cinnamon/sugar-coated tortilla.

9. Spray whipped cream around the base of the ice cream.

10. Spray an additional pile of whipped cream on top of the ice cream.

11. Put a cherry in the top pile of whipped cream.

12. Repeat for the remaining scoop of ice cream.

Serves 2.

Puerto Rican Christmas Salad

Ingredients

3 pounds potatoes

½ pound string beans

4 hard boiled eggs, sliced

2 apples

1 large onion, chopped

1 pound boneless chicken breast

3 garlic cloves, crushed

5 stuffed olives

1 can (8 ounces) red peppers

1 teaspoon salt

½ teaspoon ground pepper

1 jar (8 ounce) mayonnaise

½ cup olive oil

Procedure

1. Preheat oven to 350°F.
2. Place chicken on flat roasting pan and bake for one hour or until done.
3. Boil potatoes and cut into small pieces.
4. When the chicken is cooked, cut into small pieces.
5. Mix all the ingredients except olives and peppers and season to taste.
6. Garnish with red peppers and olives.

Optional: Form flowers with the peppers as petals and olive in the middle. Serves 12.

5 MEALTIME CUSTOMS

Most Latinos eat three meals a day. The main meal is eaten at dinnertime. Eating together with the family is important to Latinos. Many families pray together before meals.

Busy schedules sometimes keep families from eating together during the week. On Sundays, they can still gather to cook together and share food, prayer, and the latest news. Many Latino children have Sunday dinner with their aunts, uncles, grandparents, and cousins.

In the past, most Latinos ate large, home-cooked meals every day. Foods were made from traditional recipes that were hard to prepare and were time consuming. As more women have entered the work force, there is less time to cook some of these traditional foods. Also, Latinos, like other Americans, eat out more than they used to. Some even gather in restaurants for the big family dinner on Sunday.

Each Latino ethnic group has its own food customs and traditions. Cubans consider many foods symbolic. For example, sweet foods symbolize happiness. Fruits are often the main part of a Cuban meal. Puerto Ricans are known for their love of fancy meals. Many Puerto Ricans still serve a wide variety of dishes at two of their meals every day.

Gazpacho

Ingredients

3 large onions, chopped

3 large peppers, chopped

3 garlic cloves

1 sprig parsley

2 cucumbers, peeled and chopped

2 cups water

1 lemon, peeled

1 teaspoon salt

1 teaspoon pepper

3 red peppers, chopped

3 large tomatoes, chopped

1 cup tomato juice

Procedure

1. Mix all the ingredients in a blender or food processor and season to taste.

2. If desired, add 1 Tablespoon of wine vinegar and 1 teaspoon of olive oil.

3. Ladle soup into individual bowls and serve chilled.

Serves 4.

Cuban Avocado and Pineapple Salad

Ingredients

Iceberg lettuce head, shredded

2 cups pineapple chunks

1 large avocado, peeled and sliced

1 small onion, sliced thin

Olive oil, enough to lightly coat mixture

Red wine or cider vinegar, to taste

Salt and pepper, to taste

Procedure

1. Toss ingredients in a bowl and serve.

Serves 4 to 6.

Chili Corn Bread

Ingredients

1 box corn bread mix

1 or 2 ripe red tomatoes

2 to 3 teaspoons hot chili powder

Procedure

1. Prepare the corn bread mix according to the instructions on the box (do not add sugar).

2. Cut the tomatoes into small pieces and drain the excess juice and seeds.

3. Add them to the corn bread mixture along with the hot chili powder and mix well.

4. Bake the corn bread in a lightly greased bread pan according to instructions on the mix package.

Serves 6.

Tropical Fruit Salad

Ingredients

2 pounds bananas

1 can pineapple rings, cut into small pieces

1 cup raisins

3 large oranges

2 mangos cut into pieces

Procedure

1. Cut the bananas into slices about ⅓-inch thick.

2. Mix all the ingredients and serve in individual bowls.

6 POLITICS, ECONOMICS, AND NUTRITION

The Bureau of Census reports that the Hispanic population in the United States is the fastest-growing minority population, and projects that it will be the largest minority population by 2010.

A number of health concerns face the Latino population. For recent immigrants, language barriers and unfamiliarity with health care resources (or lack of health insurance) may prevent them from seeking preventive health care.

Mexican Americans and Puerto Ricans are two- to three-times more likely to develop diabetes than non-Hispanic whites. Risk factors such as family history of diabetes, obesity, and physical inactivity all increase a person's chances of developing diabetes.

7 FURTHER STUDY

Books

Illsley, Linda. *Food and Festivals: Mexico.* Austin, Tex.: Raintree Steck-Vaughn, 1999.

Menard, Valerie. *The Latino Holiday Book.* New York: Marlowe & Company, 2000.

Novas, Himilce, and Rosemary Silva, *Latin American Cooking Across the U.S.A.* New York: Knopf, 1997.

Rexach, Nilda Luz. *The Hispanic Cookbook.* New York: Citadel Press, 1995.

Web Sites

Etznab's Latino Recipes. [Online] Available http://www.geocities.com/NapaValley/7035/icecream.html (accessed April 2001).

United States
Midwest Region

Recipes

Bread Pudding 124
Midwestern Chili 125
Deviled Eggs 126
Corn on the Cob 127
Green Bean Casserole 127
Reuben Sandwich 128
Caramel Corn 128
Cornhusker's Casserole 129
Midwestern Pork Chop Dinner 130

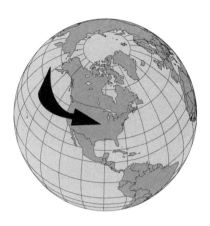

1 GEOGRAPHIC SETTING AND ENVIRONMENT

The Midwest region of the United States consists of the states in the center of the country, east of the Rocky Mountains. States considered part of the Midwest are North and South Dakota, Nebraska, Kansas, Minnesota, Wisconsin, Iowa, Missouri, and Illinois. The combined population of these states is over 28 million. (Sometimes the states just east of these—Indiana, Ohio, and Michigan, are also included when describing the Midwest.) The area is known for its plains, which are long stretches of grasslands. Historically, many tornados have touched down in the region, due to the flatness of the land and the area's climate. In Kansas, tornados are considered to be a fact of life. Dodge City, Kansas, is said to be the windiest city in the United States, with an average wind speed of 14 miles per hour. However, the Midwestern states are not solely made up of flatlands. Many states have natural and artificial lakes and streams. In fact, Minnesota has over 10,000 lakes.

Midwestern climate is highly changeable, according to season and state. The winters are generally snowy and cold, averaging around 10°F. Springs are mild, with temperatures around 70°F. Summers are hot, averaging around 80°F, and fall temperatures taper down to around 40°F to 50°F.

The climate and terrain of the Midwest are perfect for cultivating crops. The Midwest is commonly called the "breadbasket of America." Kansas is known as the Wheat State, Iowa's most famous crop is corn, and Nebraska is known as the Cornhusker State.

2 HISTORY AND FOOD

The Midwest region of the United States has many cultural influences in its cooking. Over the decades, people including Germans, British, Italian, Hungarians, and Scandinavians immigrated to the Midwest-

ern United States and made it their home. In the early 1700s, the Germans started to arrive and brought beer, sauerkraut, and sausages. They also introduced the tradition of serving meals family style—meats, relishes, soups, vegetables, and pies were set on the table all at one time. The British arrived in the late 1700s and brought *pasties* (PASS-tees), or meat pies, bread pudding, and roasts with potatoes. The Italians brought pastas and native cheeses, and the Hungarians brought goulash. *Lefse* (potato bread) and meatballs were introduced by the Scandinavians.

Bread Pudding

Ingredients

2 teaspoons shortening

5 slices day-old bread, cubed

½ cup raisins

4 eggs

2 cups milk

⅓ cup sugar

1 teaspoon vanilla

Procedure

1. Preheat the oven to 350°F.
2. Grease a small casserole or 8-inch square baking dish with shortening.
3. Place the bread cubes and raisins in a mixing bowl and gently mix. Pour into baking dish.
4. In the same mixing bowl, combine the eggs, milk, sugar, and vanilla. Stir well.
5. Pour the mixture over the bread cubes and raisins.
6. Bake for 35 to 45 minutes, or until a knife inserted in the middle comes out clean.
7. Serve warm or chilled.

Makes 4 servings.

3 FOODS OF THE MIDWEST

Foods of the Midwest are considered to be simple and hearty. Dairy products, such as milk, cheese, and eggs, are common ingredients in Midwest cooking. Main dishes may include roasts, stews, and dishes made from trout and whitefish. Rice is used in many side dishes and desserts. Wheat bread and cornbread typically accompany meals. Seasoning with spices is generally mild, and fresh herbs such as dill, parsley, and sage may be used to flavor a dish.

The Midwest is famous for its long stretches of grasslands. Corn (Iowa's most famous crop), apples, wheat, and potatoes are some examples of staple crops. Beef, pork, and poultry are produced in many Midwestern states, and trout, bass, and walleye are just a few examples of fish found in Minnesota's 10,000 lakes.

Many Midwestern foods are based on the season. In summer months (around May to August), picnic foods such as deviled eggs (Indiana is a leading state in egg production), potato and pasta salads, and fresh fruits are enjoyed. Winters once forced cooks to find methods such as smoking, pickling, and canning, to preserve food. Meatloaf (made with ground beef and breadcrumbs), chicken and noodles, and chili (a thick beef and bean stew) are hearty foods to keep people warm and full during the harsh winter weather.

3. Add oregano, bay leaves, and beef, and cook until beef is no longer pink.

4. Add 2 Tablespoons of the chili powder, tomatoes, and kidney beans.

5. Reduce heat to low and simmer, stirring occasionally, about 1 hour.

6. Add remaining chili powder and salt, vinegar, and red pepper flakes.

7. Simmer for an additional 15 minutes. Serve hot.

Makes 10 to 12 servings.

Midwestern Chili

Ingredients

4 medium onions, chopped

3 garlic cloves, crushed

¼ cup vegetable or olive oil

1 teaspoon oregano

2 bay leaves, crumbled

2 pounds ground beef

¼ cup chili powder (4 Tablespoons)

1 can (28-ounce) chopped tomatoes, do not drain

2 cans (20 ounces each) red kidney beans (do not drain)

2 teaspoons salt

3 Tablespoons apple cider vinegar

Crushed red pepper flakes, to taste

Procedure

1. In a large pot, heat the oil over medium heat.

2. Add chopped onions and garlic. Sauté onions and garlic until golden, about 10 minutes.

The city of Cincinnati, Ohio, located in the southern part of the state, and bordering the Ohio River, is famous for its unique chili, which may include such ingredients as allspice, cinnamon, or cloves, and sometimes even chocolate. Cincinnati-style chili is usually served as a topping over a bowl of spaghetti.

A typical Midwestern meal is considered "all-American." It might be roast beef, grilled steak, hamburgers, or meat loaf accompanied by potatoes (mashed or baked), green beans, corn on the cob, and apple pie for dessert. Kansas City, Missouri, is a leading producer of beef cattle and famous for its steaks. Other Midwestern favorites are chicken potpie (a creamy stew of chicken and vegetables baked in a pastry crust), potato salad, wild rice soup, and corn relish. Corn relish is made from fresh yellow corn, vinegar, and sugar, and is flavored with red peppers, onion, and celery. It is usually served with grilled or roasted meat.

Cory Langley

Candied apples—apples on sticks dipped into a sugary red or caramel coating—are a favorite fall treat, and are a common sight at county fairs and fall festivals across the Midwest.

Deviled Eggs

Ingredients

6 hard boiled eggs

2 Tablespoons mayonnaise

½ teaspoon dry mustard

Paprika

Procedure

1. Fill a large saucepan about half full with water. Add eggs.

2. Bring the water to a boil. Lower heat and simmer eggs for 15 minutes.

3. Drain eggs. Run cold water into the pan to cool the eggs. Drain and allow eggs to cool completely.

4. Carefully peel the eggs and cut in half, lengthwise.

5. Remove the egg yolks and mash them together in a small mixing bowl.

6. Stir in mayonnaise and dry mustard.

7. Spoon yolk mixture into the halved eggs and sprinkle with the paprika.

8. Refrigerate until ready to serve.

Serves 8 to 12.

Corn on the Cob

Ingredients

6 ears of corn

Salt and pepper, to taste

Butter or margarine

Procedure

1. Remove the husk from the corn.
2. Fill a large pot about half full of water.
3. Bring to a boil and add the corn.
4. Boil over high heat until corn is cooked, about 15 minutes.
5. Remove from the water and rub butter or margarine over the corn.
6. Season with salt and pepper, if desired.

Serves 6.

4 FOOD FOR RELIGIOUS AND HOLIDAY CELEBRATIONS

Christian religions dominate in the Midwest, with Christmas and Easter being the main holidays. These holidays are celebrated in generally the same way as the rest of the United States; it is a time for families to get together and visit and eat. Roasted ham or turkey is a common main course. A variety of vegetables may be served, such as potatoes, carrots, green beans, or corn. Depending on family traditions, gifts are exchanged Christmas Eve or Christmas day. Children may hunt for colored Easter eggs on Easter, go to church, and eat candy from baskets given to them by the Easter Bunny.

There are many non-religious holidays and festivals celebrated in the Midwest. Thanksgiving Day, a national holiday, commemorates the feast held between the Pilgrims and Wampanoag Indians in 1621.

Midwesterners, as most Americans, celebrate Thanksgiving with a menu that typically includes turkey and stuffing, mashed potatoes, cranberries, green bean casserole, rolls, and a variety of pies, such as pumpkin pie. Television sets are usually tuned to Thanksgiving parades in the morning and football in the afternoon.

Green Bean Casserole

Ingredients

¾ cup milk

1 can cream of mushroom soup

2 packages frozen cut green beans, thawed

1⅓ cups french fried onions (canned)

Procedure

1. Preheat oven to 350°F.
2. Combine all ingredients except ⅔ cup french fried onions in a casserole dish.
3. Bake 30 minutes.
4. Stir, then top with remaining ⅔ cup french fried onions.

Serves 6.

Food festivals are very popular in the Midwest. In early July, St. Paul (Minnesota's capital) celebrates the Taste of Minnesota Food Festival. Food stands feature roasted corn on the cob, deep-fried walleye, corn dogs, barbeque ribs and chicken, and a variety of soft drinks and beer. The festival lasts for one week and ends each night with fireworks.

The Potato Bowl festival is celebrated in Grand Forks, North Dakota. Its main attraction is free french fries. In 1999, over 3,840 pounds of potatoes were used. Activities for children included art projects, face painting, a bean bag toss, and making handprints. An estimated 3.6 million people attended the annual week-long Taste of Chicago festival in 2001. Each year, this big event attracts nearly 70 of the area's finest restaurants, as well as well-known musical acts. It is one of Illinois' top tourist attractions. Milwaukee's Summerfest, similar to the Taste of Chicago, offers visitors a variety of the area's best cuisine and musical entertainment.

5 MEALTIME CUSTOMS

Midwestern people, like many other people in the United States, usually eat three meals a day and snacks throughout.

Breakfast may be hearty, with bacon, sausage, eggs, toast or biscuits, grits or oatmeal, and coffee, or a simple doughnut or cinnamon roll with coffee.

Lunch is usually a light meal, with dinner being the main meal of the day. Lunch may be a sandwich (such as a reuben), a salad, or soup. A hamburger and french fries may be a quick lunch picked up at a fast food restaurant. Students may buy lunch at the school cafeteria, or carry a lunch, made at home, in a brown bag. Barbequed pork sandwiches, chicken nuggets, and hamburgers may be on a typical school cafeteria menu, while a sandwich, potato chips, and fruit may be brought from home.

Snacks eaten in the Midwest are similar to the rest of the United States, and may include potato chips, crackers, carmel corn, and candy.

Reuben Sandwich

Ingredients

Cooking spray

12 slices rye bread

¾ cup Russian or Thousand Island dressing

18 slices cooked corned beef

1 cup sauerkraut

12 slices swiss cheese

Procedure

1. Preheat the oven broiler.
2. Spray a broiler pan with the cooking spray.
3. On 6 of the bread slices, place 3 slices of corned beef, a heaping Tablespoon of sauerkraut, and 2 slices of cheese.
4. Place in the pan.
5. Place the other 6 slices in the pan to toast.
6. Place the pan under the broiler.
7. Wait until the cheese is melted and bread slices are lightly toasted, about 2 minutes.
8. Spread the bread slices with the dressing and place on top of the other sandwich half.
9. Cut in half and serve.

Makes 6 sandwiches.

Caramel Corn

Ingredients

8 cups popped corn

1 cup butter (2 sticks)

1 cup brown sugar, packed

½ cup corn syrup

1 teaspoon baking soda

Procedure

1. Preheat oven to 250°F.

2. Place the popped corn in a large roasting pan.

3. Place the butter, brown sugar, corn syrup, and baking soda into a large saucepan. (The baking soda will cause the mixture to foam, so an oversized saucepan is needed.)

4. Heat the butter-sugar (caramel) mixture over medium heat, stirring constantly.

5. Remove saucepan from heat and allow to cool about 5 minutes.

6. Pour caramel mixture over popcorn and stir until mixed.

7. Bake for 45 minutes, stirring every 15 minutes.

8. Remove pan from oven and pour onto wax paper.

9. Allow to cool slightly, and break apart.

Serves about 6.

Dinnertime is usually the time when family members gather to eat and talk about their day. Large dinners are traditionally cooked on Sundays. Dinner, or supper, usually consists of meat, such as beef, chicken, or pork chops, a vegetable (or vegetable casserole) such as corn, green beans, or carrots, and a starch, such as potatoes, rice, or noodles. Baked beans may also be eaten.

Cornhusker's Casserole

Ingredients

1 can (14½ ounces) yellow or white hominy (found in supermarkets), drained and patted dry

2 cups canned corn, drained and patted dry

1 cup shredded sharp cheddar cheese

4 eggs, beaten

2 cups milk

2 Tablespoons flour

1 clove garlic, minced

Salt and ground red pepper, to taste

Procedure

1. Preheat oven to 350°F.

2. Combine hominy and corn in a greased 2-quart casserole dish. Top with cheese.

3. In a mixing bowl, whisk eggs, milk, flour, and garlic.

4. Season with salt and red pepper.

5. Pour mixture over hominy and corn mixture.

6. Bake 50 to 55 minutes, or until inserted knife comes out clean.

7. Let stand 10 minutes before serving.

Makes 6 to 8 servings.

Dinner is most often eaten at home, but may also be eaten at a "sit-down" restaurant, where diners are waited on, or at a fast food restaurant. The list of fast food restaurants is endless, offering a wide variety of foods. McDonald's offers its regular fare of sandwiches and fries, along with some regional dishes. In the Midwest, for example, grits are on the breakfast menu. Kansas City, Missouri, is known for its beef cattle and its streets are lined with steak restaurants. Chicago is famous for its deep-dish pizza, which was first made there in 1943. It is baked in a deep dish, so the sides of the crust hold in more cheese and toppings than a thin-crust pizza.

Midwestern Pork Chop Dinner

Ingredients

6 pork chops

1 teaspoon vegetable oil

Salt and pepper, to taste

4 cups potatoes, peeled and sliced

2 cups carrots, sliced

2 cups onions, sliced

1½ teaspoons salt

½ teaspoon marjoram

2 cups milk

Procedure

1. Preheat oven to 350°F.
2. Heat oil in a large frying pan over medium to high heat.
3. Add pork chops and brown both sides. Season with salt and pepper.
4. In a large bowl, combine the potatoes, carrots, onion, salt, marjoram and pepper.
5. Mix lightly and place mixture into a 9x13-inch baking dish.
6. Pour milk over potato mixture and top with browned pork chops.
7. Cover baking dish with aluminum foil and bake for 1½ hours, or until pork chops and vegetables are very tender.

Serves 6.

6 POLITICS, ECONOMICS, AND NUTRITION

In general, people of the Midwest receive adequate nutrition. The foods they eat come from the land and are plentiful. A variety of crops, such as corn, potatoes, and wheat are grown, and cattle and poultry are raised in abundance. These foods supply not only the Midwest, but also the rest of the United States and abroad. These natural resources contribute to the United States being among the world's leading exporters of wheat and corn. For those who cannot afford it, the United States government provides money to pay for school lunches and nutrition programs.

7 FURTHER STUDY

Books

Adams, Marcia. Heartland: *The Best of the Old and the New from Midwest Kitchens.* New York, NY: C.N. Potter, 1991.

Andrews, Glenn. *Food from the Heartland: The Cooking of America's Midwest.* New York, NY: Prentice Hall Press, 1991.

D'Amico, Joan. *The United States Cookbook: Fabulous Foods and Fascinating Facts from all 50 States.* New York, NY: John Wiley, 2000.

Ginderson, Mary. *Pioneer Farm Cooking.* Mankato, MN. Blue Earth Books, 2000.

Mandel, Abby. *Celebrating the Midwestern Table: Real Food for Real Times.* New York, NY: Doubleday, 1996.

Web Sites

Cuisinenet.com. [Online] Available http://www.cuisinenet.com/glossary/midwest.html (accessed April 22, 2001).

Culinary History Timeline. [Online] Available http://www.connerprairie.org/diet.html (accessed April 22, 2001).

United States
Native Americans

Recipes

Popcorn 132
Succotash (Traditional Corn and Bean Stew) 133
Maple Baked Beans 134
Pumpkin-Corn Sauce... 135
Buffalo Stew... 135
Pumpkin Bread.. 136
Indian Fry-Bread... 137
Iroquois Strawberry Drink... 137
Pinole (Cornmeal Drink)... 137
Popped Wild Rice.. 138

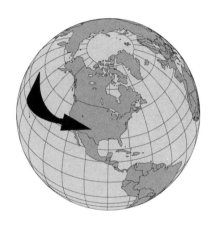

1 GEOGRAPHIC SETTING AND ENVIRONMENT

Once the sole inhabitants of North America, Native Americans were forcefully and often brutally relocated by white settlers and U.S. government policies to reservations. As of the early twenty-first century, the states with the largest populations of Native Americans are Oklahoma, California, Arizona, and New Mexico. Sometimes called American Indians, the Native Americans lived in dozens of tribal groups—from Abenaki to Zuni—scattered across North America.

2 HISTORY AND FOOD

Before Europeans settled North America, Native American tribes lived in five major parts of the United States: the Northeast, the South, the Great Plains, the Pacific Coast, and the deserts of the Southwest. Ancient artifacts show that native peoples fished off the coast of New England as long ago as 3000 B.C. Some Native American tribes were gatherers, eating the fruits and vegetables native to their regions. Other tribes practiced agriculture. They used farming methods that let them grow crops on the same soil for many years. By the time the first white settlers arrived, Native Americans knew how to grow almost 100 different kinds of crops. These were used as medicines and dyes, as well as food.

In addition to gathering and farming, most Native Americans hunted for meat. In the 1500s, the Spanish brought horses to America. Horses helped the Indians of the Great Plains hunt buffalo. Later, however, the arrival of more Europeans made it increasingly difficult for Native Americans to hunt for food. The white settlers cleared many forests where animals had lived. They

The states with the largest populations of Native Americans are Oklahoma, California, Arizona, and New Mexico.

"life." Corn was the most important dietary staple. It was served at almost every meal. Ears of corn were boiled or roasted over a fire. Corn was also pounded into flour and then cooked as cereal (mush) or baked in bread. Native Americans were also the first people to cook popcorn. According to legend, an American Indian named Quadequina brought a bowl of popcorn to a Thanksgiving dinner in 1621.

Popcorn

Ingredients

2 Tablespoons vegetable oil

⅔ cup white popcorn kernels

Procedure

1. Pour oil into a medium-size pot and heat over medium heat. (The oil is ready when a kernel of popcorn dropped into it pops right away.)

2. Pour in the popcorn and cover the pot tightly.

3. Shake the pan once or twice before the corn starts popping.

4. Keep shaking the pan until the popping sounds stop.

5. Take the pan off the stove and pour the popped corn into a bowl.

6. Add topping or seasoning to taste, then serve.

Makes about 6 cups.

also reduced the animal population by hunting, not only for meat but also for sport and to sell furs and feathers. Yet some Native Americans continued hunting buffalo for food as recently as the end of the 1800s.

3 FOODS OF THE NATIVE AMERICANS

Various seafood, especially fish, played an important dietary role in the Northeast and Pacific regions. Meat was the central dietary ingredient for the Indians of the Midwestern plains, where large herds of buffalo roamed. Deer and rabbits were also hunted. Native tribes of the Northeast hunted elk, moose, and bears.

Corn has always been a sacred food for Native Americans. Different tribes have different names for corn, but all of them mean

AP Photo/J.D. Pooley

Ears of popcorn are harvested by this farmer. The kernels will be removed from the cob later, and packaged for sale. Native Americans introduced both popcorn and wild rice to European settlers.

Succotash (Traditional Corn and Bean Stew)

Ingredients

1 butternut squash, washed

2 cans of corn

1 package (10-ounce) frozen lima beans

Salt and pepper

Butter

Procedure

1. Scoop out the seeds from the squash and cut into small pieces. Trim the peel away from the pieces and place them into a heavy kettle.

2. Add enough cold water to cover the squash.

3. Bring the mixture to a boil, reduce the heat, cover, and simmer until the squash is tender, about 30 minutes.

4. Add the corn to the squash.

5. Stir in the lima beans and continue simmering until the corn and beans are tender, about 15 minutes.

6. Drain the vegetables. Toss them with salt, pepper, and butter.

Serves 4.

Beans were also an important part of the Native American diet. Fresh or dried, they were cooked in soups and stew, mashed into cakes, and ground into flour. Other popular

Native American foods included squash, pumpkins, sunflower seeds, many types of nuts and wild berries, peanuts (first brought to America by the Spanish), and wild rice. (Wild rice is not really rice—it is a type of grass.) Indians of the Northeast tapped maple trees for sap. The sap was used to make maple syrup and maple candy. Chili peppers were also eaten by Indians in the deserts of the Southwest, where the fruit of cactus plants was used to make syrup and jam.

Maple Baked Beans

Ingredients

4 cups water

1 pound dried navy or butter beans

1 Tablespoon butter

1 medium onion, sliced

1½ teaspoons salt

1 cup maple syrup

1 teaspoon dry mustard

1 teaspoon ginger

Procedure

1. Preheat oven to 350°F.

2. Add water and beans to a large pot.

3. Bring to a boil over high heat, reduce heat, and simmer uncovered for 2 hours.

4. Drain the beans, reserving 2 cups of the liquid. (Add water to make 2 cups, if necessary.)

5. In a small skillet, melt the butter.

6. Add the onions and sauté until golden, about 7 to 10 minutes.

7. Add the onion, salt, maple syrup, dry mustard, and ginger to the beans, and transfer mixture to a large baking pot.

8. Cover the pot and bake in the middle of the oven for 2 hours.

9. Occasionally check the beans and add more water, if necessary.

10. After 2 hours, uncover the beans and bake an additional 30 to 45 minutes, or until all the liquid is absorbed.

11. Let stand about 10 minutes before serving hot.

Serves 10 to 12.

4 FOOD FOR RELIGIOUS AND HOLIDAY CELEBRATIONS

Native Americans had a number of spiritual customs connected with food. The Comanches used to thank the Creator for their food. They would hold a piece of food toward the sky and then burn it as an offering. Cherokee medicine men offered a special apology to the Corn Spirit after their people cut down the ripened corn stalks. In the Southwest, hunters tried to inhale the last breath of animals they killed so that the spirit of the animals would be kept alive.

Native tribes observed many different food taboos (forbidden foods). The Comanches would not eat fish or poultry. Many Native Americans avoided food that came in pairs because twins were thought to bring bad luck.

Native Americans celebrated the corn harvest with feasts, which might last for days. Large amounts of food and drink were consumed. In many tribes, a special festival was held as soon as the corn began to ripen. It was called the Green Corn Festival. For

Festive Clambake Menu

1 bushel steamed clams
1 dozen lobsters
1 dozen baked potatoes
2 dozen ears sweet corn
Serves 12

the Creek Indians, this festival was so important that it was considered the beginning of the new year. Other tribes celebrated the raspberry harvest or the killing of the first buffalo of the hunting season.

Some native tribes celebrated their bounty with a special festival called a potlatch. The goal of a potlatch was to use up as much of the host's wealth as possible. Guests stayed for days and received lavish gifts. It would be their turn to host a potlatch the next time.

Pumpkin-Corn Sauce

Ingredients

1 can (15-ounce) plain pumpkin, without spices

1 cup frozen or canned corn, drained well

½ teaspoon salt

2 Tablespoons honey

Procedure

1. Preheat oven to 350°F.

2. Grease a baking sheet with a small amount of oil.

3. Put the corn on the greased baking sheet and bake for 20 minutes.

4. Mix the corn, pumpkin, salt, and honey in a medium-size pot.

5. Heat the mixture over medium heat until it starts to bubble.

6. Turn the heat to low and cook for 10 minutes, stirring from time to time.

7. Serve with grilled chicken or pork.

Serves 4.

Buffalo Stew

Ingredients

4 pounds beef roast (rump or eye round)

2 Tablespoons oil

1 large onion, coarsely chopped

1 cup red wine or beef stock

1 pound mushrooms, coarsely chopped

2 Tablespoons flour

1 Tablespoon beef stock

Salt and pepper, to taste

Procedure

1. Cut the meat into bite-size chunks.

2. In a large skillet over medium heat, sauté the meat, turning constantly with a wooden spoon.

3. As the meat begins to brown, add the onion and lower the heat.

4. Season with salt and pepper, and add wine or beef stock.

5. Simmer the meat uncovered in the liquid for 40 to 50 minutes, or until the meat is tender when you stick a fork into it. (There will be about ¼ cup of liquid left.)

6. Remove the meat and onions to a platter with a slotted spoon.

7. Add the mushrooms to the cooking liquids and cook on medium heat. Reduce heat.

8. Coat meat and onions with flour and return to the pan.

9. Cook for 1 to 2 minutes, until flour cooks, then add the beef stock, salt, and pepper. Simmer until thickened slightly.

10. Ladle into bowls. Serve hot.

Serves 8 to 10.

Pumpkin Bread

Ingredients

1½ cups sugar

½ cup oil

1 cup pumpkin filling

2 eggs

⅓ cup water

¾ cup whole wheat flour

1¼ cups white flour

1 teaspoon baking soda

1 teaspoon salt

¼ teaspoon baking powder

½ cup raisins, dried apples, or dried cranberries

½ cup walnuts, chopped

½ teaspoon each cinnamon, ground cloves, and nutmeg

Procedure

1. Preheat oven to 300°F.

2. In a large bowl, combine sugar, oil, pumpkin, eggs, and water; mix well.

3. In another bowl, mix whole wheat flour, white flour, baking soda, and salt.

4. Add the dry ingredients to the pumpkin mixture and stir until moistened. Pour batter into greased loaf pan.

5. Bake for 1 hour, or until a knife inserted in the center of the loaf comes out clean.

6. Cool thoroughly before slicing.

Makes 1 loaf.

5 MEALTIME CUSTOMS

Native Americans have always been thrifty cooks. They are known for never wasting any food. In the days when they hunted buffalo, they used almost every part of the animal. Only the buffalo hearts were left behind. This was supposed to help the herd to grow again.

Traditionally, Native Americans ate one-course meals. There were no separate courses such as appetizers or desserts. Corn was an important snack between meals. Cherokee Indians ate two main meals a day. In the morning they had cornmeal mush, or cereal. They also ate it in the evening, with meat and vegetable stew or broiled meat or fish.

Hospitality has always been an important tradition among Native Americans. Guests were always served first at meals. If an Inuit Indian had only one bit of food, he would first offer it to his guest. Native Americans also made sure that the poor people in their community had enough to eat.

Modern Native Americans eat many of the same foods as other Americans. They enjoy everyday foods like hot dogs, hamburgers, potato chips, and ice cream. However, some traditional foods, such as corn, are still important. So are dishes like frybread, a popular snack and side dish. Frybread is probably the most popular traditional food still eaten by Native Americans.

It is served with meals or eaten as a snack or dessert.

Indian Fry-Bread

Ingredients

2 cups flour

1 teaspoon baking powder

½ teaspoon salt

Warm water

¼ cup vegetable oil

Procedure

1. Combine the flour, baking powder, and salt together in a bowl.

2. Slowly add the warm water while stirring.

3. Continue to add water to make a soft dough.

4. Mix and knead the dough with your hand until it is smooth. Sprinkle with flour if the dough is sticky.

5. Cover the dough with a towel and let it rest for 10 minutes.

6. Break the dough into lemon-size pieces.

7. Roll each piece into a ball and flatten into a pancake.

8. Heat the oil in a heavy frying pan.

9. Add as many pieces of bread as will fit in the pan.

10. Fry the pieces on each side until they are lightly browned.

11. Remove the brown fry-breads and place them on a plate covered with a paper towel.

12. Serve the fry-breads with salt or maple syrup.

Serves 4.

Iroquois Strawberry Drink

Ingredients

1 pint ripe strawberries (about 2 cups)

4 cups water

4 Tablespoons maple sugar (or brown sugar)

Procedure

1. Wash the strawberries and remove the stems and leaves.

2. Cut the berries into small pieces and mash them in a large bowl.

3. Stir in the water and maple sugar. (For a very smooth drink, puree the mixture in a blender.)

4. Chill in the refrigerator or serve at once.

Serves 4.

Pinole (Cornmeal Drink)

Ingredients

½ cup yellow cornmeal

2 Tablespoons honey

½ teaspoon cinnamon

1 cup boiling water

Procedure

1. Heat a heavy frying pan on medium heat.

2. When the pan is hot, sprinkle in the cornmeal to dry roast it.

3. Stir until you see the cornmeal starting to turn brown (about 6 to 8 minutes).

4. When it is brown, scrape the cornmeal into a small bowl.

5. Add the honey and cinnamon and mix well.

6. Stir 1 Tablespoon of this mix into 1 cup of boiling water, as the Native Americans did, and let it sit for 10 minutes.

Serves 1.

Popped Wild Rice

Ingredients

1 cup wild rice

3 cups water

1 teaspoon oil

½ teaspoon salt

Procedure

1. Rinse the rice well in cold water.

2. Bring the water, oil, and salt to a boil in a heavy saucepan. Stir in the rice.

3. Reduce the heat, cover, and simmer until the rice pops (about 1 hour).

4. Do not lift the cover while the rice is cooking.

Serves 4.

6 POLITICS, ECONOMICS, AND NUTRITION

Native American families are twice as likely to experience "food insecurity" (defined by the U.S. Department of Agriculture as not having access to enough food to meet basic needs) and hunger as other families. Almost one-third of Native Americans live at or below the poverty level. Poverty is the main reason Native Americans experience hunger, malnutrition, and undernutrition. The Bureau of Indian Affairs reports that unemployment and the remote location of most reservations contributes to a high percentage of Native American children (over 40 percent) living in poverty.

The United States Department of Agriculture created the Food Distribution Program on Indian Reservations (FDPIR) in the 1970s to distribute food. However, in the early years of the program, many of the food items distributed (cheese and processed meats) were high in fat. As of the early twenty-first century, the Food Distribution Program has expanded to include lower fat meats, fruit, and vegetables.

7 FURTHER STUDY

Books

Carson, Dale. *New Native American Cooking.* New York: Random House, 1996.

Erdosh, George. *Food and Recipes of the Native Americans.* New York: PowerKids Press, 1997.

Lund, Duane R. *Early Native American Recipes and Remedies.* Cambridge, Minn.: Adventure Publications, 1995.

Native American Cookbook: Lenni Lenape Historical Society. Allentown, PA: Museum of Indian Culture, n.d.

Penner, Lucille Recht. *A Native American Feast.* New York: Macmillan, 1994.

Tribal Cooking: Traditional Recipes and Favorite Stories. Lac du Flambeau, WI: Great Lakes Inter-Tribal Council, Inc., n.d.

Web Sites

Books about Native American food. [Online] Available http://www.astuk.com/products-by-keywords/native-american-food.html (accessed April 17, 2001).

The Cooking Post. [Online] Available http://www.cookingpost.com/ (accessed April 17, 2001).

National Bison Association. [Online] Available http://www.nbabison.org/membership/sale.html (accessed April 17, 2001).

Native American Cooking. [Online] Available http://www.councilfire.com/ntvfoods.htm (accessed August 1, 2001).

Native Way Cookbook. [Online] Available http://222.wisdomkeepers.org/nativeway (accessed August 1, 2001).

United States
Northeast Region

Recipes

Indian Pudding 140
Succotash 141
Johnnycakes 141
Maple Butter 142
Boston Baked Beans 143
Coffee Milkshake 144
New England Clam Chowder 144
New England Boiled Dinner 144
Hot Cranberry Punch 146
Honey-Baked Apples 146

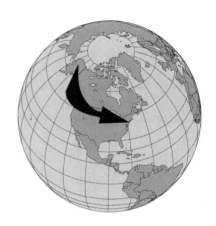

1 GEOGRAPHIC SETTING AND ENVIRONMENT

The Northeastern region of the United States, often referred to as "New England," consists of Connecticut, Maine, Massachusetts, New Hampshire, Rhode Island, and Vermont. Most of these states border the Atlantic Ocean on their eastern coasts. The combined population of these states is more than 14 million people.

Besides the Atlantic Ocean waters, states such as New Hampshire and Maine have thousands of lakes and ponds, which are protected by the Executive Office of Environmental Affairs.

2 HISTORY OF FOOD

Long before the British first established permanent settlements in what was to be called New England, the Native American tribes of North America had already occupied the land for hundreds of years. In fact, much of what the European settlers learned about harvesting crops and surviving in a new land was adapted from the Native Americans. Crops such as beans and squash are native to the Indians and are still evident in modern-day New England dishes, such as baked beans and succotash (a corn and bean dish). Maize ("Indian corn") was first domesticated in Mexico, but was introduced to the Native Americans nearly 400 years before the arrival of the first settlers.

When the first settlers, the Pilgrims, arrived off of Cape Cod, Massachusetts (which was named for its abundance of cod fish), in the 1620s, they brought from England such foods as meat and vegetables. Local tribes were kind to the Pilgrims and helped them plant seeds for harvesting

one of the most important cooking utensils in the colonial kitchen, allowing several items to be cooked at the same time. Baking was also important. A sheet of tin was initially used to reflect the sun's heat onto foods to heat them. However, Dutch ovens (portable metal covered cooking pots) set over an open fire and permanent brick ovens were used later. Most of what people ate was prepared at home (although shops carried baked goods and imported items). "Eating out" was not common, as most taverns were used mostly to socialize and drink.

By the 1800s, Irish families, Acadians from French Canada, Scandinavians, Central European Jews, Eastern and Western Europeans, and those from the Middle Eastern nations began immigrating to New England. With the introduction of new immigrant groups came new traditions, tastes, and foods. Immigrants from Southeast Asia, Latin America, and the Caribbean soon followed, making the New England diet a melting pot of international cuisines.

crops such as cranberries, corn, and tomatoes, taught them how to catch lobsters and clams, and taught them how to raise turkeys (called "turkie-birds" by the settlers). The Pilgrims were also introduced to such native dishes as Indian pudding, Boston brown bread, New England Clam Chowder, and maple syrup. In return, the Europeans introduced many foods to the Indians, including almonds, apples, apricots, garlic, lemons and limes, peaches, rice, sugarcane, wheat, cattle (beef, cheese, and milk), and pigs (pork, ham, and bacon).

During the 1600s, most colonists ate from carved round or square wooden bowls known as trenchers. Within 100 years, bowls and plates made of pewter replaced trenchers. Early colonists ate with knives and spoons, with the fork first introduced in 1633. Linen napkins were often kept in high supply due to frequent messes when having to eat with fingers. The iron kettle pot was

Indian Pudding

Ingredients

3 cups milk

⅓ cup molasses

⅓ cup yellow cornmeal

1 egg, beaten

¼ cup sugar

2 teaspoons butter

½ teaspoon ginger

½ teaspoon cinnamon

¼ teaspoon salt

Typical Colonial New England Meal

Dried, salted codfish

Bacon

Cabbage and turnips

Brown biscuits with butter

Apples

White crackers

Indian pudding

Beer

Procedure

1. Preheat oven to 300°F.

2. In a deep skillet, combine the milk and molasses.

3. Using a wooden spoon, blend in the cornmeal.

4. Cook this mixture over medium heat for about 10 minutes, stirring frequently. It will gradually become thick and hard to stir.

5. Remove from heat and let the mixture cool slightly.

6. In a mixing bowl, combine the egg, sugar, butter, spices, and salt.

7. Add the hot cornmeal mixture a few spoonfuls at a time, stirring until smooth.

8. Pour into a 2-quart casserole dish and bake uncovered for about 1½ hours. Indian pudding is great served hot with ice cream or whipped cream.

Serves 6.

Succotash

Ingredients

2 cups lima beans, fresh or frozen

2½ cups yellow corn kernels

3 Tablespoons butter

1 teaspoon sugar

¾ teaspoon salt

¼ teaspoon pepper (optional)

¾ cup heavy cream

Procedure

1. Cook the beans by covering with boiling, salted water in a saucepan for 7 to 8 minutes. They should be tender but still firm.

2. Add the corn and cook for 5 more minutes.

3. Drain the corn and beans and set aside.

4. Melt the butter in a heavy skillet over medium heat.

5. Add the drained corn and beans and stir to coat.

6. Add the remaining ingredients and stir until they are well blended. Succotash goes well with sliced tomatoes, biscuits, and baked apples sweetened with maple syrup.

Serves 4 to 6.

Johnnycakes

These used to be called "journey cakes" in colonial days because they were made to take on long journeys.

Ingredients

7 Tablespoons cornmeal

1 Tablespoon sugar

½ teaspoon salt

½ cup milk

Procedure

1. Place the cornmeal, sugar, and salt in a bowl and pour boiling water over them to scald the cornmeal.

2. Beat the mixture to a smooth consistency, then beat in the milk.

3. Grease a heated griddle, drop the batter by spoonfuls on the griddle, and fry until golden brown on each side. For thinner johnnycakes, flatten each cake with a spatula.

4. Serve warm with maple syrup.

Serves 4 to 6.

Maple Butter

Ingredients

1 cup maple syrup

½ stick butter, softened

Procedure

1. In a mixing bowl, thoroughly combine the maple syrup with the butter until well blended.

2. Place in a container and store in the refrigerator until ready to serve.

3. Serve on toast or crackers.

EPD Photos

An employee at Woodman's restaurant in Essex, Massachusetts, scoops fried clams into a box. Woodman's is believed to be the first place to serve fried clams. People in the Northeast enjoy clams in many forms—steamed, fried, and in chowders.

3 FOODS OF THE NORTHEAST

When most people picture the foods eaten in the New England states, the simple and hearty foods eaten by early colonists probably come to mind. Many of the same foods of hundreds of years ago continue to be grown and produced, including cranberries in Massachusetts and Rhode Island, dairy and sheep farming (especially in Vermont), and maple syrup throughout forested areas.

However, 200 years of immigrants migrating to the region have introduced a variety of international foods into New England's cuisine. In the countryside of Maine, New Hampshire, and Vermont, Scottish and Welsh settlers' descendents continue to bake scones (biscuit-like pastries) and oatmeal bread and grow a variety of vegetables. French Canadians introduced split pea soup and pork pies to the region, and Germans in central Massachusetts and Maine still make sauerkraut and a variety of sausages.

Each state in New England has its own unique foods that it contributes to the cuisine of the region as a whole. Connecticut adds milk, eggs, apples, pears, mushrooms, and beef. Its long coastline gives the state a successful fishing industry that includes clams, oysters, scallops, and a variety of fish. The world's first lollipop was made in the city of New Haven in 1908. Maine is the country's leading producer of blueberries and lobster (over 90 percent of U.S. lobsters are from Maine's waters). More potatoes are grown in Aroostock County in Maine than in any other county in the country.

Cranberries require an abundance of water to grow, and the "Bay State" of Massachusetts has plenty (it is the country's leading producer of the fruit). In addition, the first commercial yogurt was produced in the northeast city of Andover, and baked beans are Boston's renowned dish. New Hampshire is dotted with dairy cows that produce large amounts of milk. Potatoes, apples, and the production of maple syrup are also popular. Seafood, poultry, eggs, and milk are most common in Rhode Island. Clams are its specialty, as demonstrated by its famous clambakes each year. Vermont's maple syrup production (the largest of any state) is nationally recognized. Dairy products and apples are also produced on the state's abundance of farms. The popular Ben & Jerry's ice cream was first made in the city of Burlington.

As a whole, New Englanders are best known for the wide variety of seafood the North Atlantic Ocean has to offer. New England Clam Chowder and Maine lobster are two popular seafood dishes. Seasonal fruits such as apples, pumpkins, and a variety of berries are often included in meals, particularly as ingredients in fruit pies (which may be served for dessert along with puddings and milkshakes called frappes). The boiled dinner, a one-dish meal of boiled beef, cabbage, carrots, and potatoes, is a New England original. After a large meal, tea (an influence from the British), coffee, or a New England wine or beer may be served.

Boston Baked Beans

Ingredients

1 onion, peeled, halved, and cut into small pieces

2 cans (16-ounce each) navy beans

1 can (15-ounce) pinto beans

⅓ cup ketchup

3 Tablespoons brown sugar

2 Tablespoons molasses

1 Tablespoon spicy brown mustard

Procedure

1. Preheat oven to 400°F.

2. Spray a sauté pan with cooking spray and heat over medium heat.

3. Add the onion pieces and sauté until soft, about 5 minutes.

4. Open the 3 cans of beans and empty them into a sieve in the sink, rinsing them under cold, running water.

5. In a 2-quart casserole dish, stir together the onions, beans, ketchup, brown sugar, molasses, and mustard.

6. Cover and bake for 30 minutes until the mixture is bubbly.

Makes 6 servings.

Coffee Milkshake

Ingredients

1 cup brewed or instant coffee, cooled

1 cup 2 percent milk

1 Tablespoon light vanilla syrup

3 scoops coffee ice cream

4 ice cubes

Procedure

1. Put the coffee, milk, vanilla syrup, and ice cream in a blender and mix well.

2. Add the ice cubes and blend until the mixture is smooth.

3. Pour into 4 tall glasses.

Makes 4 servings.

New England Clam Chowder

Ingredients

1 can (10¾-ounce) condensed cream of celery soup

1 can (10¾-ounce) condensed cream of potato soup

1 can (10¾-ounce) New England Clam Chowder

2 cans (6½-ounce each) minced clams, with juice

1 quart half-and-half cream

1 pint heavy whipping cream

Procedure

1. In a slow cooker, mix together cream of celery soup, cream of potato soup, New England clam chowder, 1 can undrained clams, 1 can drained clams, half-and-half, and heavy whipping cream.

2. Cook on low for 6 to 8 hours.

Serves 6.

New England Boiled Dinner

Ingredients

4 pounds corned beef (brisket is preferred)

8 small white onions

8 parsnips

8 carrots

8 potatoes

1 cabbage, cored and cut into eighths

Procedure

1. Wash the beef under running water.

2. Place in a large kettle, cover with water, and slowly bring to a boil, cooking for 5 minutes.

3. Remove debris, cover, and simmer for 2½ hours.

4. Skim excess fat off liquid, then bring meat to a rolling boil; add whole onions, parsnips, carrots, and potatoes, and cook gently, uncovered, about 20 minutes.

5. Add cabbage and cook for 20 more minutes, or until vegetables are tender.

6. Place meat on a hot, large platter and arrange vegetables around it. Garnish with parsley.

Serves 8.

A Typical Christmas Menu

Baked honey ham
Apple, cranberry, and walnut salad
Mashed potatoes
Cabbage
Buttermilk biscuits
Hot cranberry punch
Eggnog Custard Pie

4 FOOD FOR RELIGIOUS AND HOLIDAY CELEBRATIONS

The United States was partially founded by those who were seeking religious freedom. The Pilgrims, who settled in New England in the early 1620s, had separated themselves from the Protestant Church of England. They were known as separatists. As a result of this early influence, much of New England today is Protestant, although influences from other countries have brought Catholicism and Judaism to the area as well. Because the majority of the population is Christian, such holidays as Easter and Christmas are widely celebrated. Thanksgiving originally was the Pilgrims' celebration of their first year in the New World. It has become a national holiday now celebrated by all Americans for everything their country means to them, including food on the table. The historic Thanksgiving feast in 1621 lasted three days and included venison (deer), wild turkey, bass, cod, and maize (corn).

Secular (nonreligious) holidays are also widely celebrated, often in the form of festivals throughout New England. Many festivals honor the harvest of a specific crop or the abundance of seafood off New England's shores.

Connecticut's Southington Apple Harvest Festival is the first two weekends in October, celebrating the rich tastes of the state's autumn apple harvest. The city of Norwalk participates in the Norwalk Seaport Association's Oyster Festival each September. For three days, nearly 100,000 visitors come to the festival to enjoy live entertainment, art and craft shows, and a diverse selection of food. Oyster boats and tall ships line the waterfront while oysters and clams are eaten in abundance.

One of New Hampshire's largest annual events is the two-day Seafood Festival each fall. The city of Hampton Beach hosts more than 50 restaurants and 60 caterers, who compete for prizes for the best food, including best New England Clam Chowder and most creative dish. Maine's famous lobsters are honored each year during the Maine Lobster Festival in the city of Rockland. The event celebrates the importance of the lobster to the region. Festival participants enjoy an abundance of lobster, as well as a parade and a variety of marine displays. At the end of the five-day festival, The Great International Lobster Race takes place. Contestants compete to run over partially submerged lobster crates floating in the city's harbor.

Hot Cranberry Punch

Ingredients

4 cups cranberry juice

4 cups apple juice

¼ cup freshly squeezed lemon juice

Sugar (optional)

2 cinnamon sticks

2 cloves

2 lemons, thinly sliced

Cranberries, whole

Apple slices

Procedure

1. Mix all of the ingredients in a pot, except for the cranberries and apple slices, over medium heat.

2. Reduce heat to low and gently simmer until completely warmed.

3. Garnish with cranberries and apple wedges.

4. To serve chilled, simmer for 10 to 15 minutes, then chill for at least 2 hours. Serve with frozen whole cranberries instead of ice cubes.

Serves 15.

Honey-Baked Apples

Ingredients

4 large tart apples

4 Tablespoons honey

3 Tablespoons orange juice

1 Tablespoon walnuts, chopped

Sugar

Nutmeg

Procedure

1. Preheat oven to 400°F.

2. Core the apples, being careful not to cut all the way through; trim off a ½-inch band of skin around the middle.

3. Combine the honey, orange juice, and nuts, and divide equally to fill the apple centers.

4. Set the apples in a baking dish, pouring in boiling water to ¼-inch depth.

5. Bake for 50 to 60 minutes, or until the apples are tender.

6. Sprinkle the tops with a little sugar and freshly grated nutmeg, then put the apples under the broiler to glaze. Bring to the table hot.

Serves 4.

5 MEALTIME CUSTOMS

New Englanders typically eat three meals a day. Blueberry pancakes or waffles topped with fresh fruit and homemade maple syrup are popular breakfast dishes, and bacon, sausage, or eggs often accompany them. Toast with butter or homemade preserves with freshly squeezed juice may also be served. A national restaurant chain founded in Massachusetts, Dunkin Donuts, is a popular establishment to purchase coffee, donuts, and other morning or afternoon pastries.

On the weekdays, people on the go often grab lunch at a restaurant, occasionally from a deli, a seafood or steak restaurant, or possibly from one of many national fast food chains. Children may purchase lunch at school or prepare one at home and bring it with them to eat. Peanut butter and jelly, meat and cheese, and grilled cheese sandwiches are most popular. Most lunches will also include fruit (often an apple or banana) and a snack such as potato chips or pretzels. To drink, milk is most commonly served in school cafeterias, although soda and fruit juices are also popular among children.

Dinners may include several courses, including an appetizer, fresh bread with butter, salads, the main meal, and dessert. Appetizers are commonly soups, particularly cream-based chowders made with seafood and vegetables (such as potatoes and celery).

Desserts are likely to follow dinner after a short break to digest some of the food. During this break, freshly brewed coffee and tea are often enjoyed, particularly when guests are visiting. Popular desserts are fruit pies, sweet puddings, and ice cream. New Englanders consume more ice cream than any other region in the country.

6 POLITICS, ECONOMICS, AND NUTRITION

In general, the people living in Northeastern United States receive adequate nutrition and have a large amount of natural resources. Because of its coastline, Connecticut has a wide variety of fish and seafood including clams, oysters, scallops, and flounder. These foods, caught from the Atlantic Ocean, are considered low in fat and rich in iron. Maine is also a top fishing state and is famous for its lobster. Rhode Island fishermen pull in large amounts of tuna and striped bass.

Not only is fish and seafood plentiful along the coastal Northeastern states, but fruits and vegetables are grown as well. In north Maine, more potatoes are grown in Aroostock County than any other county in

the United States. Maine is also among the top producers of blueberries, and Massachusetts grows more cranberries than any other state. Such fruits provide a variety of vitamins and nutrients, including Vitamin C.

For those who cannot afford it, the United States government provides money and programs to assist needy families. New Englanders, however, earn about $5,000 more in annual income than the national average.

7 FURTHER STUDY

Books

Beilenson, Evelyn L. *Early American Cooking: Recipes from America's Historic Sites*. White Plains, New York: Peter Pauper Press, Inc., 1985.

D'Amico, Joan and Karen Eich Drummond. *The United States Cookbook*. New York: John Wiley & Sons, Inc., 2000.

Jones, Judith and Evan. *The L.L. Bean Book of New New England Cookery*. New York: Random House, 1987.

Kent, Deborah. *How We Lived in Colonial New England*. Tarrytown, New York: Marshall Cavendish Corporation, 2000.

Kirlin, Katherine S. and Thomas M. *Smithsonian Folklife Cookbook*. London: Smithsonian Institution Press.

Klein, Ted. *Celebrate the States: Rhode Island*. Tarrytown, New York: Marshall Cavendish Corporation, 1999.

Sherrow, Victoria. *Celebrate the States: Connecticut*. Tarrytown, New York: Marshall Cavendish Corporation, 1998.

Web Sites

Creative Cuisine. [Online] Available http://www.creativecuisine.com (accessed April 24, 2001).

Ethnic Food and the Making of Americans. [Online] Available http://

www.hup.harvard.edu/Featured/
We_Are_What_We_Eat/dailymeals.html
(accessed April 24, 2001).

Sallys Place. [Online] Available http://www.sallys-
place.com/food/ethnic_cusine/us.htm
(accessed April 24, 2001).

Soup Recipes. [Online] Available http://
www.souprecipe.com (accessed April 24,
2001).

Welcome to America the Bountiful. [Online]
Available http://www.lib.ucdavis.edu/exhibits/
food/ (accessed April 24, 2001).

United States
Southern Region

Recipes

Chess Pie 150
Old Fashioned Turnip Soup 151
Cornbread 152
Southern Fried Chicken 152
Chicken and Sausage Gumbo 153
Creole Seasoning 153
Sweet Potato Pie 154
Fruitcake Cookies 154
Mardi Gras King Cake 155
Collard Greens with Hamhocks 157
Sweet Tea 157
Pralines 157

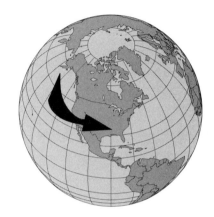

1 GEOGRAPHIC SETTING AND ENVIRONMENT

The South is distinctive in its customs, food, and even dialect and accent. More than any other regional group, people born and raised as Southerners tend to think of themselves as Southerners all their lives, no matter where they live. By most geographic definitions, the northern border of the South is marked by the Ohio River and is straddled by the nation's capital, Washington, D.C.

In alphabetical order, the states in this region are Alabama, Arkansas, Florida, Georgia, Kentucky, Louisiana, Mississippi, North Carolina, Oklahoma, South Carolina, Tennessee, Texas, Virginia, and West Virginia. Some people also consider Maryland part of the "South."

2 HISTORY AND FOOD

The population of the Southern United States is made up of many different peoples who came to the region in a variety of ways, each contributing to what is now called "Southern cooking." American Indians, native to the region, taught European settlers to grow and cook corn, a grain unknown in Europe at the time. Spanish explorers in the 1500s brought pigs with them, introducing pork to the region. West Africans carried some of their traditional foods with them, such as watermelon, eggplant, collard greens, and okra, when they were brought to the United States by force as slaves beginning in the 1600s. Creoles, known for their unique use of spices, are descended from French and Haitian immigrants who later mingled with Spanish settlers in the New Orleans area. "Cajuns,"

SOUTHERN & CREOLE

The first African American, and the only ex-slave, known to have written a cookbook was Abby Fisher. Her book, *What Mrs. Fisher Knows About Old Southern Cooking*, was published in 1881 and includes many recipes that would now be considered soul food.

Chess Pie

No one knows for sure how chess pie got its name. Although there are many recipe variations, all have eggs, sugar, and butter in the filling, and many contain buttermilk.

Ingredients

½ cup butter

½ cup brown sugar

1 cup white sugar

3 eggs

1 Tablespoon vinegar

½ teaspoon vanilla

1 Tablespoon cornmeal

9-inch pie crust, unbaked

Procedure

1. Preheat oven to 350°F.
1. Melt the butter and add the brown and white sugar to it. Stir well to combine.
2. Add other ingredients and stir gently to mix. Do not beat the mixture.
3. Pour into unbaked pie shell and bake for about one hour, until a knife inserted in the center comes out clean (with no custard sticking to it).
4. Cool on a wire rack and serve.

Serves 6 to 8.

also recognized for their unique style of cooking, were originally Acadians, French settlers in Nova Scotia who were driven out by the British in 1755 and made their way to New Orleans. In Louisiana, crawfish (resemble miniature lobsters) and catfish are popular, prepared in dozens of different ways. Fried catfish is popular all across the South. Texas's spicy and flavorful "Tex-Mex" cuisine reflects the state's close proximity to the spicy cuisine of Mexico.

The American Civil War (1861–1865) had a major impact on the South and its food. Many plantations and farms were destroyed during the conflict. To survive, Southerners ate whatever they could grow or find, and nothing went to waste. When the economy began to recover, most African Americans were not allowed to share in the newfound wealth and continued to eat the simple foods that were available during the war. This type of simple and inexpensive food became known later as "soul food."

Old Fashioned Turnip Soup

Ingredients

2 pounds veal bones

1 pound turnips

½ gallon water

Salt and pepper, to taste

Procedure

1. Place veal bones in a large pot with ½ gallon of water.
2. Boil the water and veal bones until the water is reduced by half the amount.
3. Put the turnips in the pot with the bones and boil until the turnips are soft.
4. Pour off the liquid, then add salt and pepper to taste. Serve hot.

Makes 4 servings.

Because kitchens only had wood-burning stoves in the late 1800s, recipes did not give baking temperatures or times. Bakers simply had to guess how long something would take to bake and keep checking it. Even if they had baked something many times before, the fire could be hotter or cooler each time, so baked goods had to be checked frequently to make sure they did not burn.

EPD Photos

The turnip, popular for generations in the South, is the main ingredient in Old-Fashioned Turnip Soup.

3 FOODS OF THE SOUTHERN UNITED STATES

The staple food of the Southern United States is corn—it is used in grits (hulled and coarsely ground corn cooked to a thick–soup consistency and eaten at breakfast), a wide variety of breads and cakes, and as a breading on fried foods. Corn is native to the United States and was introduced to European settlers by American Indians. Another staple food in the South is pork, originally brought to America by Spanish explorers in the 1500s. Chitterlings (pronounced CHIT-lins), made from pig intestines, were traditionally seen as a "poor person's" food, but have recently begun to appear in fine restaurants. Barbecued meat, usually pork, on a grill is a Southern tradition.

Besides grits, most people also think of southern-fried chicken when they hear "Southern cooking." Traditionally served for Sunday dinner, fried chicken has become a stereotype of Southern food, popularized by Colonel Sanders' Kentucky Fried Chicken. Other meats, such as steak, are also "chicken-fried" in the South by breading and frying them. Cornbread, made from cornmeal, is typically eaten with a Southern meal.

Okra, black-eyed peas, and collard greens are all common Southern-grown vegetables that were brought to the region by African slaves. The name for meat stew, gumbo, often thickened with okra, comes from a West African word for okra, *quingombo*. Jambalaya, a pork and rice stew from the Creole and Cajun New Orleans region, takes its name from the French and Spanish words for ham: *jambon* and *jamón*, respectively. Crawfish, catfish, and shrimp are enjoyed all across the South.

Favorite desserts in the South include chess pie, sweet potato pie, pecan pie, key lime pie, and watermelon, which is also the most popular melon in the United States.

Cornbread

Ingredients

1½ cups white or yellow cornmeal

½ cup flour

2 teaspoons baking powder

1 teaspoon sugar

1 teaspoon salt

¼ teaspoon baking soda

¼ cup, plus 1 to 2 Tablespoons vegetable oil, shortening or bacon grease

1½ cups buttermilk

2 large eggs

Procedure

1. Preheat oven to 425°F.

2. Combine cornmeal, flour, baking powder, sugar, salt and baking soda in large mixing bowl.

3. Add ¼ cup oil, buttermilk and eggs, stirring with a wooden spoon until just mixed.

4. In a medium-sized skillet with an oven-proof handle, add the 1 to 2 tablespoons oil and heat until very hot.

5. Quickly pour the batter into the hot skillet, and with a potholder, transfer the skillet to the oven.

6. Bake for 20 to 25 minutes or until golden brown and center springs back when lightly pressed. Best served warm.

Makes 8 servings.

Southern Fried Chicken

Ingredients

3-pounds chicken pieces (any combination of breasts, wings, drumsticks, and thighs)

1 cup flour

Salt and black pepper, to taste

½ cup milk

Vegetable shortening, melted

2 teaspoons bacon grease

Procedure

1. Rinse the chicken under running water.

2. In a plastic bag, combine the flour, salt, and pepper and shake until well blended.

3. Pour the milk into a bowl.

4. Place a large cast-iron skillet on the stove at moderate heat.

5. Fill the skillet half full of melted shortening and add the bacon grease.

6. Dip some of the chicken pieces into the milk and then put them in the plastic bag. Shake vigorously to coat evenly.

7. Remove the chicken pieces from the bag, shake the excess flour back into the bag, and then arrange the pieces in the hot oil, making sure not to crowd the pan.

8. Fry 15 to 20 minutes until golden brown and crisp, turn over with tongs, and reduce heat to low to moderate, frying another 15 minutes until golden brown.

9. Drain on another paper bag or paper towels.

10. Repeat the procedure with the rest of the chicken pieces, adding shortening and bacon grease, if necessary.

Serves 4 or more.

Chicken and Sausage Gumbo

Ingredients
½ cup oil

½ cup flour

1 large onion, chopped

1 bell pepper, chopped

2 stalks celery, chopped

3 cloves garlic, minced

2 quarts chicken stock

1 bay leaf

1 teaspoon Creole seasoning (see recipe), or to taste

½ teaspoon dried thyme

Salt and pepper, to taste

1 pound andouille or smoked sausage, cut into ½-inch pieces

½ chicken, cut into pieces

4 green onions, tops only, chopped

⅓ cup fresh parsley, chopped

Procedure

1. Brown the sausage in a skillet over medium heat. Remove from the pan and set aside.

2. Season the chicken with salt, pepper, and Creole seasoning, and brown quickly in the remaining sausage grease in the frying pan.

3. Remove the chicken and carefully discard the grease.

4. In a large pot, heat the oil over medium heat and add the flour, stirring constantly. This roux (sauce) should become a dark reddish-brown color.

5. Add the vegetables and stir quickly. Continue to cook, stirring constantly, for about 4 minutes.

6. Add the stock, seasonings, chicken, and sausage.

7. Bring to a boil, then cook for about 1 hour, skimming fat off the top as needed.

8. Add the chopped onion tops and parsley, and heat for 5 more minutes.

9. Serve over rice in large, shallow bowls.

Serves about 6.

Creole Seasoning

Ingredients
2 teaspoons onion powder

2 teaspoons garlic powder

2 teaspoons dried oregano

2 teaspoons dried basil

1 teaspoon dried thyme

1 teaspoon black pepper

1 teaspoon white pepper

1 teaspoon cayenne pepper

5 teaspoons sweet paprika

Procedure

1. Combine the ingredients and mix well with a wooden spoon.

2. Use to season dishes such as chicken and sausage gumbo (see recipe).

Sweet Potato Pie

Ingredients

1 stick margarine

2 cups sweet potatoes, cooked and mashed

2 cups sugar

1 small can evaporated milk

2 pie crusts, unbaked

1 teaspoon vanilla extract

3 eggs

1½ teaspoons cinnamon

Procedure

1. Preheat oven to 350°F.

2. (To cook sweet potatoes, peel them and chop into small chunks, then boil until soft, about 25 minutes.) Mix mashed sweet potatoes, sugar, and margarine until creamy.

3. Add remaining ingredients and mix well.

4. Pour into piecrusts and bake for 1 hour.

Makes 2 pies.

4 FOOD FOR RELIGIOUS AND HOLIDAY CELEBRATIONS

Most US Southerners are Christian, for whom the main holidays are Christmas and Easter. It is a longstanding tradition in the South to make fruitcake for Christmas. The Claxton Fruitcake Company in Georgia sells more than 200 tons of fruitcake each year. The typical main dish for both holidays is ham. Southerners are known for their country ham, a hindquarter of a year-old hog that is preserved with either salt or sugar, smoked, and then aged for a year or more.

Another Christian holiday that receives special treatment in the South is Mardi Gras (French for "Fat Tuesday"), the day of feasting before Lent begins. New Orleans is famous for its Mardi Gras celebration, which lasts several days and involves parades, balls, music, and lots of food. One traditional element of the feast is the King Cake in which a small figurine or dried bean is baked inside. Whoever gets the piece with the figurine in it is crowned king or queen for the day.

Fruitcake Cookies

Ingredients

1 pound margarine or butter

1 pound brown sugar

3 eggs

1 Tablespoon milk

5 cups flour

1 can shredded coconut

1 teaspoon baking soda

1 pound raisins

1 pound nuts (pecans or walnuts), chopped

1 pound candied cherries, available in most supermarkets

1 pound candied pineapple, diced, available in most supermarkets

Procedure

1. Preheat oven to 375°F.

2. Measure 4 cups flour and mix with baking soda.

3. Combine fruit, coconut, and nuts and mix with remaining 1 cup flour in a separate mixing bowl.

4. Cream the butter, sugar, and milk together.

5. Add the eggs one at a time.

6. Beat in flour and baking soda mixture gradually, switching to a wooden spoon or spatula if batter becomes too stiff for the electric mixer.

7. Stir fruit, coconut, and nut mixture into batter.

8. Drop by teaspoonful onto greased cookie sheet.

9. Bake for 10 minutes.

Makes about 3 dozen.

Mardi Gras King Cake

Ingredients

1 package dry yeast

¼ cup warm water

6 teaspoons milk, boiled then cooled

4 to 5 cups flour

½ pound butter

¾ cup sugar

¼ teaspoon salt

4 eggs

2 teaspoons butter, melted

Small plastic figurine or bean (optional)

Light corn syrup, for topping

Colored sugar crystals (green, yellow, purple), for topping

Procedure

1. Preheat oven to 325°F.

2. Dissolve yeast in warm water.

3. Add milk and about ½ cup of flour.

4. In a large bowl, blend butter, sugar, salt, and eggs.

5. Add yeast mixture and mix thoroughly.

6. Gradually add 2½ cups of flour to make a stiff dough.

7. Place in a large greased bowl and brush with melted butter.

8. Cover with a damp cloth and allow to rise until double in size, about 3 hours.

9. When risen, punch down.

10. Use 1 cup or more of flour to knead dough and roll into a 4-foot long rope.

11. Form into an oval on a 14- x 17-inch greased cookie sheet, connecting ends of the rope with a few drops of water.

12. Press the figurine (or bean) in the dough from underneath.

13. Cover with a damp cloth and let rise until double in size, about 1 hour.

14. Bake for 35 to 45 minutes or until lightly browned.

15. Brush top of cake with corn syrup and sprinkle with colored sugar.

5 MEALTIME CUSTOMS

The main meal of the day in the Southern United States used to be at midday and was called "dinner." The smaller evening meal was referred to as "supper." In recent years, the main meal has moved to the evening, though most Southerners still call it "dinner." During the 1800s, the era of large plantations, guests would often come to visit for days or weeks at a time. Hospitality is very important to Southerners, and hosts prepare huge meals for their guests. A dinner menu from the mid-1800s may have included five kinds of meat, cucumbers and tomatoes, hot rolls, and five different desserts, plus three beverages. The African slaves did not share in this abundance of food, but lived on small amounts of salt pork, cornbread, and hominy (corn mush), plus whatever greens they could grow them-

Two Tennessee cooks prepare kettles of fried catfish at the World's Biggest Fish Fry held over four days in Paris, Tennessee. Nearly 12,000 pounds of catfish were fried during festival.

selves. This meager diet became the basis for what is known today as "soul food."

Southerners' favorite beverages are iced tea, usually loaded with sugar and called "sweet tea," and soft drinks, many of which were invented in the South. Coca-Cola was developed in 1886 in Atlanta, Georgia. Pepsi was created 10 years later in North Carolina. Dr. Pepper first appeared in Waco, Texas, in 1885, and Mountain Dew was first produced in either Virginia or Tennessee around 1961. Other Southern-made soft drinks include Royal Crown Cola, Nehi fruit-flavored drinks, Barq's root beer, and Gatorade. The South continues to be the largest consumer, as well as producer, of soft drinks. In the 1990s, North Carolina was the number one soft-drink consumer of the 50 states with over 50 gallons consumed per person per year.

Other snack foods native to the South include corn dogs (hot dogs breaded with cornmeal), pralines (almond or pecan clusters), and the Moon Pie (a chocolate-coated marshmallow sandwich cookie), invented at the Chattanooga Bakery in Tennessee in 1917.

Collard Greens with Hamhocks

Ingredients

1 to 2 medium smoked hamhocks, or 1 pound smoked pork neckbones

2 pounds collard greens, or 3 to 4 large bunches (if fresh greens are not available, use frozen)

1 teaspoon salt

Hot sauce (optional)

Procedure

1. Put hamhocks or neckbones in large pot of water.

2. Boil for about 1½ hours, adding more water as needed.

3. If using fresh greens, rinse well.

4. Stack greens and roll together.

5. Slice rolled greens into thin strips.

6. When hamhocks begin to fall apart, add greens to pot. Add as many as you can, then let them wilt down to make room to add more. Continue until all greens are in the pot. (If using frozen greens, simply pour them right from the package into the pot when hamhocks begin to fall apart.)

7. Add salt, cover, and cook for 30 minutes over medium heat, stirring every few minutes.

8. When greens are tender, serve with slotted spoon so liquid drains out. Sprinkle hot sauce on greens, if desired.

Sweet Tea

Ingredients

3 to 4 cups water

3 family-sized tea bags

¼ teaspoon baking soda

1 to 1⅓ cups of sugar

Procedure

1. Bring 3 to 4 cups water to a boil.

2. Add baking soda and tea bags to the water.

3. Remove from heat and cover.

4. Allow to set for 10 to 15 minutes.

5. Pour into a gallon pitcher and add sugar.

6. Add cold water to make 1 gallon.

7. Refrigerate.

Serves 4 to 6.

Pralines

Ingredients

1 cup light brown sugar

1 Tablespoon flour

⅓ teaspoon salt

1 egg white

1 teaspoon vanilla extract

2 cups chopped pecans

Procedure

1. Preheat oven to 275°F.

2. Combine the sugar, flour, and salt in a mixing bowl.

3. Beat egg white until stiff in a separate bowl.

4. Add vanilla extract to egg white.

5. Fold in flour mixture and pecans.

6. Drop by teaspoonfuls onto a greased cookie sheet.

7. Bake for 30 to 35 minutes.

8. Cool and remove cookies from sheet.

Makes 2 to 3 dozen.

6 POLITICS, ECONOMICS, AND NUTRITION

People living in the Southern states generally receive adequate nutrition in their diets. Traditional Southern cooking is high in fat and calories, and many modern Southerners are striving for a healthier lifestyle, reserving the delicious fried and sugary foods for special occasions and celebrations.

Southern teens and adults are slightly more likely than people from other parts of the United States to smoke cigarettes. This is due in part to the role tobacco farming has played in the economies of such states as Kentucky, Tennessee, Virginia, and North and South Carolina.

7 FURTHER STUDY

Books

Edge, John T. *A Gracious Plenty: Recipes and Recollections from the American South.* New York, Putnam, 1999.

Edge, John T. *Southern Belly: The Ultimate Food Lover's Companion to the South.* Athens, GA: Hill Street Press, 2000.

Egerton, John, Ann Bleidt Egerton, and Al Clayton. *Southern Food: At Home, on the Road, in History.* Chapel Hill: University of North Carolina, 1993.

Hayes, Isaac. *Cooking with Heart and Soul.* New York: Putnam Publishing Group, 2000.

Lundy, Ronni. *Butter Beans to Blackberries: Recipes from the Southern Garden.* New York: North Point Press, 1999.

Miller, Joni. *True Grits: The Southern Foods Mail-Order Catalog.* New York: Workman Publishing, 1990.

Reed, John Shelton, and Dale Volberg Reed. *1001 Things Everyone Should Know about the South.* New York: Doubleday, 1996.

Web Sites

AnythingSouthern.com: The Online Gateway to the South. [Online] Available at http://www.anythingsouthern.com (accessed April 12, 2001).

Chitterling Site, The (or The Soul Food Site). [Online] Available at http://www.chitterlings.com (accessed April 12, 2001).

Civil War Interactive. [Online] Available at http://civilwarinteractive.com (accessed April 12, 2001).

CooksRecipes.com. [Online] Available http://www.cooksrecipes.com (accessed April 17, 2001).

Creole and Cajun Recipe Page, The. [Online] Available at http://www.gumbopages.com/recipe-page.html (accessed April 13, 2001).

DixieDining.com. [Online] Available at http://www.dixiedining.com (accessed April 12, 2001).

Gritlit.com: More Southern food than you can shake a stick at. [Online] Available at http://www.gritlit.com (accessed April 12, 2001).

Grits. [Online] Available at http://www.grits.com (accessed April 12, 2001).

Origins of Southern Food, Fall 1996: Applied Anthropology course project at the University of West Florida in Pensacola. [Online] Available at http://www.uwf.edu/tprewitt/sofood (accessed April 11, 2001).

SouthernFood.com. [Online] Available at http://www.southernfood.com (accessed April 12, 2001).

Southern Foodways Alliance. [Online] Available at http://www.southernfoodways.com (accessed April 12, 2001).

Southern U.S. Cuisine. [Online] Available at http://southernfood.about.com/food/southernfood (accessed April 12, 2001).

United States
Western Region

Recipes

Chuck Wagon Brisket 161
Cranberry Salsa 162
Fortune Cookies 163
Marinated Artichokes 163
Broiled Salmon Steaks 164
Chinese Peanut Sauce 164
Apple Crisp 165
Parsley New Potatoes 165
Blueberry Muffins 165

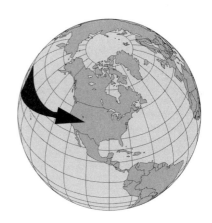

1 GEOGRAPHIC SETTING AND ENVIRONMENT

The Western region of the United States may be defined as including the states west of the Rocky Mountains. These include California, Oregon, and Washington bordering the Pacific Ocean on their western coasts; moving east, Montana, Idaho, Nevada, Utah, and Arizona form the basin and plateau region and feature some of the most dramatic scenery in the United States, with canyons (including the Grand Canyon), the Great Salt Lake, and the deserts of the southwest. The combined population of these states is about 42 million, the majority of whom (about 33 million) live in California.

The environment of this region is varied, but one problem that affects most Western states is the availability of fresh water. In urban areas, air pollution inspired government regulations in the 1970s, 1980s, and 1990s to help curb smog-producing emissions from industrial and consumer sources (especially from automobiles). California has stringent auto emissions regulations. Phoenix, Arizona, also has problems with air quality.

2 HISTORY AND FOOD

As pioneers began moving west, they expected living to be difficult. Traveling with horses, livestock, and their families, the pioneers encountered challenges both from the harsh environment and with the Native Americans already living in this region. While some Native American tribes were friendly, others regarded the white pioneer settlers as invaders. Disease and lack of adequate food and water were trials that the pioneers confronted as they traveled from eastern towns and villages to the open spaces of the West. Drought was a regular

AP Photos/L.M. Otero

Nopales, or prickly pear cactus, appears in the bowl behind a display of foods. All dishes contain nopales: nopales and eggs (bottom left); beef and nopales stir fry (top left); cactus juice (bottom center); nopales salsas and nopales avocado dip (bottom right). Dishes made using nopales are rarely seen outside the Western United States.

happening on the prairie, which made life hazardous for those making a long westward journey.

Despite these hardships, the pioneers enjoyed social gatherings. Shooting contests, riding and cattle-roping competitions, and other games that made use of the pioneer skills were organized. Some pioneer men, many of whom traveled without their families, also liked to gamble, playing poker in the saloons that grew up around settlements.

Most women did not get involved in the competitive sports, but socializing was important to them. Women would meet to "put up" (can) stores of food for the long winter months, gather for "sewing bees" when they would make quilts or do mending. Carding and spinning of wool and weaving cloth were also done, often meeting together as a group. Men and women would join together for dancing parties and harvest socials; many of their activities included food.

Chuck Wagon Brisket

Brisket was roasted all day over a low campfire until the cowboys returned for their evening meal.

Ingredients

2–4 pounds lean beef brisket

½ cup white sugar

¼ cup salt

Ground pepper, to taste

2 cups barbeque sauce

½ cup white vinegar

1 cup catsup

1 18-ounce jar of grape jelly

Procedure

1. Coat brisket with sugar, salt, and pepper. Let meat marinate in this combination in the refrigerator overnight.

2. Combine barbecue sauce, vinegar, catsup, and jelly in a saucepan and heat until jelly melts completely.

3. Line a baking dish with a sheet of foil long enough to wrap back over the top of the brisket.

4. Place brisket in foil-lined baking dish. Pour cooking sauce over brisket.

5. Wrap foil around sauce-covered brisket, and pinch foil edges together.

6. Preheat oven to 325°F.

7. Roast for about 2 hours in the oven. Reduce heat to 200°F and roast an additional 4 hours.

8. Remove brisket carefully from oven with mitts. Place on a large cutting board.

9. Cut meat crosswise into thin slices. Place on serving platter and cover with foil to keep warm.

Serves 8 to 10.

The foods of these early pioneer days combined the recipes brought by families from the East, as well as contributions from the Spanish and Native American inhabitants of the region. Ranchers raised cattle on vast tracts of lands, and often took their meals over an open campfire while tending to the herds. A chuckwagon—a large cart that carried the supplies and utensils for cooking—often accompanied the ranchers as they traveled with the herd. The foods prepared for these men, known as cowboys, were hearty and filling.

As farmers began planting crops that grew well in this region and women became adept at cooking the foods of the area—such as buffalo and deer—recipes and eating habits were transformed.

In the late nineteenth century, workers were needed to build both the cities of the West and the transcontinental railroad to bring more people from the East. Immigration from Asia, especially from China, brought new foods and cooking styles. In the twentieth century other Asian groups (Japanese, Koreans, and Vietnamese) and Mexicans immigrated to the West, and contributed their own influences on the style of cooking. While meals still centered around meat, especially beef, cooks began including the vegetables and grains of Asia and Mexico in their recipes.

In the late twentieth century healthy lifestyles became a focus of many Western citizens, and the Western region seemed to take the lead in learning how to eat healthier and live a healthier lifestyle. Many people became vegetarians (those who do not eat meats and animal products), preparing meals from legumes (beans), rice, and vegetables.

3 FOODS OF THE WESTERN REGION

The foods found in the West are varied. The Pacific Northwest has fruit orchards—pears, cherries, apples, blueberries, and grapes. Northern California, Oregon, and Washington, are all home to wineries and produce much of the fresh fruit that is sold throughout the United States.

California produces almost 100 percent of the artichokes consumed in the United States, and is also a top producer of dried fruits like raisins, prunes, dates, apricots, and figs. The coastal waters of the Pacific Ocean provide abundant seafood, including Dungeness crab, calamari (octopus), and salmon. Relishes and salsas are popular accompaniments to many dishes, and combine the influences of the many ethnic groups who live in the coastal states.

Idaho is home to vast potato farms, and the Idaho potato is stocked by almost every supermarket in the United States. Reflecting the Americans' love for potatoes that are quick and easy to prepare, about three-fourths of Idaho's potato crop is now processed and sold as frozen french fries, instant mashed potatoes, or similar products. In Idaho, fur-trapping was one of the first occupations. Today it is also famous for gold and silver mines, and beautiful mountains and rivers.

Meat, especially beef, is produced on the vast tracts of ranch land that make up large sections of sparsely populated states such as Arizona, Wyoming, Montana, and Colorado. (Ranches in Arizona and Wyoming average over 3,700 acres each.)

In the desert regions, one might find foods, jellies, and candies made from the prickly pear cactus, or *nopales*. These foods are rarely seen outside the Southwestern region where the prickly pear cactus grows in the hot, dry desert landscape.

Cranberry Salsa

Ingredients

1 package fresh or frozen cranberries

⅓ cup sugar

¼ cup thinly sliced green onions

¼ cup chopped fresh cilantro

1 lime, grate the peel, then squeeze for juice (You may substitute a lemon.)

1 or 2 jalapeño chilies, seeded and finely diced

1 teaspoon ginger

Procedure

1. Coarsely chop cranberries with a knife or in the food processor.

2. Combine chopped cranberries with all other ingredients.

3. Mix well in food processor.

4. Use as a dip with tortilla chips or to accompany chicken or fish.

Makes 1-2 cups

Fortune Cookies

Chinese immigrants introduced the fortune cookie first to California.

Ingredients

1 egg white

¼ teaspoon vanilla extract

1 pinch of salt

¼ cup white flour

¼ cup white sugar

Clean strips of white paper, about 4 inches long and ½ inch wide

Procedure

1. Write fortunes on strips of paper.

2. Preheat oven to 400°F. Generously grease 2 cookie sheets.

3. Mix the egg white and vanilla until foamy, but not stiff.

4. Sift together flour, salt, and sugar.

5. Blend dry mixture into egg mixture.

6. Place teaspoon-sized portions of batter on the cookie sheets, at least 4 inches apart. Use the bottom of the spoon to make round shapes of about 3 inches in diameter. Make sure batter is spread evenly.

7. Bake just 3 or 4 cookies at a time, because cookies must be formed while still warm from the oven. (While one batch of cookies is baking, prepare the next one.)

8. Bake cookies for 5 minutes or until golden-colored on the edge. The center will remain pale.

9. Remove the cookies from the oven and with a wide spatula quickly remove and place upside down on a wooden board.

10. Quickly place one fortune in the center of each cookie.

11. Fold the cookie in half. Place the folded edge across the rim of a glass and pull the pinted edges down, one on the inside of the cup and one on the outside.

12. Place folded cookies into the cups of a muffin tin or an empty egg carton to hold their shape.

13. Allow the cookie to cool completely in the muffin tin to set the shape.

Makes 1 dozen cookies.

Marinated Artichokes

Ingredients

1 to 2 pounds small artichokes

3 cups water

2 Tablespoons lemon juice

⅓ cup red wine vinegar

⅓ cup olive oil

1½ teaspoon salt

Ground pepper, to taste

4 medium cloves garlic, peeled

Procedure

1. Cut off the tips and stems of the artichokes. Remove any outer leaves with scissors or paring knife.

2. Combine all remaining ingredients in an uncovered saucepan. Add prepared artichokes.

3. Heat mixture over medium-high heat until the liquid begins to boil. Lower heat and simmer the mixture for about 30 minutes.

4. Remove from heat and cool to room temperature. Serve artichokes at room temperature or chilled.

Makes 4 servings.

Broiled Salmon Steaks

Ingredients

4 salmon steaks, ¾ inches thick

1 teaspoon salt

Ground pepper, to taste

¾ stick butter (6 Tablespoons)

1 Tablespoon vegetable oil

½ Tablespoon dill or parsley

1 lemon, quartered

Procedure

1. Preheat broiler.
2. Rinse salmon steaks under cold running water and pat dry. Lightly sprinkle with salt and pepper.
3. In small saucepan melt butter over low heat. Set aside.
4. Lightly coat broiler pan with vegetable oil. Lay fish on the pan.
5. Brush fish generously with melted butter. Broil for 5 minutes, brushing with melted butter after 2 to 3 minutes.
6. Wearing oven mitts, remove pan from oven and carefully turn fish over. Brush with more butter and return to oven.
7. Broil as you did the first side. To test for doneness, carefully remove pan from oven (wearing the mitts). Using a fork, pull some fish away. The fish flesh should look opaque and light pink, not translucent and glassy, and the flesh will flake away easily.
8. If the fish is not done, return to oven and broil for another 1 to 3 minutes. Overcooking will dry the fish out.
9. Serve, garnish with remaining melted butter, dill or parsley, and lemon wedges.

Makes 4 servings.

Chinese Peanut Sauce

Use as a dip for fresh raw vegetables, as a dressing for cold or hot noodles, or as a sauce for freshly cooked fish.

Ingredients

½ cup peanut butter, chunky or smooth

½ cup hot water

2 Tablespoons soy sauce

2 Tablespoons sugar

3 medium cloves of garlic, peeled and minced

1 teaspoon cider vinegar

1–2 Tablespoons fresh cilantro, minced

Cayenne pepper, to taste

Procedure

1. Place peanut butter in a small bowl. Add the hot water, stirring with a small spoon or whisk until evenly blended.
2. Stir in remaining ingredients. Mix well.
3. Cover tightly and put in the refrigerator.
4. Let sauce come to room temperature to serve.

Makes 1 cup.

In the cool, wet climate of the Northwest region, apples have become an important food product for the state of Washington. This orchard crop dominates the state's agricultural economy. Washington is the nation's leading producer of apples.

Apple Crisp

Crunchy apples from Washington state are the inspiration for many baked apple dishes.

Ingredients for bottom

About 10 medium-sized Granny Smith or Golden Delicious apples, peeled, cored, and sliced.

½ cup white sugar

¼ cup brown sugar, light or dark

¼ cup lemon juice

1 teaspoon cinnamon

Ingredients for topping

½ cup white flour

¾ cup white sugar

½ stick butter, at room temperature

Procedure

1. Preheat oven to 350°F.
1. Place sliced apples in a bowl. Toss with the sugars and cinnamon
2. Place apple mixture in an 8-inch or 9-inch square baking dish.
3. Sprinkle with the lemon juice. Set aside.
4. To make topping, combine flour and sugar. With fork, add butter. Mixture will be crumbly.
5. Sprinkle topping over apples in pan.
6. Bake for 45 minutes, or until apples are soft and topping is browned.

Serves 6 to 8.

Parsley New Potatoes

Ingredients

1 Tablespoon salt

12 small new potatoes of about the same size, scrubbed clean

1 stick butter

¼ cup finely–chopped fresh parsley, or 2 Tablespoons dried parsley

½ fresh lemon, cut into four wedges, optional

Procedure

1. Pour 3 quarts of water into large pot, add the salt, and bring to a rolling boil.
2. Gently, and carefully, drop the potatoes into the boiling water.
3. Boil for 15 to 20 minutes. Test doneness with fork. (Fork should pierce the potato easily.)
4. Place cooked potatoes in a colander in the sink, allowing them to drain.
5. Melt butter in a skillet, add the cooked potatoes, shaking until well-covered.
6. Sprinkle on the parsley.
7. Serve with the lemon wedges on the side.

Serves 4.

Blueberry Muffins

Ingredients

1 cup blueberries, washed and drained

1¾ cups plus 2 Tablespoons flour

1 Tablespoon baking powder

1 teaspoon salt

½ cup white sugar

1 egg

1 cup milk

½ stick butter, melted and cooled

Paper baking cups

Procedure

1. Preheat oven to 400°F
2. Line each cup of muffin tin with a paper baking cup.

EPD Photos.

Blueberry muffins are easy to make and may be enjoyed anytime—for breakfast, with lunch or dinner, or as an afterschool or bedtime snack.

6. Sprinkle the remaining 2 Tablespoons of flour over the blueberries and add them to the batter, stirring gently.

7. Spoon batter into the baking cups, filling each about ¾ full.

8. Bake 18 to 20 minutes, or until the tops are dry and the muffins slightly shrunk from the sides of the muffin tin.

9. Remove tin from the oven, and turn muffins out of the pan. Allow to cool slightly.

Serves 12.

4 FOOD FOR RELIGIOUS AND HOLIDAY CELEBRATIONS

Western citizens celebrate all the usual American holidays—Fourth of July, Halloween, and Thanksgiving. Religious holidays such as Christmas and Easter (Christian); *Rosh Hashanah, Yom Kippur,* and *Hanukkah* (Jewish), and *Ramadan* and *Eid al-Fitr* (Muslim) are celebrated by people who practice those religions.

Two holidays celebrated in the Western region reflect the influence of Hispanic and Asian immigrants to the area. A special celebration influenced by the immigration of Mexicans into the United States is *Cinco de Mayo* (Fifth of May). Latino Americans hold festivals where special food, such as guacamole, Mexican rice, refried beans, burritos, and tamales, are served.

Cinco de Mayo remembers the victory of the Mexican army over the French forces in the Battle of Puebla on May 5, 1862. To the Mexicans and Mexican Americans, this event is regarded as a symbol of their resistance to European domination. In the United

3. Sift 1¾ cups of the flour with the baking powder, salt, and sugar into a large mixing bowl.

4. In a smaller mixing bowl beat the egg with a fork or whisk until frothy. Add milk and melted butter to the egg mix, and stir to combine.

5. Add the liquid mixture to the flour mixture. Stir gently with a wooden spoon to blend. Do not beat; the batter will be a little lumpy.

States, this holiday was celebrated as early as 1863 in San Francisco, California.

With the influx of Asians into the Western region, especially northern California, came celebrations long-practiced in Asia. One holiday of special note is the Chinese New Year. Because the Chinese New Year is based on the lunar (moon) calendar, it is celebrated on the occasion of the first new moon of the year. Chinese New Year can fall anytime between January 21 and February 19. For its celebrants, Chinese New Year is the beginning of the Spring Festival. The New Year is celebrated for fifteen days. On the last day, called Lantern Day, children march in parades carrying brightly colored, glowing paper lanterns.

Chinese New Year is a time of family reunions, thanksgiving, and remembering one's ancestors. When families gather there are always special foods that are prepared and eaten. One special dish is called *jai*, which is a vegetarian dish of root and fibrous vegetables. Each vegetable ingredient has a special meaning and is included in the dish for a purpose. Many holiday practices are based on traditions and superstitions. Vegetables prepared for New Year represent good luck, happiness, and prosperity for the coming year. It is considered unlucky to include any white ingredients, such as tofu or bean sprouts.

Other foods for New Year's celebrations include whole fish (for abundance); chicken (for prosperity); head, tail, and feet of the chicken (for completeness); and uncut noodles (for long life).

Chinese New Year's traditions require that the entire house be cleaned before the celebration and all brooms and mops put away. To use a broom or mop on New Year's would be to "sweep away" the good luck. Another popular custom is to wear and decorate with the color red, as this color is considered lucky. Although many modern Chinese Americans are not superstitious, they carry on the traditional practices in celebration of the New Year with family and friends..

5 MEALTIME CUSTOMS

Westerners generally eat three meals each day, like most Americans. However, because of the intense heat in the desert regions, lunch may be more leisurely, and features a lighter menu of cool foods (such as salads and fresh fruits) accompanied by refreshing lemonade, limeade, or iced tea.

6 POLITICS, ECONOMICS, AND NUTRITION

Westerners generally receive adequate nutrition in their diets, although recent immigrants sometimes experience difficulties finding adequate resources for shopping for and preparing food from their native countries. With an abundance of rich soil and farming land, the region produces nutritious fruit and vegetable crops. Westerners in general are among the most active and health-conscious of all Americans.

7 FURTHER STUDY

Books

Altman, Linda Jacobs. *Celebrate the States: California.* New York: Benchmark Books, 1997.

Braun, Matthew. *Matt Braun's Western Cooking.* Chicago: Contemporary Books, 1998.

D'Amico, Joan and Karen Eich Drummond. *The United States Cookbook.* New York: John Wiley & Sons, Inc., 2000.

Kirlin, Katherine S. and Thomas M. *Smithsonian Folklife Cookbook.* London: Smithsonian Institution Press.

Linsenmeyer, Helen Walker. *From Fingers to Finger Bowls: A Lively History of California Cooking.* San Luis Obispo, CA: EZ Nature Books, 1990.

Web Sites

Lone Hand Western. [Online] Available http://www.lonehand.com/ (accessesed August 17, 2001).

Northwest Palate. [Online] Available http://www.nwpalate.com/ (accessed August 17, 2001).

Nutritiously Gourmet. [Online] Available http://www.nutritiouslygourmet.com/ (accessed August 17, 2001).

Western Recipes. [Online] Available http://www.cowboyshowcase.com/recipes.htm (accessed August 17, 2001).

Vietnam

Recipes

Nuoc Cham (Dipping Sauce) 171
Pho Bo (Beef Noodle Soup)....................................... 172
Coconut Custard.. 174
Canh Bi Ro Ham Dua (Braised Pumpkin) 174
Banh Chuoi Nuong (Banana Cake).......................... 175
Caphe (Vietnamese Coffee)..................................... 176
Soda Chanh (Lemon Soda) 176
Spring Rolls 177

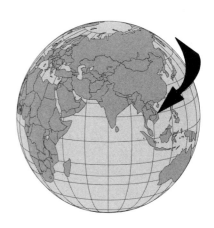

1 GEOGRAPHIC SETTING AND ENVIRONMENT

Vietnam is a long, narrow country in Southeast Asia. China borders it to the north; Cambodia, Laos, and the Gulf of Thailand to the west; and the South China Sea (which the Vietnamese call "the East Sea") to the east. Covering a total of 327,500 square kilometers (126,500 square miles), Vietnam is approximately the same size as Italy and Japan.

The geography of Vietnam plays an important role in the country's cuisine. Rice, the mainstay of the Vietnamese diet, is grown throughout the country but particularly in the Red River delta in the north and Mekong River delta in the south. In fact, the Vietnamese people say that their country resembles a bamboo pole (the narrow central region) with a basket of rice at each end.

Although three-quarters of the land in Vietnam is hilly or mountainous, the long seacoast and many inland waterways provide fish and other aquatic species that are staples in the Vietnamese diet. Vietnamese cuisine varies somewhat by region, with Chinese influences (such as stir fries, noodles, and use of chopsticks) in the north, as well as Cambodian (Khmer) and French influences in the south.

Climate affects the availability of ingredients, which in turn affects the types of dishes that dominate a particular region. During the winter months in the north, families gather around a big bowl of seasoned broth and cook vegetables and meat in it for sustenance and warmth. A fish dish called *cha ca,* which is cooked in a similar fashion, is also quite common. The charcoal brazier (small barbecue-like heat source) that keeps the broth boiling sits on the table and keeps the entire family warm.

In the south, where the climate is conducive to a long growing season and where more ingredients are available, the typical diet contains a wide variety of fruits and vegetables. In the south, sugar and sugarcane are used more often than in the north. A popular dish in the south is *cha tom* (shrimp wrapped in sugarcane). Reflecting

crops. This type of farming, known as shifting cultivation (or "slash and burn"), is practiced most often in the north and in other countries around the world.

Too much fishing has depleted the number of fish in the waters surrounding Vietnam, and the coastal marine environment is also threatened by oilfield development in the south.

Safe drinking water is another problem in Vietnam. According to UNICEF, only 45 percent of Vietnam's inhabitants have access to safe drinking water and only 29 percent have access to adequate sanitation. In recent years, the government and other organizations have begun programs to slow the pace of environmental degradation by educating citizens about sanitation and sustainable agriculture practices.

the tropical climate, foods in the south are cooked for a shorter length of time than in the north. In the north, there are many stir-fries and slow-cooking stews whereas in the south most foods are quickly grilled or eaten raw.

Vietnam is one of the most densely populated countries in the world, with a rapidly growing population, estimated in 2000 to be 76 million people. As the population increases, more land is cleared for agriculture. Estimates in 2001 indicated that less than 20 percent of the land remained forested and 40 percent was considered useless for growing crops. Farmers trying to clear land quickly burn the vegetation to make way for crops. They then overuse the land until it is no longer fertile or suitable for

2 HISTORY AND FOOD

Neighbors have influenced the Vietnamese people in regards to what they eat and how they cook. People from Mongolia who invaded Vietnam from the north in the tenth century brought beef with them. This is how beef became part of the Vietnamese diet. Common Vietnamese beef dishes are *pho bo* (Beef Noodle Soup) and *bo bay mon* (Beef Cooked Seven Ways). The Chinese who dominated Vietnam for 1,000 years taught the Vietnamese people cooking techniques such as stir frying and deep frying, as well as the use of chopsticks. In the south, neighboring Laos, Cambodia, and Thailand introduced such ingredients as flat, Cambodian-style egg noodles, spices, chili, and coconut milk.

Beginning in the sixteenth century, explorers and traders introduced foods such as potatoes, tomatoes, and snow peas. When the French colonized Vietnam (1858–1954), they introduced foods such as baguettes (French bread), pâté, coffee with cream, milk, butter, custards, and cakes. In the 1960s and 1970s (Vietnam War era), the U.S. military introduced ice cream to Vietnam when it contracted with two U.S. dairies to build dozens of ice cream factories.

3 FOODS OF THE VIETNAMESE

Plain rice (*com trang*) is at the center of the Vietnamese diet. Steamed rice is part of almost every meal. The Vietnamese prefer long-grain white rice, as opposed to the short-grain rice more common in Chinese cooking. Rice is also transformed into other common ingredients such as rice wine, rice vinegar, rice noodles, and rice paper wrappers for spring rolls.

Rice is also used to make noodles. There are four main types of rice noodles used in Vietnamese cooking. *Banh pho* are the wide white noodles used in the quintessential Vietnamese soup, *pho*. *Bun* noodles (also called rice vermicelli) look like long white strings when cooked. *Banh hoi* are a thinner version of bun noodles. In addition, there are dried glass, or cellophane, noodles (*mien* or *bun tao*) made from mung bean starch.

Just as essential to Vietnamese cuisine as rice and noodles is *nuoc mam*, a salty fish sauce that is used in most Vietnamese recipes (just as salt is used in most Western dishes). Nuoc mam is produced in factories along the coast of Vietnam. Anchovies and salt are layered in wooden barrels and then allowed to ferment for about six months. The light-colored, first-drained sauce is the most desirable. It is also the most expensive and reserved primarily for table use. Less expensive *nuoc mam* is used in cooking. When shopping for *nuoc mam*, one should look for the words *ca com* on the label, which indicates the highest quality.

The most popular condiment is *nuoc cham* (dipping sauce), which is as common in Vietnam as ketchup is in North America. Saucers filled with *nuoc cham* are present at practically every meal, and diners dip everything from spring rolls to meatballs into it. The recipe that follows can be adjusted to suit individual tastes by using more or less red pepper and *nuoc mam*. *Nuoc cham* is quite simple to make and will keep in the refrigerator for up to 30 days. A few spoonfuls over a bowl of plain rice can be considered an authentic Vietnamese peasant meal.

Nuoc Cham (Dipping Sauce)

Ingredients
1 teaspoon crushed red pepper flakes
1 Tablespoon distilled white vinegar
½ cup *nuoc mam* (fish sauce), available at Asian markets
½ cup fresh lime juice
4 cloves garlic, minced
½ cup sugar

Procedure
1. In a small bowl, soak the red pepper flakes in the vinegar for 10–15 minutes.
2. In a second bowl, combine the fish sauce, lime juice, garlic, and sugar.

3. Stir in 1½ cups boiling water and the pepper-vinegar mixture.

4. Stir until the sugar is dissolved. Allow to cool. Serve at room temperature.

5. Store in a jar in the refrigerator for up to 30 days.

Fish and other aquatic animals, such as squid and eel, are central to the Vietnamese diet. Beef, pork, and chicken are also important, but are consumed in smaller quantities. The unique flavorings in Vietnamese cooking are created with a variety of spices and seasonings, including mint leaves, parsley, coriander, lemon grass, shrimp, fish sauces (*nuoc nam* and *nuoc cham*), peanuts, star anise, black pepper, garlic, shallots, basil, rice vinegar, sugar, green onions, and lime juice. To provide a contrast in texture and flavor to the spicy meat components of a meal, vegetables are often left raw and cut into small pieces (usually cut at an angle, or julienne), especially in the south. Cool, crunchy foods include cucumbers and bean sprouts. The typical Vietnamese meal includes meat and vegetables, either eaten with chopsticks and rice or rolled into rice paper or (red) leaf lettuce and dipped into an accompanying sauce. Traditional preparation techniques are determined by eating habits, geography, and economics.

Pho bo (Beef Noodle Soup) is the signature dish of Vietnamese cuisine. It is often eaten for breakfast, purchased from sidewalk vendors on the way to work or school. *Pho bo* is also a common home-cooked meal, and it is a fun dish to prepare for a group. Seated around a table with dishes of ingredients in the center, each person is

Food Words in Vietnamese

pho (fol) = soup

bo (ball) = beef

ga (gaw) = chicken

gao (gow) = uncooked rice

com (gum) = cooked rice

nuoc mam (nook mum) = fish sauce

bun (poom) = noodles

cuon (coom) = salad or lettuce

given a bowl of spicy beef broth. Then, each selects his or her vegetables and noodles to add to the broth. No two bowls of *pho bo* are alike.

Dessert is not as common in Vietnam as it is in North America, except perhaps for a piece of fresh fruit. One exception is sweet coconut custard, which might follow a celebratory meal.

Pho Bo (Beef Noodle Soup)

Broth ingredients

3 cans beef broth (low-salt suggested)

2 carrots, julienne

4 slices fresh ginger, chopped

1 cinnamon stick

1 star anise

2 whole cloves

2 cloves garlic

Cory Langley

Planting and harvesting rice is labor intensive.

2 teaspoons black peppercorns

3 Tablespoons fish sauce

Accompaniments ingredients

½ pound roast beef (may be purchased from a deli), sliced into very thin bite-sized strips

1 onion, thinly sliced

2 cups fresh bean sprouts

¼ cup chopped cilantro

1 bunch fresh basil, coarsely chopped

2 or more chilies, sliced at a diagonal

2 limes, cut into wedges

1 package rice noodles, cooked

Procedure

1. Make broth by pouring contents from three cans of broth into a large saucepan.

2. Add carrots, ginger, cinnamon, star anise, cloves, garlic, and peppercorns.

3. Simmer covered for 20 minutes.

4. Add fish sauce and simmer about 5 more minutes.

5. Strain by pouring through a colander.

6. To serve, arrange the following on a platter: beef, onion, bean sprouts, cilantro, basil, chilies, lime wedges, and noodles.

7. Ladle the broth into bowls, and serve.

8. Each person chooses items from the platter to add to his or her bowl of broth.

Coconut Custard

Ingredients

5 eggs

1 cup coconut milk

1 cup granulated sugar

1 teaspoon vanilla

Procedure

1. Beat eggs, sugar, coconut milk, and vanilla until frothy.

2. Pour into ramekins (small baking cups).

3. Place in a steamer over boiling water.

4. Cover and cook about 20 minutes or until set. Chill.

Serves 4.

4 FOOD FOR RELIGIOUS AND HOLIDAY CELEBRATIONS

Of the many influences that China has had on Vietnam, the most profound is probably the introduction of Buddhism. The widespread practice of Buddhism in Vietnam has led to the development of one of the world's most sophisticated style of vegetarian cooking (*an chay*), particularly in the coastal city of Hue, which is home to many Buddhists.

On the first and middle days of each lunar month (the full moon and a sliver moon), many Vietnamese do not eat meat, seafood, chicken, or eggs. On these days, the street vendors have numerous vegetarian dishes available. Following is a recipe for a traditional Buddhist vegetarian dish.

Canh Bi Ro Ham Dua (Braised Pumpkin with Coconut Milk)

Ingredients

2 cups peeled and cubed pumpkin (¾-inch cubes)

2 cups thin coconut milk

2 cups cubed sweet potato (¾-inch cubes)

½ cup wood ear or shiitake mushrooms

¼ cup thick coconut cream

½ raw peanuts, soaked in warm water

½ cup thinly sliced zucchini

1 teaspoon sugar

Salt, to taste

Fresh cilantro leaves

Procedure

1. In a deep saucepan, bring coconut milk and pumpkin to a boil.

2. Cook for about 10 minutes, until pumpkin is half done (still too firm to be easily pierced with a knife).

3. Add the sweet potatoes and mushrooms.. Reduce heat and simmer until sweet potatoes are tender.

4. Add thick coconut cream, peanuts, and zucchini. Bring to a boil again, then remove from heat. Season with salt and sugar.

5. Serve garnished with fresh cilantro leaves.

Tet Nguyen Dan (often referred to simply as *Tet)* is the Lunar New Year, perhaps the most important holiday of the year. The New Year does not fall on the same date every year, although it is always in January or February. The official holiday lasts three days, but it is often celebrated for a full seven days. In many ways, the *Tet* "holiday season" is not unlike the December "holiday season" in North America.

Tet Nguyen Dan literally means "first morning of the first day of the new period." It is believed that the course of these few days determines the events of the coming year. People stop quarreling; children vow to behave; and families make special efforts to gather together. Prior to the celebration, homes are cleaned and painted and decorated with yellow *hoa mai* (peach blossoms. Many *Tet* traditions concern *Tao Quan*, the Spirit of the Hearth or the Kitchen God. It is believed that the Kitchen God leaves the household during *Tet* to report on the family to the Emperor of Jade. (Cleaning is avoided during *Tet,* so good luck will not be "swept away.") New clothes are purchased, and old debts are repaid. Many superstitions and traditions revolve around *Tet,* the Vietnamese Lunar New Year. One such belief is that when a watermelon is cut open, the redder the flesh, the more luck the family will have in the upcoming year. Families construct a *Cay Neu* (New Year's tree) from a bamboo pole stripped of its leaves except a few at the top and then decorated with red paper. (Red is believed to ward off evil.) The *Cay Neu* stands in front of their homes to protect them from evil spirits while *Tao Quan* is away.

Families prepare and partake in feasts that include such rare treats as *sup bao ngu* (abalone soup) and *canh vay ca* (shark's fin soup). People carry gifts of food to family and friends. The following recipe for banana cake might be considered the Vietnamese equivalent of fruitcake.

Banh Chuoi Nuong (Banana Cake)

Ingredients
1¼ pounds ripe banana, sliced on the diagonal

1 cup sugar

1 cup coconut milk

½ teaspoon vanilla

7 slices white bread

2 Tablespoons melted butter

Procedure
1. Preheat oven to 350ºF.
2. In a mixing bowl, sprinkle ½ cup of the sugar over the sliced bananas. Set aside.
3. In a saucepan, cook ½ cup of the sugar in the coconut milk until dissolved; then stir in the vanilla.
4. Soak the bread in this sweetened coconut milk.
5. Grease a 12-square-inch nonstick baking pan and arrange ⅓ of the bananas on the bottom.
6. Cover with half of the soaked bread, ⅓ more bananas, another layer of bread, and then finish with bananas. Drizzle the melted butter on top.
7. Cover with foil and bake for one hour. Allow to stand for 12 hours before cutting.
8. Serve with vanilla ice cream.

Serves 16 to 20.

5 MEALTIME CUSTOMS

Vietnamese meals are rarely divided into separate courses. Rather, all the food is served at once and shared from common dishes set out on a low table. The family sits on mats on the floor, and each person has a rice bowl, chopsticks, and soup spoon. Family members use the narrow end of the chopsticks to bring food to the mouth and the wide end to serve from the common dishes. Certain foods, such as spring rolls, are picked up and eaten out of the hand. Most meals include soup, a stir-fry or other main dish, a light salad, and a variety of side dishes.

Snacks are often purchased from street vendors. Popular handheld snacks include spring rolls or pork meatballs on a stick. These foods and *pho* (beef noodle soup) are the equivalent of fast food in Vietnamese cities. Also common between meals are sweet fruits and ice cream, introduced during the Vietnam War era (1960s and 1970s). Another "imported" snack food is a baguette with pâté, a holdover from the years when Vietnam was a colony of France.

Tea (*che* or *tra*) is the most common beverage in Vietnam. It is common practice to prepare enough tea for the whole day first thing in the morning because traditional Vietnamese hospitality dictates that one must be able to serve tea immediately if unexpected visitors drop by. Tea is served before and after meals, but not during. Vietnamese prefer green (unfermented) tea, but the black tea more familiar to Westerners is available in cities.

Although most Vietnamese prefer tea, coffee is grown in Vietnam and is readily available in cities. Served both hot and cold, *caphe* is a well-known Vietnamese beverage consisting of coffee with sweetened condensed milk (recipe follows). Fresh coconut milk is another popular drink that is widely available from street vendors, who simply cut the top off a young coconut and then serve it with a straw. A particularly refreshing beverage on a hot day is *soda chanh* (lemon soda).

Caphe (Vietnamese Coffee)

Ingredients

½ cup sweetened condensed milk

3 to 4 cups hot, strongly brewed French-roast coffee

Procedure

1. Pour 2 Tablespoons of condensed milk into the bottom of each of four clear glass coffee cups.

2. Slowly fill each cup with the coffee, making sure not to disturb the layer of milk at the bottom. Serve immediately.

3. Each person stirs his/her own milk into the coffee before drinking.

4. For iced coffee, pour the condensed milk into the bottom of four tall glasses.

5. Fill the glasses to overflowing with ice cubes, then slowly pour in the coffee.

Serves 4.

Soda Chanh (Lemon Soda)

Ingredients

For simple syrup:

2 cups sugar (to make 1 cup simple syrup)

2 cups water

For soda:

½ cup freshly squeezed lemon juice

Ice cubes or crushed ice

6 cups sparkling water or club soda

Procedure

1. To make the simple syrup, combine 2 cups of sugar and 2 cups of water in a saucepan.

2. Bring to a boil over medium heat, stirring occasionally until the sugar is dissolved.

3. Continue cooking without stirring for about 5 minutes, until the mixture is clear and the consistency of light syrup.

4. Remove pan from heat and allow to cool completely.

5. Either use immediately or pour into a clean, dry jar and refrigerate, covered tightly, until ready to use. Makes about 2½ cups.

6. To make lemon soda: In a pitcher, combine 1 cup simple syrup and lemon juice. Stir to mix well.

7. Fill six glasses with crushed ice; then pour ¼ cup of lemon syrup in each glass. Fill the rest of the way with sparkling water, stir, and serve immediately.

Serves 6.

In southern Vietnam, it is impolite for visitors to refuse a meal. If guests are not hungry, they may excuse themselves by explaining that they have eaten very recently, and then sit down with the hosts and keep them company during the meal. Polite guests will take a small amount so as not to insult their hosts.

In northern Vietnam, the situation is reversed. Invitations to join someone for a meal should always be refused unless they have been repeated many times. This custom most likely stems from the fact that, historically, people in the north did not have enough food to feed an extra mouth. Even though invitations are extended out of courtesy, a guest is expected to refuse them.

Vietnamese city dwellers frequently eat meals outside the home. For example, *pho bo* is available on almost every street corner in the morning, and there are spring rolls or pork meatball kabobs later in the day. The cost of meals outside the home can vary widely depending on the type of establishment in which they are purchased. A street vendor meal (the Vietnamese equivalent of "fast food") might cost US$1 to 2, whereas a meal in a sit-down restaurant ranges from US$4 to 8 per person. At the most exclusive restaurants, an elaborate meal could run as high as US$40 per person.

A typical "lunchbox" type item in Vietnam would be spring rolls, which can be prepared in advance and wrapped in plastic wrap to be eaten out of hand later.

Spring Rolls

Ingredients

3 Tablespoons soy sauce

2 Tablespoons minced garlic

2 Tablespoons honey

1 pound pork tenderloin, trimmed

1½ pound medium shrimp

½ pound rice vermicelli (*Bun* noodles)

2 heads Boston lettuce

2 large carrots, peeled and shredded

¾ fresh mint leaves, shredded

¾ cup fresh cilantro leaves, shredded

35 round rice paper wrappers (8-in diameter)

EPD Photos

Spring roll.

6. Poach the shrimp in boiling water until pink; then peel, slice in half lengthwise, and devein. Set aside.

7. Heat water in a saucepan to cook the rice vermicelli. Soften the vermicelli in hot water; then cook until just tender.

8. Rinse under cold water and drain. Set aside.

9. Separate the lettuce leaves; rinse, dry, and remove the tough center ribs.

10. In a large bowl, toss together the pork, rice vermicelli, carrots, mint, and cilantro.

11. Fill a roasting pan with hot water.

12. Dip one rice paper wrapper into the hot water; then place it on a dishtowel.

13. Arrange a lettuce leaf on the lower third of the wrapper; then spoon 2 Tablespoons of the pork filling onto the lettuce.

14. Fold the bottom edge over the filling and tuck in the sides.

15. Place 2 shrimp halves, cut side down, on top; then roll up into a tight cylinder.

16. As the spring rolls are completed, place them on a serving platter and cover with a damp towel to keep them from drying out.

17. These can be prepared ahead of time and wrapped in plastic wrap until ready to eat.

Serves 15 to 35.

6 POLITICS, ECONOMICS, AND NUTRITION

Vietnam's population is growing rapidly, and the farmers must work hard to produce enough food. Vietnam produces about 25 million tons of rice per year, making it the world's third-largest exporter of this commodity (after Thailand and the United States). Agricultural products include rice, corn, potatoes, soybeans, coffee, tea,

Procedure

1. Preheat oven to 375°F.

2. In a small bowl, mix together soy sauce, garlic, and honey.

3. Place the pork tenderloin in a foil-lined baking pan. Pour the soy sauce-garlic marinade over the meat and turn to coat.

4. Roast about 35 minutes or until the pork is thoroughly cooked.

5. Allow to cool; then slice into 1½-inch-long strips.

bananas, poultry, pork, fish, cashews, and sugarcane.

Socio-economics determines how much protein is in the Vietnam diet. The poorest Vietnamese eat less beef, pork, fish, and poultry than do the upper classes. Consequently, iron-deficiency anemia and other dietary deficiencies are more common among the rural poor. City dwellers tend to fare better economically and are more likely to have access to refrigeration, safe drinking water, and sanitation.

7 FURTHER STUDY

Ferro, Jennifer. *Vietnamese Foods and Culture.* Vero Beach, FL: Rourke Press, 1999.

Halvorsen, Francine. *Eating Around the World in Your Neighborhood.* New York: John Wiley & Sons, 1998.

Jeys, Kevin, Emily Kendrick, and Taran March, Eds. *Vietnam, Cambodia and Laos Handbook.* Chico, CA: Moon Publications, 1996.

Robinson, Daniel. *Vietnam, Laos & Cambodia: A Travel Survival Kit.* Berkeley, CA: Lonely Planet Publications, 1991.

Shalant, Phyllis. *Look What We've Brought You from Vietnam: Crafts, Games, Recipes, Stories, and Other Cultural Activities from Vietnamese Americans.* 2nd ed. New York: J. Messner, 1998.

Tran, Diana My. *The Vietnamese Cookbook.* Sterling, VA: Capital Books, 2000.

Trang, Corinne. *Authentic Vietnamese Cooking: Food from a Family Table.* New York: Simon & Schuster, 1999.

Web Sites

Embassy of the Socialist Republic of Vietnam in the United States. [Online] Available http://www.vietnamembassy-usa.org/ (accessed July 17, 2000).

Vietspace. [Online] Available http://kicon.com (accessed July 17, 2000).

VNN Media. "Vietnam News Network." [Online] Available http://www.vnn-news.com/ (accessed July 17, 2000).

Zimbabwe

Recipes

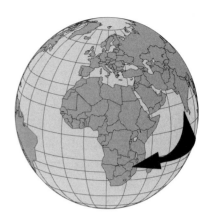

Mapopo (Papaya) Candy.................................... 182
Roasted Butternut Squash 182
Sadza 183
Dovi (Peanut Butter Stew)............................... 183
Cornmeal Cake 184
Zimbabwe Greens.. 185
Rock Shandy 186

1 GEOGRAPHIC SETTING AND ENVIRONMENT

A landlocked country of south-central Africa, Zimbabwe (formerly known as Rhodesia) lies between the Zambezi River on the north and the Limpopo River on the south. It has an area of 390,580 square kilometers (150,804 square miles), slightly larger than the state of Montana. Most of Zimbabwe is rolling plateau, called veld. The highveld (or high plateau) stretches from southwest to northeast, ending in the Inyanga mountains. On either side of the highveld is the middleveld. The lowveld is made up of wide, grassy plains in the basins of the Zambezi and the Limpopo rivers. Among the most serious of Zimbabwe's environmental problems is erosion of its agricultural lands and expansion of the desert. Air and water pollution result from the combined effects of transportation vehicles, mining, fertilizers, and the cement industry.

2 HISTORY AND FOOD

Zimbabwe (zihm-BAHB-way) literally means "House of Stone." This name comes from the 800-year-old stone ruins left by the Shona people. The descendents of the Shona people make up 77 percent of the Zimbabwean population in the twenty-first century; the other 18 percent are Ndebele (eng-duh-BEH-leh).

By 1300, gold was discovered in the Zimbabwe area and the value of the land for farming was discovered. The Shona and Ndebele peoples alternately held power over the area until the Europeans arrived in the 1850s. The British gained control of the Zimbabwe area (then called Rhodesia) until 1923. As a result, food unadorned with spices, commonly associated with British cooking, infiltrated Zimbabwean cuisine with sugar, bread, and tea.

The Lipopo and Zambesi rivers outline the border of Zimbabwe and supply the soil

Mapopo (Papaya) Candy

Ingredients

1 papaya (approximately 1 pound)

2 cups sugar

Lemon peel, grated

½ teaspoon mint, dried or fresh

Procedure

1. Peel the papaya and wash well. Slice into little strips.
2. Place the papaya, mint, grated lemon and sugar over low heat until the sugar dissolves.
3. Cook for 10 minutes, then set aside for half an hour.
4. Reheat over medium heat until the mixture crystallizes.
5. Remove from heat and, using a spoon and fork, mold into ball or stick shapes.

Roasted Butternut Squash

Ingredients

1 large butternut squash

3 Tablespoons butter

Cinnamon, to taste

Procedure

1. Preheat oven to 425°F.
2. Remove the skin of the squash with a vegetable peeler, and cut into large chunks, discarding the seeds.
3. Place the chunks onto a large piece of foil and place the butter on top.
4. Bring up the edges of the foil around the squash and seal tightly.
5. Place on cookie sheet and roast for 20 to 25 minutes, or until the squash is tender and lightly browned.

with moisture and nutrients needed to grow crops. These crops, such as squash, corn, yams, pumpkins, peanuts, and *mapopo* (papaya), flourish during the summer and autumn months, but can be destroyed in the dry winter months. To preserve food for consumption during the winter months, Zimbabweans dry various produce and meats after the rainy season. Tiny dried fish called *kapenta* are a common snack. Another dried specialty is *biltong*, which is sun-dried, salted meat cut into strips similar to beef jerky. Beef or game, such as kudo and springbok (both members of the antelope family), may be used.

6. Sprinkle cinnamon on top to taste.

Serves 4 to 6.

3 FOODS OF THE ZIMBABWEANS

The cornmeal-based dietary staple of Zimbabwe is also the national dish, called *sadza*. *Sadza* to the Zimbabweans is like rice to the Chinese, or pasta to Italians. In fact, *sadza re masikati,* or "sadza of the afternoon" simply means lunch. *Sadza re manheru,* or "sadza of the evening" means dinner. *Sadza* is made from cornmeal or maize, and eaten with relish. Relish can be any kind of vegetable stew, but *nyama,* (meat), such as beef or chicken, is common among families who can afford it. *Sadza* is cooked slowly until thick, like porridge.

Other traditional foods are peanuts, beans, butternut squash, gem squash, green maize (or corn on the cob), and cucumbers. Avocados are plentiful and cheap. *Bowara,* or pumpkin leaves, can be eaten fresh and are commonly mixed into stews, like *dovi* (peanut butter stew).

Meat and game such as beef, springbok (African gazelle), kudu (large antelope), and goat are eaten, the larger game reserved for special occasions. At more expensive restaurants, crocodile tail, shoulder of impala (a type of antelope), and warthog may be on the menu.

During the summer, open-air markets sell dried mopane worms (spiny caterpillars) and flying ants by the pound. Both can be eaten fried and are said to taste chewy and salty. Flying ants fly in dense clouds around any source of light during the summer, and can be eaten live. The wings are torn off, then the bodies are eaten. The taste is considered slightly buttery.

Sadza

Ingredients

4 cups water

2½ cups white cornmeal (regular cornmeal may be used)

Procedure

1. Bring 3 cups of the water to a boil in a large pot.

2. Combine 1½ cups of the cornmeal with the remaining 1 cup water.

3. Reduce heat to medium to low and add the cornmeal mixture to the boiling water, stirring constantly with a wooden spoon. Cook for about 5 minutes.

4. Slowly adding the remaining 1 cup of cornmeal. When the mixture is very thick and starts to pull away from the sides of the pan, transfer to a serving bowl or plate.

5. Use a wooden spoon to shape the mixture into a round shape.

6. You may use wet hands to help shape the *sadza*.

Serves 4 to 6.

Dovi (Peanut Butter Stew)

Ingredients

2 medium onions, finely chopped

2 Tablespoons butter

2 cloves garlic, crushed

1 teaspoon salt

½ teaspoon pepper

½ teaspoon cayenne pepper

2 green bell peppers, chopped

1 chicken, cut into pieces (may use skinless, boneless chicken if preferred)

3 to 4 tomatoes

6 Tablespoons creamy peanut butter

½ pound fresh spinach, or 1 package frozen spinach

Procedure

1. Cook onions with butter in a big stew pot until browned.

2. Add garlic, salt, and seasonings.

3. Stir, adding green peppers and chicken.

4. Once the chicken is browned, add the tomatoes and mash them with a fork.

5. Add 2 cups water and simmer for 5 to 10 minutes. Add half the peanut butter to the pot, lower heat, and continue to simmer.

6. In a separate pan, cook the spinach. If using fresh spinach, wash the leaves, add about 2 Tablespoons of water to a saucepan with the spinach and heat over medium low until spinach leaves are limp and tender. If using frozen spinach, cook according to package directions.

7. Add the rest of the peanut butter to the spinach and heat for 5 minutes.

8. Serve the stew and the greens together.

Serves 6 to 8.

Cornmeal Cake

Ingredients

1 cup cornmeal

4 cups milk

2 eggs, beaten

¾ cup butter or margarine

½ cup sugar

1 Tablespoon vanilla extract

½ cup sour cream

Procedure

1. Measure milk into a saucepan and bring just to a boil. Remove from heat and allow to cool for about 10 minutes.

2. Add eggs, ½ cup butter or margarine, and sugar to the in a saucepan. Bring to a boil and remove from heat.

3. Add cornmeal, stirring constantly to prevent lumps.

4. Return to low heat and continue cooking for 20 minutes, or until thickened, stirring constantly to prevent sticking. Add vanilla extract and stir well.

5. Preheat oven to 350°F.

6. Melt remaining ¼ cup butter and pour into 8-inch cake pan. Swirl pan to coat bottom and sides.

7. Pour cornmeal mixture into pan and bake for 30 minutes, or until cake is golden brown. Cake is done when a toothpick is inserted into the middle of the cake and it comes out clean.

8. Remove cake from oven and cover top with sour cream.

9. Return to oven for 15 minutes, or until top is bubbly and lightly browned.

10. Serve cake while still warm.

Serve 12 to 16.

4 FOOD FOR RELIGIOUS AND HOLIDAY CELEBRATIONS

Meat or game is generally eaten on special occasions. The kind of meat provided by the host signifies the importance of the celebration. The bigger the occasion, the bigger the roast that is served. Christmas is an example of such an occasion.

Seventy-five percent of Zimbabweans are Christians, so Christmas is widely celebrated. Because Zimbabwe is in the southern hemisphere, Christmas overlaps with the festivities associated with the summer harvest, so many fresh vegetables such as leafy greens and young corn are eaten as well as the *sadza* staple. Starting weeks in advance, everyone begins to gather loaves of bread, jam, tea, and sugar for the Christmas dinner. Fresh fruit is also plentiful and accompanies the roast, which may be ox, goat, ostrich, kudu, or even warthog. The roast is sometimes prepared whole on a spit over an open fire when the feast is a village affair.

Zimbabwe Greens

Collard greens are not native to Zimbabwe, but are the most comparable to Zimbabwean greens.

Ingredients

1 bunch collard greens, washed

1 cup water

1 large tomato, chopped

5 green onions, sliced

3 Tablespoons creamy peanut butter

Salt, to taste

Procedure

1. Remove the tough stems, then shred the greens. Place in a saucepan with the water.

2. Bring to a boil and cook, stirring occasionally, just until the greens are crunchy-tender, about 2 to 3 minutes.

3. Place a strainer or colander over a large bowl and drain the greens, reserving the cooking liquid in the bowl.

4. Return the greens to the saucepan and add the tomato and onions.

5. Cook over medium heat, stirring constantly, about 4 to 5 minutes.

6. Combine the peanut butter with ¾ cup of the cooking liquid reserved from the greens, then add to vegetables.

7. Heat, stirring constantly, until greens have a creamy consistency, adding more reserved liquid or water if mixture seems too thick. Add salt to taste.

Serves 6 to 8.

5 MEALTIME CUSTOMS

Before eating a meal, a dish of water is placed on the dining table for diners to clean their hands. *Rudyi* is the Shona word for right hand, which means the "one used for eating." Even if a person is left-handed, it is considered impolite to eat with the left hand. Zimbabweans typically sit in a circle on the floor and eat food from one dish or bowl. The practice of sharing is the communal way of eating, so diners have to pace themselves accordingly while eating with others. Older children, learn to pace themselves at the same rate as their younger siblings so that they will not eat too much or too fast and everyone will have a fair share. Guests, however, are served instead of helping themselves. It is considered polite to leave a small amount of food on your plate to show that you have been more than sufficiently provided for.

In general, wooden plates and spoons are used along with Western utensils. In some rural areas, Zimbabweans eat with their fingers. When eating *sadza*, Zimbabweans clean their hands, then using their right hand, pinch off a chunk from the bowl and roll it into a ball in their palm. They dip the ball into relish and bite off a piece, then roll it again and continue the process.

Three meals are typically eaten a day. Breakfast is simple and may consist of *sadza*, porridge made from cornmeal or oatmeal, cereal or bread, and tea. Sometimes leftovers from the dinner before are eaten.

Lunch and dinner are simple as well. *Sadza* with relish is common, served with vegetables and meat, if available. Sour milk and sugar sometimes replace meat or vegetables with *sadza*. Rock shandy, a refreshing beverage, is a mix of lemonade, soda water, and bitters (made from herbs and other plant extracts and used to flavor drinks). Foreign food such as macaroni and cheese and mashed potatoes are now part of Zimbabwean staples.

Certain taboos are associated with Zimbabwean food. For instance, the Ndebele people discourage eating corn out of season. Many ethnic groups do not eat an animal, plant, or other forms of food that bears their family name. For example, if a family name is Nkomo (cattle: cow or oxen), they should not eat beef.

Rock Shandy

Ingredients

Ice

2 Tablespoons lemon or lime juice

3 dashes Angostura bitters (can be found in any supermarket)

Cold soda (sparkling) water

Procedure

1. Half fill a tall glass with ice.
2. Add the lemon or lime juice and Angostura bitters.

3. Fill the glass with sparkling water and serve.

Makes one serving.

6 POLITICS, ECONOMICS, AND NUTRITION

About 39 percent of the population of Zimbabwe are classified as undernourished by the World Bank. This means they do not receive adequate nutrition in their diet. Of children under the age of five, about 16 percent are underweight, and more than one-fifth are stunted (short for their age).

In the early 1990s, drought severely affected the output of almost every crop, including wheat, cotton, oilseed, coffee, and sugar. In years with adequate rainfall, Zimbabwe is one of Africa's largest corn exporters; however, corn production only produced 1,418,000 tons in 1998, down from 2,609,000 tons in 1996. Despite the drop in production, Zimbabwe continues to grow a wide variety of crops to help feed its people. Nearly three-quarters of the population have access to safe drinking water, but only about half have adequate sanitation.

7 FURTHER STUDY

Books

Hafner, Dorinda. *A Taste of Africa.* Hong Kong: Simon & Schuster, 1993.

Hultman, Tami. *The Africa News Cookbook.* New York: Hamilton Printing Company, 1986.

Isaacson, Rupert. *Zimbabwe, Botswana & Namibia.* London: Cadogan Books, PLC, 1998.

Pinchuck, Tony. *The Rough Guide to Zimbabwe and Botswana.* London: Viking Penguin, 1996.

Web Sites

The Citizens Network for Foreign Affairs (CNFA). [Online]. Available http://www.cnfa.com/AVP/

africa/zimess.htm#contacts (accessed March 19, 2001).

Diane's Gourmet Corner. [Online]. Available http://belgourmet.com/cooking/links/zimb.html (accessed March 19, 2001).

Just Think. [Online] Available http://www.justthink.org/ZEEP/perpectives.html (accessed March 19, 2001)

Lonely Planet. [Online] Available http://www.lonelyplanet.com/destinations/africa/

zimbabwe/culture.htm (accessed March 19, 2001).

New Africa. [Online] Available http://www.newafrica.com/travel/Zimbabwe/ (accessed March 19, 2001)

Plan International. [Online]. Available http://www.plan-international.org/international/about/where/articles.html?pk=493&pu=474 (accessed March 19, 2001).

Index

This index contains terms and recipes from all four volumes of this encyclopedia. The volume number is enclosed in brackets. The volume number is followed by the page number. For example, the reference [4]84 means that the indexed term can be found in volume 4 on page 84. Entries in boldface type indicate main entries and main recipe categories. Recipe categories include Appetizers, Beverages, Breads, Cookies and sweets, Desserts, Main dishes, Salads, Sandwiches, Side dishes, Snacks, Soups, Stews, and Vegetables.

A

Aaloo Bukhary Ki (Plum Chutney, Pakistan) [3]86
Aboriginals (Canada) [1]77
 Bannock [1]80
 Man-O-Min [1]80
 Saskatoon Berry Snack [1]79
 Wild Rice Cakes [1]81
Aborigines and Bush Tucker (Australia) [1]29
 Billy Tea [1]31
 Damper [1]32
 Damper European Style [1]32
 Macadamia and Fruit Snack [1]33
 Macadamia Nut Cookies [1]33
Abyssinia see Ethiopia
Acaçá (Afro-Brazilians, Brazil) [1]51
Aceitunas Alinadas (Marinated Olives, Cuba) [1]119
Aceitunas Alinadas (Marinated Olives, Spain) [4]9
Adas Bil Hamod (Lentils with Lemon Juice, Iraq) [2]96
Adobong Hiponsa Gata (Shrimp Adobo in Coconut
 Milk, Philippines) [3]107
African Americans (United States) [4]77
 Baked Macaroni and Cheese [4]82
 Collard Greens [4]78
 Fried Apples [4]83
 Fried Bologna [4]84
 Hush Puppies [4]78
 Kwanzaa Brownies [4]83
 Molasses Water [4]79
 Potato Salad [4]81
 Red Beans and Rice [4]80
 Sweet Potato Pie [4]80

 Tomato, Cucumber, and Onion Salad [4]84
Afro-Brazilians (Brazil) [1]45
 Acaçá [1]51
 Angu de Milho [1]49
 Brazilian Black Beans [1]49
 Empadas [1]50
 Moqueca [1]47
 Moqueca aos Ovos [1]47
 Olho de Sogra [1]51
 Quiabo [1]46
 Quindins [1]48
 Rice, Basic [1]46
Ahweh (Arabic Coffee, Lebanon) [3]34
Akara (Fritters, Ghana) [2]19
Alfajores de Maizena (Corn Starch Cookies, Argentina)
 [1]17
Algeria [1]1
 Algerian Cooked Carrot Salad [1]7
 Banadura Salata B'Kizbara [1]5
 Chlada Fakya [1]8
 Cucumber & Yogurt Soup [1]8
 Etzai [1]4
 Fresh Sweet Dates [1]3
 Saffron and Raisin Couscous with Fresh Mint [1]2
 Sahlab [1]4
Algerian Cooked Carrot Salad (Algeria) [1]7
Almond Candies (Mazapanes, Spain) [4]6
Almond Kisses (Hungary) [2]55
Almost Ting (Jamaica) [2]150
Aloko (Fried Bananas, Côte d'Ivoire) [1]104
Ambrosia (Brazil) [1]38

Amish and Pennsylvania Dutch (United States) [4]87
Cream of Cabbage Soup [4]89
Old-Fashioned Spicy Lemonade [4]93
Peachy Baked Apples [4]91
Peanut Butter and Molasses Spread [4]93
Pork Chops with Sauerkraut and Potatoes [4]89
Shoofly Pie [4]89
Snow Ice Cream [4]93
Spicy Oven-Fried Chicken [4]91
Strawberry Jam [4]93
Sugar Cookies [4]92
Angu de Milho (Afro-Brazilians, Brazil) [1]49
ANZAC Biscuits (Australia) [1]22
Apfelpfannkuchen (Apple Pancakes, Germany) [2]5
Apfelschörle (Germany) [2]7
Appetizers
Australian Meat Pie (Australia) [1]21
Baked Papas Skins (Peru) [3]92
Bocaditos (Argentina) [1]14
Bruschetta (Italy) [2]141
Buffalo Chicken Wings (Great Lakes, United States) [4]100
Ceviche (Peru) [3]99
Chicken Satay (Thailand) [4]38
Chopped Chicken Liver (Jewish Americans, United States) [4]107
Clam Chowder (Northeast Region, United States) [4]144
Cornish Pasty (Great Lakes, United States) [4]103
Cream of Cabbage Soup (Amish and Pennsylvania Dutch, United States) [4]89
Cuban Avocado and Pineapple Salad (Latino Americans, United States) [4]121
Deviled Eggs (Midwest Region, United States) [4]126
Dolma (Iran) [2]82
Empanadas (Argentina) [1]13
Feta Cheese and Vegetable Tray (Iran) [2]91
Fish Boil (Great Lakes, United States) [4]97
French-Canadian Creton (Canada) [1]71
Fried Wonton (China) [1]101
Fromage (France) [1]156
Ful Mudammas (Egypt) [1]132
Gazpacho (Latino Americans, United States) [4]120
Guacamole (Guatemala) [2]33
Guacamole (Latino Americans, United States) [4]117
Haysa Al-Tumreya (Saudi Arabia) [3]135
Herring Dip (Jewish Americans, United States) [4]113

Hummus (Great Lakes, United States) [4]99
Hummus (Saudi Arabia) [3]140
Jansson's Frestelse (Sweden) [4]14
Kutya (Ukraine) [4]63
Lettuce Dipped in Honey and Vinegar Dressing (Iran) [2]88
Macadamia and Fruit Snack (Aborigines and Bush Tucker, Australia) [1]33
Maple Butter (Northeast Region, United States) [4]142
Marinated Artichokes (Western Region, United States) [4]163
Matzo Brie (Jewish Americans, United States) [4]112
Mealie Soup (South Africa) [3]153
Miso Soup (Japan) [2]156
Nam Pla Prig (Thailand) [4]37
New England Clam Chowder (Northeast Region, United States) [4]144
Old Fashioned Turnip Soup (Southern Region, United States) [4]151
Peanut Butter and Molasses Spread (Amish and Pennsylvania Dutch, United States) [4]93
Pepinos Rellenos (Guatemala) [2]36
Poa Pee (Thailand) [4]39
Popcorn (Native Americans, United States) [4]132
Ramen (Japan) [2]161
Salsa Cruda (Latino Americans, United States) [4]116
Spring Roll (Vietnam) [4]177
Swedish Meatballs (Great Lakes, United States) [4]102
Tapas (Spain) [4]8, [4]9
Toast with Vegemite or Milo Spread (Australia) [1]27
Traditional Biltong and Dried Fruit Snack (South Africa) [3]152
Apple and Carrot Tsimmes (Jewish Americans, United States) [4]111
Apple Cake (Ireland) [2]111
Apple Cake (Russia) [3]130
Apple Crisp (Western Region, United States) [4]165
Apple Pancakes (Germany) [2]5
Apple Sauerkraut (Great Lakes, United States) [4]101
Arabic Coffee (Lebanon) [3]34
Arabic Coffee (Saudi Arabia) [3]141
Arachid Sauce (Côte d'Ivoire) [1]110
Argentina [1]11
Alfajores de Maizena [1]17
Bocaditos [1]14
Carbonada Criolla [1]12

Argentina *(continued)*

Chimichurri [1]13

Dulce de Leche [1]17

Empanadas [1]13

Fruit Salad with Frozen Yogurt [1]15

Submarino [1]16

Arni Souvlakia (Lamb on Skewers, Greece) [2]24

Arroz Blanco (White Rice, Mexico) [3]53

Arroz con Leche (Rice Pudding, Peru) [3]99

Arroz con Leche (Rice Pudding, Chile) [1]90

Arroz con Leche (Rice Pudding, Cuba) [1]120

Arroz Guatemalteco (Guatemalan-Style Rice) [2]34

Artsoppa (Pea Soup, Sweden) [4]20

Aterkek Alecha (Vegetable Stew, Ethiopia) [1]148

Australia [1]19

Aborigines and Bush Tucker [1]29

ANZAC Biscuits [1]22

Australian Meat Pie [1]21

Billy Tea [1]31

Black Australian Coffee [1]22

Chocolate Crackles [1]27

Christmas Shortbread [1]24

Damper Aboriginal Style [1]32

Damper European Style [1]32

Grated Carrot, Apple, and Raisin Salad [1]20

Lamingtons [1]23

Macadamia and Fruit Snack [1]33

Macadamia Nut Cookies [1]33

Pavlova [1]24

Quick No-Cook Mini-Pavlova [1]25

Toast with Vegemite or Milo Spread [1]27

Australian Meat Pie (Australia) [1]21

Avgolemono (Egg-Lemon Soup, Greece) [2]22

Avocado Chili Sauce (Peru) [3]93

Avocado Drink (Indonesia) [2]74

Avocado Soup, Chilled (Côte d'Ivoire) [1]109

Avocado with Groundnut Dressing (Côte d'Ivoire) [1]111

B

Baat Bo Fon (Rice Pudding, China) [1]97

Badam Pistaz Barfi (Islands of the Pacific) [2]118

Baguette (French Bread, France) [1]152

Baguette Sandwich (France) [1]153

Baigan Bhartha (Eggplant Puree, India) [2]60

Baked Kibbeh (Lebanon) [3]31

Baked Macaroni and Cheese (African Americans, United States) [4]82

Baked Papas (Potato) Skins (Peru) [3]92

Baked Papaya Dessert (Islands of the Pacific) [2]121

Baked Ripe Banana (Jamaica) [2]150

Baked Yams (Côte d'Ivoire) [1]109

Baklava (Egypt) [1]134

Bamia (Sweet and Sour Okra, Egypt) [1]137

Banadura Salata B'Kizbara (Tomato and Coriander Salad, Algeria) [1]5

Banana and Pineapple Salad (Cameroon) [1]58

Banana Bread (Guatemala) [2]37

Banana Cake (Vietnam) [4]175

Banana Cakes, Fried (Indonesia) [2]77

Banana Frita (Brazil) [1]42

Banana with Coconut Milk (Thailand) [4]41

Bananas and Sweet Potatoes (Islands of the Pacific) [2]118

Bananas, Baked Ripe (Jamaica) [2]150

Bananas, Fried (Brazil) [1]42

Bananas, Fried (Côte d'Ivoire) [1]104

Bananas, Fried (Tanzania) [4]28

Banh Chuoi Nuong (Vietnam) [4]175

Bannann Peze (Fried Plantains, Haiti) [2]43

Bannock (Aboriginals, Canada) [1]80

Barm Brack (Ireland) [2]108

Barros Jarpa (Ham and Cheese Sandwich, Chile) [1]89

Basturma (Kazakhstan) [3]2

Baursaki (Fried Doughnuts, Kazakhstan) [3]4

Bean Goulash with Beef (Czech Republic) [1]126

Beef Noodle Soup (Vietnam) [4]172

Beef Sukiyaki (Japan) [2]157

Beef with Fruit (Iraq) [2]94

Beet Soup (Russia) [3]129

Berbere (Spice Paste, Ethiopia) [1]144

Berry Punch (Chile) [1]90

Beverages

Ahweh (Lebanon) [3]34

Almost Ting (Jamaica) [2]150

Apfelschörle (Germany) [2]7

Berry Punch (Chile) [1]90

Billy Tea (Aborigines and Bush Tucker, Australia) [1]31

Black Australian Coffee (Australia) [1]22

Café de Olla (Mexico) [3]48

Caphe (Vietnam) [4]176

Chai (Tanzania) [4]24

Chai Po-Russki (Russia) [3]131

Chocolate Mexicana (Mexico) [3]53

Beverages (*continued*)

Coffee Milkshake (Northeast Region, United States) [4]144

Cola de Mono (Chilean Eggnog) [1]87

Crème de Vie (Cuba) [1]120

Dugh (Iran) [2]86

Es Avocad (Indonesia) [2]74

Es Pokat (Indonesia) [2]74

Etzai (Algeria) [1]4

Ginger Beer (Liberia) [3]42

Glühwein (Germany) [2]7

Guaraná (Brazil) [1]40

Hot Christmas Punch (Guatemala) [2]36

Hot Cranberry Punch (Northeast Region, United States) [4]146

Irea (Egypt) [1]138

Iroquois Strawberry Drink (Native Americans, United States) [4]137

Jamaican Fruit Drink (Jamaica) [2]149

Laban Drink (Saudi Arabia) [3]138

Lassi (Pakistan) [3]88

Lemon Grass Tea (Liberia) [3]42

Limoonada (Lebanon) [3]35

Mango Juice (Haiti) [2]42

Mango-Orange Drink (Tanzania) [4]28

Maté (Brazil) [1]40

Molasses Water (African Americans, United States) [4]79

Moroccan Mint Tea [3]58

Naneli Limonata (Turkey) [4]49

Old-Fashioned Spicy Lemonade (Amish and Pennsylvania Dutch, United States) [4]93

Pineapple Nog (Haiti) [2]46

Pineapple-Orange Drink (Brazil) [1]43

Pineapple Sherbet (South Africa) [3]158

Pinole (Native Americans, United States) [4]137

Ponche (Chile) [1]90

Qahwa (Saudi Arabia) [3]141

Rock Shandy (Zimbabwe) [4]186

Sahlab (Algeria) [1]4

Sbiten (Russia) [3]128

Shai (Egypt) [1]134

Soda Chanh (Vietnam) [4]176

Soo Chunkwa (Korea) [3]18

Spiced Cocoa (Haiti) [2]41

Submarino (Argentina) [1]16

Svart Vinbärsglögg (Sweden) [4]18

Sweet Tea (Southern Region, United States) [4]157

Té con Leche (Chile) [1]84

Tea with Milk (United Kingdom) [4]75

Teh Halia (Indonesia) [2]77

Tropical Fruit Shake (Islands of the Pacific) [2]121

Tsokolate (Philippines) [3]108

Wassail (United Kingdom) [4]74

Bigos (Polish Hunter's Stew, Poland) [3]114

Billy Tea (Aborigines and Bush Tucker, Australia) [1]31

Birthday Cake (Chile) [1]87

Birthday Noodles with Peanut Sauce (China) [1]99

Biscotti (Italy) [2]139

Bisteeya (Morocco) [3]59

Black Australian Coffee (Australia) [1]22

Black Beans (Brazil) [1]49

Black Beans and Rice (Cuba) [1]114

Black Currant Glögg (Sweden) [4]18

Blandad Fruktsoppa (Swedish Fruit Soup) [4]15

Blintzes (Israel) [2]124

Bliny (Russian Pancakes, Russia) [3]125

Bliny Filling (Russia) [3]126

Blue Cheese, Apple, and Walnut Spread (Spain) [4]8

Blueberry Muffins (Western Region, United States) [4]165

Bobotie (South Africa) [3]157

Bocaditos (Finger Sandwiches, Argentina) [1]14

Boiled Cassava (Cameroon) [1]59

Boiled Rice (Japan) [2]155

Bolo Polana (Cashew Nut and Potato Cake, Mozambique) [3]71

Borscht (Beet Soup, Russia) [3]129

Boston Baked Beans (Northeast Region, United States) [4]143

Braised Pumpkin with Coconut Milk (Vietnam) [4]174

Bratwurst (Sausage, Germany) [2]4

Brazil [1]37

Acaçá (Afro-Brazilians) [1]51

Afro-Brazilians [1]45

Ambrosia [1]38

Angu de Milho (Afro-Brazilians) [1]49

Banana Frita [1]42

Basic Rice [1]46

Brazilian Black Beans (Afro-Brazilians) [1]49

Corn Cake [1]41

Empadas (Afro-Brazilians) [1]50

Feijoada [1]38

Maté [1]40

Moqueca (Afro-Brazilians) [1]47

Moqueca aos Ovos (Afro-Brazilians) [1]47

Olho de Sogra (Afro-Brazilians) [1]51

Orange Salad [1]39

Brazil *(continued)*

Pepper-Scented Rice [1]41

Pineapple-Orange Drink [1]43

Pudim (Custard) [1]42

Quejadinhas [1]43

Quiabo (Afro-Brazilians) [1]46

Quindins (Afro-Brazilians) [1]48

Rice, Basic (Afro-Brazilians) [1]46

Brazilian Black Beans (Afro-Brazilians) [1]49

Breads

Baguette (France) [1]152

Bannock (Aboriginals, Canada) [1]80

Barm Brack (Ireland) [2]108

Blueberry Muffins (Western Region, United States) [4]165

Bread Pudding (Midwest Region, United States) [4]124

Bruschetta (Italy) [2]141

Chapatti (Tanzania) [4]27

Chili Corn Bread (Latino Americans, United States) [4]121

Cornbread (Southern Region, United States) [4]152

Damper (Aborigines and Bush Tucker, Australia) [1]32

Damper European Style (Aborigines and Bush Tucker, Australia) [1]32

Date Nut Bread (Tanzania) [4]30

Fatir (Saudi Arabia) [3]134

Gari Biscuits (Ghana) [2]17

Hush Puppies (African Americans, United States) [4]78

Indian Fry-Bread (Native Americans, United States) [4]137

Injera (Ethiopia) [1]146

Irish Soda Bread (Ireland) [2]105

Italian Christmas Bread (Italy) [2]138

Italian Easter Bread (Italy) [2]138

Johnnycakes (Northeast Region, United States) [4]141

Kategna (Ethiopia) [1]144

Kimaje (Saudi Arabia) [3]137

Matzo Brie (Jewish Americans, United States) [4]112

Pain Haïtien (Haiti) [2]46

Pita Bread (Lebanon) [3]28

Potica (Slovenia) [3]147

Pumpkin Bread (Native Americans, United States) [4]136

Rågbröd (Sweden) [4]20

Rice Bread (Liberia) [3]41

Rosca de Reyes (Mexico) [3]49

Rye Bread (Germany) [2]5

Scones (Ireland) [2]110

Scones (United Kingdom) [4]71

Simit (Turkey) [4]51

Bread Pudding (Midwest Region, United States) [4]124

Broad Beans in Sauce (Egypt) [1]132

Broiled Salmon (Japan) [2]162

Broiled Salmon Steaks (Western Region, United States) [4]164

Brown-Stewed Fish (Jamaica) [2]146

Bruschetta (Toasted Bread, Italy) [2]141

Bûche de Noël (Yule Log, France) [1]156

Buffalo Chicken Wings (Great Lakes, United States) [4]100

Buffalo Stew (Native Americans, United States) [4]135

Bulgar Wheat Salad (Saudi Arabia) [3]139

Bulgur Pilavi (Cracked Wheat Pilaf, Turkey)

Bunuelos (Fried Fritters, Guatemala) [2]35

Butter Tarts (French Canadians, Canada) [1]71

Butternut Squash, Roasted (Zimbabwe) [4]182

C

Cabbage Pirozhki or Piroghi (Russia) [3]126

Cabbage Rolls, Stuffed (Poland) [3]116

Cabbage Rolls, Stuffed (Ukraine) [4]60

Café de Olla (Spiced Coffee, Mexico) [3]48

Calalou (Meat and Vegetable Stew, Côte d'Ivoire) [1]109

Cameroon [1]53

Banana and Pineapple Salad [1]58

Boiled Cassava [1]59

Easy Fufu [1]55

Ndole [1]56

Safou a la Sauce Tomate [1]54

Traditional Fufu [1]56

Canada [1]61

Aboriginals (Canada) [1]77

Butter Tarts (French Canadians) [1]71

Canada Day Cake [1]65

Canadian Bacon with Maple Glaze [1]63

Candlemas Pancakes (French Canadians) [1]74

Crêpes de la Chandeleur (French Canadians) [1]74

Creton (Spicy Pork Pate, (French Canadians) [1]71

Doughboys (Dumplings, (French Canadians)) [1]70

French Canadians 1[69

French-Canadian Creton [1]71

Canada (*continued*)

French Pea Soup (French Canadians) [1]70

Man-O-Min (Aboriginals, Canada) [1]80

Maple Sundae [1]67

Maple Syrup Upside-Down Cake [1]67

Pudding au Chomeur (French Canadians) [1]72

Quebec Poutine (French Canadians) [1]75

Ragoût de Boulettes (French Canadians) [1]74

Tarte au Sucre (French Canadians) [1]72

Tourtière (French Canadians) [1]73

Saskatoon Berry Snack (Aboriginals, Canada) [1]79

Sauteed Fiddleheads [1]63

Sweet Corn Pancakes [1]64

Wild Rice Cakes (Aboriginals, Canada) [1]81

Canada Day Cake (Canada) [1]65

Canadian Bacon with Maple Glaze (Canada) [1]63

Candied Citrus Peels (Iraq) [2]101

Candlemas Pancakes (Canada) [1]74

Canh Bi Ro Ham Dua (Vietnam) [4]174

Cannoli (Italy) [2]141

Caphe (Vietnam) [4]176

Caramal Custard (Peru) [3]102

Caramel Corn (Midwest Region, United States) [4]128

Carbonada Criolla (Stew with Meat, Vegetables, and Fruit, Argentina) [1]12

Carrot Bredie (South Africa) [3]154

Cassava and Plantains, Boiled (Côte d'Ivoire) [1]106

Cassava *see also* Yucca

Cauliflower Cheese, Sunday Lunch (United Kingdom) [4]74

Cellophane Noodles, Mixed Vegetables with (Korea) [3]22

Ceviche (Marinated Seafood, Peru) [3]99

Chai (Tea, Tanzania) [4]24

Chai Po-Russki (Tea, Russian-Style) [3]131

Champ (Ireland) [2]106

Chancho en Piedra (Chili and Tomato Spread, Chile) [1]89

Chapatti (Fried Flat Bread, Tanzania) [4]27

Chap Ch'ae (Mixed Vegetables with Cellophane Noodles, Korea) [3]22

Charoset (Jewish Americans, United States) [4]110

Charoseth (Israel) [2]131

Cheese and Pear Sandwich (Sweden) [4]22

Cheese Sandwich, Baked (Mozambique) [3]68

Cheesecake (Poland) [3]117

Cheesecake, New York (Jewish Americans, United States) [4]113

Chess Pie (Southern Region, United States) [4]150

Chicken, Grilled on Skewers (Japan) [2]161

Chicken, Grilled Skewered (Iran) [2]85

Chicken Karaii (Pakistan) [3]86

Chicken Kiev (Ukraine) [4]61

Chicken Paprikas (Czech Republic) [1]126

Chicken and Rice (Saudi Arabia) [3]136

Chicken Satay (Thailand) [4]38

Chicken and Sausage Gumbo (Southern Region, United States) [4]153

Chicken Tajine with Almonds and Prunes (Morocco) [3]56

Chicken Tandoori (India) [2]63

Chicken Teriyaki (Japan) [2]157

Chickpea, Feta, and Olive Salad (Morocco) [3]62

Chile [1]83

Arroz con Leche [1]90

Barros Jarpa [1]89

Chancho en Piedra [1]89

Cola de Mono [1]87

Ensalada Chilena [1]84

Pastel de Choclo [1]84

Ponche [1]90

Té con Leche [1]84

Tomaticán [1]86

Torta de Cumpleaños [1]87

Chili Corn Bread (Latino American, United States, United States) [4]121

Chili and Soy Sauce (Indonesia) [2]74

Chilled Avocado Soup (Côte d'Ivoire) [1]109

Chimichurri (Dipping Sauce, Argentina) [1]13

China [1]93

Baat Bo Fon (Rice Pudding) [1]97

Birthday Noodles with Peanut Sauce [1]99

Eggdrop Soup [1]96

Fried Rice [1]97

Fried Wonton [1]101

Fu Yund Don [1]101

Spiced Chicken [1]99

Sweet and Sour Pork [1]96

Wonton Soup [1]95

Chinchin (Nigeria) [3]81

Chinese Peanut Sauce (Western Region, United States) [4]164

Chlada Fakya (Fresh Fruit Medley, Algeria) [1]8

Choclo con Queso (Corn on the Cob with Cheese, Peru) [3]95

Chocolate Crackles (Australia) [1]27

Chocolate Mexicana (Hot Chocolate Drink, Mexico) [3]53

Ch'o Kanjang (Vinegar Soy Sauce, Korea) [3]24

Chopped Chicken Liver (Jewish Americans, United States) [4]107

Christmas Bread, Italian [2]138

Christmas Cake, Jamaican [2]148

Christmas Shortbread (Australia) [1]24

Chuck Wagon Brisket (Western Region, United States) [4]161

Churros (Spain) [4]7

Cinnamon Beverage (Egypt) [1]138

Citrus Peels, Candied (Iraq) [2]101

Clam Chowder (Northeast Region, United States) [4]144

Coconut Bean Soup (Tanzania) [4]25

Coconut and Cheese Snacks [1]43

Coconut-Chicken Soup (Thailand) [4]43

Coconut Chips (Jamaica) [2]146

Coconut Custard (Vietnam) [4]174

Coconut, Fresh Grated (Islands of the Pacific) [2]115

Coconut Macaroons (Brazil) [1]48

Coconut Milk (Indonesia) [2]71

Coconut Milk (Islands of the Pacific) [2]115

Coffee, Arabic (Saudi Arabia) [3]141

Coffee Milkshake (Northeast Region, United States) [4]144

Coffee, Vietnamese [4]176

Cola de Mono (Chilean Eggnog) [1]87

Colcannon (Ireland) [2]107

Cold Tomato Soup (Spain) [4]3

Coleslaw, Red (Germany) [2]9

Collard Greens (African Americans, United States) [4]78

Collard Greens with Hamhocks (Southern Region, United States) [4]157

Cookies and sweets

Alfajores de Maizena (Argentina) [1]17

Almond Kisses (Hungary) [2]55

ANZAC Biscuits (Australia) [1]22

Apple Crisp (Western Region, United States) [4]165

Badam Pistaz Barfi (Islands of the Pacific) [2]118

Baklava (Egypt) [1]134

Barm Brack (Ireland) [2]108

Baursaki (Kazakhstan) [3]4

Biscotti (Italy) [2]139

Buneolos (Guatemala) [2]35

Butter Tarts (French Canadians, Canada) [1]71

Caramel Corn (Midwest Region, United States) [4]128

Cheesecake (Poland) [3]117

Chinchin (Nigeria) [3]81

Chocolate Crackles (Australia) [1]27

Christmas Shortbread (Australia) [1]24

Churros (Spain) [4]7

Cornmeal Cookies (Côte d'Ivoire) [1]105

Dulce de Leche (Argentina) [1]17

Easy Lebanese Baklava (Lebanon) [3]32

Filhos de Natal (Mozambique) [3]70

Firifiri (Islands of the Pacific) [2]121

Fortune Cookies (Western Region, United States) [4]163

Fruitcake Cookies (Southern Region, United States) [4]154

Gizzada (Jamaica) [2]151

Groundnut Toffee (Ghana) [2]15

G'shur Purtaghal (Iraq) [2]101

Halva (Turkey) [4]50

Honey-Baked Apples (Northeast Region, United States) [4]146

Hungarian Butter Cookies (Hungary) [2]54

Indian Fry-Bread (Native Americans, United States) [4]137

Johnnycakes (Northeast Region, United States) [4]141

Ka'ak Cookies (Lebanon) [3]34

Kaymakli Kuru Kayisi (Turkey) [4]46

Kourabiethes [2]27

Kwanzaa Brownies (African Americans, United States) [4]83

Lamingtons (Austalia) [1]23

Lebkuchen (Germany) [2]6

Locum (Turkey) [4]52

Lokma (Turkey) [4]53

Lussekatter (Sweden) [4]17

Macadamia and Fruit Snack (Aborigines and Bush Tucker, Australia) [1]33

Macadamia Nut Cookies (Aborigines and Bush Tucker, Australia) [1]33

Malasadas (Mozambique) [3]69

Mandelbrot (Israel) [2]132

Maple Butter (Northeast Region, United States) [4]142

Mapopo (Zimbabwe) [4]182

Mathis (India) [2]67

Matzo Brie (Jewish Americans, United States) [4]112

Mazapanes (Spain) [4]6

Mescouta (Morocco) [3]58

Mexican Fried Ice Cream (Latino Americans, United States) [4]119

Cookies and sweets *(continued)*
    Mincemeat Pies, Individual (United Kingdom) [4]73
    Moravske Vano ni Kukyse (Czech Republic) [1]127
    Moroccan String of Doughnuts [3]63
    Nanaimo Bars (Canada) [1]65
    New York Cheesecake (Jewish Americans, United
        States) [4]113
    Papaya Candy (Zimbabwe) [4]182
    Papparkakor (Sweden) [4]16
    Pavlova (Australia) [1]24
    Pisang Goreng (Indonesia) [2]77
    Polvoron (Philippines) [3]110
    Potica (Slovenia) [3]147
    Pralines (Southern Region, United States) [4]157
    Pumpkin Bread [4]136
    Quick No-Cook Mini-Pavlova (Australia) [1]25
    Quindins (Brazil) [1]48
    Sesame Candy (Israel) [2]127
    Shoofly Pie (Amish and Pennsylvania Dutch, United
        States) [4]89
    Simit (Turkey) [4]51
    Slovenian Almond Bars (Slovenia) [3]148
    Springerle [4]101
    Strawberry Jam (Amish and Pennsylvania Dutch,
        United States) [4]93
    Sugar Cookies (Amish and Pennsylvania Dutch,
        United States) [4]92
    Sugared Almonds (Lebanon) [3]34
    Sweet Peanut Mochi (Japan) [2]159
    Sweet Potato Pie (African Americans, United States)
        [4]80
    Sweet Potato Pie (Southern Region, United States)
        [4]154
    Uli Petataws (Indonesia) [2]73
Corn and Meat Pie (Chile) [1]84
Cornbread (Southern Region, United States) [4]152
Cornbread Stuffing (Ukraine) [4]61
Corn Cake (Brazil) [1]41
Corned Beef with Cabbage (Ireland) [2]106
Cornhusker's Casserole (Midwest Region, United
    States) [4]129
Cornish Pasties (United Kingdom) [4]69
Cornish Pasty (Great Lakes, United States) [4]103
Cornmeal Cake (Zimbabwe) [4]184
Cornmeal Cookies (Côte d'Ivoire) [1]105
Cornmeal Drink (Native Americans, United States)
    [4]137
Cornmeal Porridge (Haiti) [2]47
Cornmeal Porridge (South Africa) [3]158

Corn on the Cob (Midwest Region, United States)
    [4]127
Corn on the Cob (South Africa) [3]157
Corn on the Cob with Cheese (Peru) [3]95
Corn Rice (Indonesia) [2]79
Corn Soup (South Africa) [3]153
Corn Starch Cookies (Argentina) [1]17
Côte d'Ivoire [1]103
    Aloko [1]104
    Arachid Sauce [1]110
    Avocado with Groundnut Dressing [1]111
    Baked Yams [1]109
    Calalou [1]109
    Chilled Avocado Soup [1]109
    Cornmeal Cookies [1]105
    Fufu (Boiled Cassava and Plantains) [1]106
    Kedjenou [1]107
    Melon Fingers with Lime [1]106
Couscous Dessert, Sweet (Algeria) [1]5
Cranberries, Frosted (Russia) [3]130
Cranberry Salsa [4]162
Cream of Cabbage Soup (Amish and Pennsylvania
    Dutch, United States) [4]89
Creamy Dipping Sauce (Sweden) [4]13
Crème de Vie (Cuban Eggnog) [1]120
Creole Seasoning (Southern Region, United States)
    [4]153
Crêpes de la Chandeleur (Candlemas Pancakes, Canada)
    [1]74
Croque-Monsieur (Ham and Cheese Sandwich) [1]154
Cuba [1]113
    Aceitunas Alinadas [1]119
    Arroz Con Leche [1]120
    Crème de Vie [1]120
    Ensalada Cubana [1]119
    Flan [1]117
    Fried Plantains [1]115
    Helada de Mango [1]118
    Moors and Christians [1]114
    Tuna in Sauce [1]117
    Yucca [1]117
Cuban Avocado and Pineapple Salad (Latino Americans,
    United States) [4]121
Cuban Beans and Rice (Latino Americans, United
    States) [4]117
Cucumber and Tomato Salad (Iran) [2]85
Cucumber and Yogurt Soup (Algeria) [1]8
Cucumber Relish (Komkomer Sambal, South Africa)
    [3]156

Cucumber Relish (South Africa) [3]156
Cucumber Salad (Thailand) [4]39
Cucumber Sandwiches (United Kingdom) [4]71
Cucumber Soup (Guatemala) [2]34
Cucumber with Yogurt (Lebanon) [3]29
Curry Chicken (Jamaica) [2]150
Custard (Brazil) [1]42
Custard, Baked (Cuba) [1]117
Czech Republic [1]123
    Fazolovy Gulás S Hovemzim Masem [1]126
    Knedlíky [1]125
    Kure Na Paprice [1]126
    Mala Sousta Se Syre [1]129
    Moravske Vano ni Kukyse [1]127
    Topinky S Vejci [1]128

D

Dabo Kolo (Little Fried Snacks, Ethiopia) [1]147
Dal (Lentils, India) [2]62
Damper (Aboriginal Style, Aborigines and Bush Tucker, Australia) [1]32
Damper (European Style, Aborigines and Bush Tucker, Australia) [1]32
Dandelion Salad (Slovenia) [3]147
Date Cookies (Morocco) [3]58
Date Nut Bread (Tanzania) [4]30
Dates (Iraq) [2]95
Dates, Fresh Sweet (Algeria) [1]3
Dates, Stuffed, and Walnuts (Algeria) [1]6
Deep-Fried Potatoes (Slovenia) [3]145
Denakil Desert [1]143
Desser Miveh (Persian Fruit Salad, Iran) [2]91
Desserts
    Alfajores de Maizena (Argentina) [1]17
    Ambrosia (Brazil) [1]38
    ANZAC Biscuits (Australia) [1]22
    Apfelpfannkuchen (Germany) [2]5
    Apple and Carrot Tsimmes (Jewish Americans, United States) [4]111
    Apple Cake (Ireland) [2]111
    Apple Cake (Russia) [3]130
    Apple Crisp (Western Region, United States) [4]165
    Arroz con Leche (Chile) [1]90
    Arroz con Leche (Cuba) [1]120
    Arroz con Leche (Peru) [3]99
    Baat Bo Fon (China) [1]97
    Baked Papaya Dessert [2]121

Baked Ripe Banana (Jamaica) [2]150
Baklava (Egypt) [1]134
Banana with Coconut Milk [4]41
Banh Chuoi Nuong (Vientam) [4]175
Barm Brack (Ireland) [2]108
Baursaki (Kazakhstan) [3]4
Blandad Fruktsoppa (Sweden) [4]15
Blintzes (Israel) [2]124
Bliny (Russia) [3]125
Bliny Filling (Russia) [3]126
Blueberry Muffins (Western Region, United States) [4]165
Bolo Polana (Mozambique) [3]71
Bread Pudding (Midwest Region, United States) [4]124
Bûche de Noël (France) [1]156
Canada Day Cake (Canada) [1]65
Cannoli (Italy) [2]141
Charoset (Jewish Americans, United States) [4]110
Cheesecake (Poland) [3]117
Chess Pie (Southern Region, United States) [4]150
Chlada Fakya [1]8
Chocolate Crackles (Australia) [1]27
Christmas Shortbread (Australia) [1]24
Coconut Custard (Vietnam) [4]174
Coconut Macaroons [1]48
Coffee Milkshake (Northeast Region, United States) [4]144
Corn Cake (Brazil) [1]41
Cornmeal Cake (Zimbabwe) [4]184
Cornmeal Cookies (Côte d'Ivoire) [1]105
Crêpes de la Chandeleur (Canada) [1]74
Dried Fruit Compote (Poland) [3]118
Dulce de Leche (Argentina) [1]17
Dutch Pancakes (Great Lakes, United States) [4]98
Easy Lebanese Baklava [3]32
Filhos de Natal (Mozambique) [3]70
Firifiri (Islands of the Pacific [2]121
Flan (Cuba) [1]117
Flan (Peru) [3]97
Flan (Spain) [4]4
Fortune Cookies (Western Region, United States) [4]163
Fresh Sweet Dates (Algeria) [1]3
Fried Apples (African Americans, United States) [4]83
Frozen Orange Delight (Peru) [3]95
Fruit Salad with Frozen Yogurt (Argentina) [1]15

Desserts *(continued)*

Fruitcake Cookies (Southern Region, United States) [4]154

Gizzada (Jamaica) [2]151

Groundnut Toffe (Ghana) [2]15

Halva (Turkey) [4]50

Helado de Mango (Cuba) [1]118

Honey-Baked Apples (Northeast Region, United States) [4]146

incemeat Pies, Individual (United Kingdom) [4]73

Indian Pudding (Northeast Region, United States) [4]140

Irish Christmas Cake [2]109

Jamaican Christmas Cake [2]148

Johnnycakes (Northeast Region, United States) [4]141

Kelewele (Ghana) [2]15

Kheer (India) [2]65

Kheer (Pakistan) [3]88

Khoshaf (Egypt) [1]138

Klyukva S Sakharom (Russia) [3]130

Kwanzaa Brownies (African Americans, United States) [4]83

La Galette des Rois (France) [1]157

Lamingtons (Austalia) [1]23

Lebanese Rice Pudding [3]28

Lebkuchen (Germany) [2]6

Leche Flan (Peru) [3]102

Locum (Turkey) [4]52

Lokma (Turkey) [4]53

Ma'mounia (Iraq) [2]98

Macadamia Nut Cookies (Aborigines and Bush Tucker, Australia) [1]33

Maja Blanco (Peru) [3]105

Makiwnyk (Ukraine) [4]63

Maple Sundae (Canada) [1]67

Maple Syrup Upside-Down Cake (Canada) [1]67

Mardi Gras King Cake (Southern Region, United States) [4]155

Matzo Brie (Jewish Americans, United States) [4]112

Melon Fingers with Lime (Côte d'Ivoire) [1]106

Melopitta (Greece) [2]26

Mexican Fried Ice Cream (Latino Americans, United States) [4]119

Mhalbi (Morocco) [3]63

Mousse au Chocolat (France)) [1]155

Muhallabi (Turkey) [4]48

Nanaimo Bars (Canada) [1]65

New Year's Honey Cake (Israel) [2]130

New York Cheesecake (Jewish Americans, United States) [4]113

Noodle Kugel (Jewish Americans, United States) [4]107

Olho de Sogra (Brazil) [1]51

Pan de Banano (Guatemala) [2]37

Pashka (Russia) [3]128

Pavlova (Australia) [1]24

Peachy Baked Apples (Amish and Pennsylvania Dutch, United States) [4]91

Peanut Butter and Molasses Spread (Amish and Pennsylvania Dutch, United States) [4]93

Picarones (Peru) [3]93

Pierogi (Poland) [3]115

Pineapple Sherbet (South Africa) [3]158

Pisang Goreng (Indonesia) [2]77

Plättar (Sweden) [4]19

Potica (Slovenia) [3]147

Pralines (Southern Region, United States) [4]157

Pudding au Chameur [1]72

Pudim (Brazil) [1]42

Pumpkin Bread [4]136

Quick No-Cook Mini-Pavlova (Australia) [1]25

Rosca de Reyes (Mexico) [3]49

Rose Hip Soup [4]12

San Ka Ya (Thailand) [4]40

Sarikayo Telor (Indonesia) [2]74

Shahi Tukra (Pakistan) [3]84

Shalotka (Russia) [3]130

Shir-Berenj (Iran) [2]88

Shoofly Pie (Amish and Pennsylvania Dutch, United States) [4]89

Slovenian Almond Bars (Slovenia) [3]148

Snow Ice Cream (Amish and Pennsylvania Dutch, United States) [4]93

Springerle (Great Lakes, United States) [4]101

Stuffed Dates and Walnuts [1]6

Sugar Cookies (Amish and Pennsylvania Dutch, United States) [4]92

Sweet Couscous Dessert (Algeria) [1]5

Sweet Peanut Mochi (Japan) [2]159

Sweet Potato Pie (African Americans, United States) [4]80

Sweet Potato Pie (Southern Region, United States) [4]154

Sweet Potato Pudding (Tanzania) [4]31

Tarte au Sucre (Canada) [1]72

Tropical Fruit Dessert (Islands of the Pacific) [2]121

Desserts *(continued)*
Tropical Fruit Salad (Latino Americans, United States) [4]121
Deviled Eggs (Midwest Region, United States) [4]126
Dhal (Lentil Stew, Pakistan) [3]85
Dip for Dates (Saudi Arabia) [3]135
Dipping Sauce (Argentina) [1]13
Dipping Sauce (Vietnam) [4]171
Dodo (Fried Plantains, Nigeria) [3]80
Doi Inthanon [4]35
Dolma (Stuffed Grape Leaves, Iran) [2]82
Doughboys (Dumplings, Canada) [1]70
Doughnuts (Mozambique) [3]69
Dovi (Peanut Butter Stew, Zimbabwe) [4]183
Dried Fruit Compote (Poland) [3]118
Dublin Coddle (Ireland) [2]110
Dugh (Sparkling Yogurt Drink, Iran) [2]86
Dulce de Leche (Milk Jam, Argentina) [1]17
Dumpling, Potato (Germany) [2]4
Dumpling, Potato (Ukraine) [4]58
Dumplings, Czech (Czech Republic) [1]125
Dutch Pancakes (Great Lakes, United States) [4]98

E

Easter Bread, Italian [2]138
Easy Fufu (Cameroon) [1]55
Easy Lebanese Baklava (Lebanon) [3]32
Efo (Greens Stew) [3]80
Egg Fu Yung (China) [1]101
Egg Rolls, Thai [4]39
Eggdrop Soup (China) [1]96
Eggnog, Cuban [1]120
Eggplant Puree (India) [2]60
Eggs on Toast (Czech Republic) [1]128
Egypt [1]131
Baklava [1]134
Bamia [1]137
Ful Mudammas [1]132
Gebna Makleyah [1]135
Irea [1]138
Koshaf [1]138
Koushari [1]133
Lettuce Salad [1]138
Shai [1]134
Spinach with Garlic [1]139
Empadas (Little Baked Pies, Brazil) [1]150
Empanadas (Little Meat Pies, Argentina) [1]13

Ensalada Chilena (Chilean Salad) [1]84
Ensalada Cubana Tipica (Cuban Salad) [1]119
Es Avocad (Indonesian Avocado Drink) [2]74
Es Pokat (Indonesian Avocado Drink) [2]74
Ethiopia [1]143
Aterkek Alecha [1]148
Berbere [1]144
Dabo Kolo [1]147
Injera [1]146
Kitfo [1]147
Lab [1]146
Niter Kebbeh [1]145
Etzai (Mint Tea, Algeria) [1]4

F

Fancy Rice (India) [2]65
Fatir (Flat Bread, Saudi Arabia) [3]134
Fava Bean Spread (Israel) [2]126
Fazolovy Gulás S Hovemzim Masem (Czech Republic) [1]126
Feijoada (Brazil) [1]38
Felafel (Israel) [2]128
Feta Cheese and Vegetable Tray (Iran) [2]91
Fettucine Alfredo (Italy) [2]136
Filhos de Natal (Christmas Fritters, Mozambique) [3]70
Finger Sandwiches (Argentina) [1]14
Firifiri (Tahitian Sugared Doughnuts) [2]121
Fish Boil (Great Lakes, United States) [4]97
Flan (Cuba) [1]117
Flan (Peru) [3]97
Flan (Spain) [4]4
Flat Bread (Saudi Arabia) [3]134, [3]137
Fortune Cookies (Western Region, United States) [4]163
France [1]151
Baguette [1]152
Baguette Sandwich [1]153
Bûche de Noël [1]156
Croque-Monsieur [1]154
Fromage [1]156
La Galette des Rois (France) [1]157
Mousse au Chocolat [1]155
Quiche au Saumon et Crevettes [1]155
Soupe à l'Oignon Gratinée [1]153
French Canadians (Canada) 1[69
Butter Tarts [1]71
Crêpes de la Chandeleur [1]74
Creton (Spicy Pork Pate, Canada) [1]71

French Canadians *(continued)*
Doughboys (Dumplings) [1]70
French Pea Soup [1]70
Pudding au Chomeur [1]72
Quebec Poutine [1]75
Ragoût de Boulettes [1]74
Tarte au Sucre [1]72
Tourtière [1]73
French Pea Soup (Canada) [1]70
French-Style Lettuce Salad (Haiti) [2]40
Fresh Fruit Medley (Algeria) [1]8
Fresh Grated Coconut (Islands of the Pacific) [2]115
Fried Apples (African Americans, United States) [4]83
Fried Baby Carrots (Morocco) [3]61
Fried Banana Cakes (Indonesia) [2]77
Fried Bananas or Plantains (Tanzania) [4]28
Fried Bologna (African Americans, United States) [4]84
Fried Noodles (Japan) [2]158
Fried Plantains (Cuba) [1]115
Fried Plantains (Latino Americans, United States)
[4]117
Fried Rice (China) [1]97
Fried Wonton (China) [1]101
Frijoles (Beans, Mexico) [3]47
Frijoles Negros Volteados (Fried Black Beans, Guate-
mala) [2]33
Frijoles Refritos (Refried Beans, Mexico) [3]47
Frittata (Italy) [2]140
Fritters (Lokma), Turkey [4]53
Fromage (Cheese Board, France) [1]156
Frosted Cranberries (Russia) [3]130
Frouta Ke Yaourti (Fruit Salad, Greece) [2]29
Frozen Orange Delight (Peru) [3]95
Fruit Salad (Greece) [2]29
Fruit Salad with Frozen Yogurt (Argentina) [1]15
Fruit Soup (Blandad Fruktsoppa, Sweden) [4]15
Fruitcake Cookies (Southern Region, United States)
[4]154
Fu Yung Don (Egg Fu Yung, China) [1]101
Fufu (Côte d'Ivoire) [1]106
Fufu (Ghana) [2]14
Ful Mudammas (Broad Beans in Sauce, Egypt) [1]132

G

G'shur Purtaghal (Candied Citrus Peels, Iraq) [2]101
Gado Gado (Vegetable Salad with Peanut Sauce, Indonesia) [2]78

Garam Masala (Spice Mixture, India) [2]60
Gari Biscuits (Ghana) [2]17
Garlic Bread, Toasted (Italy) [2]141
Gazpacho (Cold Tomato Soup, Spain) [4]3
Gazpacho (Latino Americans, United States) [4]120
Gebna Makleyah (Oven-Fried Cheese, Egypt) [1]135
Geel Rys (Yellow Rice, South Africa) [3]156
German Christmas Cookies (Great Lakes, United States)
[4]101
German Potato Salad (Great Lakes, United States) [4]98
Germany [2]1
Apfelschörle [2]7
Bratwurst [2]4
Glühwein [2]7
Kartoffelknödeln [2]4
Lebkuchen [2]6
Red Coleslaw [2]9
Rye Bread [2]5
Soft Pretzels [2]9
Spargelgemuse [2]5
Weisse Bohnensuppe [2]3
Ghana [2]11
Akara [2]19
Fufu [2]14
Gari Biscuits [2]17
Groundnut Stew [2]18
Groundnut Toffee [2]15
Kelewele [2]15
Kenkey [2]19
Oto [2]17
Pepper Soup [2]19
Yams [2]12
Ginger Beer (Liberia) [3]42
Ginger Cookies (Sweden) [4]16
Ginger Drink (Korea) [3]18
Ginger Tea, Hot (Indonesia) [2]77
Githeri (Kenya) [3]14
Gizzada (Jamaica) [2]151
Glazed Carrots (Sweden) [4]13
Glögg, Black Currant (Sweden) [4]18
Glühwein (non-alcoholic, Germany) [2]7
Goat Soup (Liberia) [3]43
Gohan (Boiled Rice, Japan) [2]155
Golabki (Stuffed Cabbage Rolls, Poland) [3]116
Golaz (Goulash, Slovenia) [3]144
Goulash (Slovenia) [3]144
Grated Carrot, Apple, and Raisin Salad Australia) [1]20

Great Lakes (United States) [4]101
Apple Sauerkraut [4]101
Buffalo Chicken Wings [4]100
Cornish Pasty [4]103
Dutch Pancakes [4]98
Fish Boil [4]97
German Potatoi Salad [4]98
Hummus [4]99
Macaroni and Cheese [4]99
Ojibwa Wild Rice [4]96
Potato Lefse [4]102
Springerle [4]101
Swedish Meatballs [4]102
Greece [2]21
Avgolemono [2]22
Frouta Ke Yaourti [2]29
Greek Salad [2]28
Greek Salad Dressing [2]28
Kourabiethes [2]27
Melopitta [2]26
Moussaka [2]23
Tzatziki [2]28
Greek Salad [2]28
Greek Salad Dressing [2]28
Green Bean Casserole (Midwest Region, United States) [4]127
Green Bean Salad (South Africa) [3]154
Greens, Zimbabwe [4]185
Grilled Skewered Chicken (Iran) [2]85
Ground Meat Stew (South Africa) [3]157
Groundnut Stew (Ghana) [2]18
Groundnut Toffee (Peanut Toffee, Ghana) [2]15
Guacamole (Guatemala) [2]33
Guacamole (Latino Americans, United States) [4]117
Guaraná (Brazil) [1]40
Guatemala [2]31
Arroz Guatemalteco [2]34
Bunuelos [2]35
Cucumber Soup [2]34
Frijoles Negros Volteados [2]33
Garlic Butter [2]37
Guacamole [2]33
Hot Christmas Punch [2]36
Mantequilla de ajo casera [2]37
Pan de Banano [2]37
Pepinos Rellenos [2]36
Picado de Rabano [2]33
Spanish Tortilla [2]33
Gulyás (Hungarian Goulash) [2]51

H

Haggis (United Kingdom) [4]68
Haiti 2[39]
Bannann Peze [2]43
Cornmeal Porridge [2]47
French-Style Lettuce Salad [2]40
Haitian Fruit Salad [2]44
Mango Juice [2]42
Pain Haïtien [2]46
Pineapple Nog [2]46
Riz Djon-Djon [2]44
Riz et Pois Rouges [2]44
Spiced Cocoa [2]41
Ti-Malice [2]47
Haitian Fruit Salad [2]44
Halva (Turkey) [4]50
Ham and Cheese Sandwich (Chile) [1]89
Ham and Cheese Sandwich (France) [1]154
Harira (Morocco) [3]61
Hasselbackspotatis (Roasted Potatoes, Sweden) Sweden
Hawayij (Spice Blend, Saudi Arabia) [3]134
Haysa Al-Tumreya (Dip for Dates, Saudi Arabia) [3]135
Helado de Mango (Tropical Mango Sherbet) [1]118
Herring Dip (Jewish Americans, United States) [4]113
Hin Pap (White Rice, Korea) [3]21
Hispaniola [2]39
Holubtsi (Stuffed Cabbage Rolls, Ukraine) [4]60
Honey-Baked Apples (Northeast Region, United States) [4]146
Hot Chocalate Drink (Mexico) [3]53
Hot Christmas Punch (Guatemala) [2]36
Hot Cranberry Punch (Northeast Region, United States) [4]146
Hot Ginger Tea (Indonesia) [2]77
Houbova Polevka Myslivecka (Hunter's Mushroom Soup, Czech Republic) [1]124
Huevos Rancheros (Ranch-Style Eggs, Mexico) [3]50
Hummus (Great Lakes, United States) [4]99
Hummus (Saudi Arabia) [3]140
Hummus be Tahini (Lebanon) [3]36
Hungarian Butter Cookies (Hungary) [2]54
Hungarian Cold Plate [2]56
Hungary [2]49
Almond Kisses [2]55
Gulyás [2]51
Hungarian Butter Cookies [2]54
Hungarian Cold Plate [2]56

Hungary *(continued)*
Paprika Chicken [2]52
Pork Cutlets with Potatoes [2]53
Pörkölt [2]51
Small Dumplings [2]56
Stuffed Green Peppers [2]52
Summer Cucumber Soup [2]57
Hunter's Mushroom Soup (Czech Republic) [1]124
Hush Puppies (African Americans, United States) [4]78

I

India [2]59
Baigan Bhartha [2]60
Dal [2]62
Fancy Rice [2]65
Garam Masala [2]60
Kheer [2]65
Mathis [2]67
Palak Bhaji [2]62
Tandoori Chicken [2]63
Vegetable Sandwich [2]67
Indian Fry-Bread (Native Americans, United States)
[4]137
Indian Pudding (Northeast Region, United States)
[4]140
Indonesia [2]69
Es Avocad [2]74
Es Pokat [2]74
Gado Gado [2]78
Nasi Goreng [2]71
Nasi Jagung [2]79
Nasi Kuning [2]78
PIsang Goreng [2]77
Sambal Kecap [2]74
Sankayo Telor [2]74
Tahu Goreng [2]75
Teh Halia [2]77
Uli Petataws [2]73
Injera (Ethiopian Bread) [1]146
Iran [2]81
Dolma (Stuffed Grape Leaves) [2]82
Dugh [2]86
Iranian Rice Cakes (Iran) [2]88
Kebab Morgh [2]85
Maast [2]91
Shirazi [2]85
Shir-Berenj [2]88

Yogurt and Mint Sauce [2]83
Iranian Rice Cakes (Iran) [2]88
Iraq [2]93
Adas Bil Hamod [2]96
Beef with Fruit [2]94
G'shur Purtaghal [2]101
Kebabs [2]99
Khubaz [2]99
Kibbe Batata [2]100
Ma'Mounia [2]98
Ma'mounia [2]98
Red Lentil Soup [2]96
Yalanchi (Iraq) [2]97
Irea (Cinnamon Beverage, Egypt) [1]138
Ireland [2]103
Apple Cake [2]111
Barm Brack [2]108
Champ [2]106
Colcannon [2]107
Corned Beef with Cabbage [2]106
Dublin Coddle [2]110
Irish Christmas Cake [2]109
Irish Soda Bread [2]105
Scones [2]110
Traditional Irish Stew [2]105
Irio (Kenya) [3]10
Irish Christmas Cake (Ireland) [2]109
Irish Soda Bread (Ireland) [2]105
Iroquois Strawberry Drink (Native Americans, United
States) [4]137
Islands of the Pacific [2]113
Badam Pistaz Barfi [2]118
Baked Papaya Dessert [2]121
Bananas and Sweet Potatoes [2]118
Firifiri [2]121
Fresh Grated Coconut [2]115
Papaya Chicken and Coconut Milk [2]118
Poisson Cru [2]116
Roast Pork [2]117
Tropical Fruit Dessert [2]121
Tropical Fruit Shake [2]121
Israel [2]123
Blintzes [2]124
Charoseth [2]131
Fava Bean Spread [2]126
Felafel [2]128
Fresh Oranges [2]124
Israeli Vegetable Salad [2]129
Mandelbrot [2]132

Israel *(continued)*
New Year's Honey Cake [2]130
Pita Sandwiches [2]131
Shakshooka [2]126
Tahini Sauce [2]128
Israeli Vegetable Salad (Israel) [2]129
Isu (Spiced Boiled Yams) [3]76
Italian Christmas Bread [2]138
Italian Easter Bread [2]138
Italy [2]133
Biscotti [2]139
Bruschetta [2]141
Cannoli [2]141
Fettucine Alfredo [2]136
Italian Christmas Bread [2]138
Italian Easter Bread [2]138
Pasta e Fagioli [2]135
Polenta [2]136
Saltimbocca all Romana [2]137
Ivory Coast see Côte d'Ivoire
Iyan (Pounded Yams, Nigeria) [3]79

J

Jamaica [2]143
Almost Ting [2]150
Baked Ripe Banana [2]150
Brown-Stewed Fish [2]146
Coconut Chips [2]146
Curry Chicken [2]150
Gizzada [2]151
Jamaican Christmas Cake [2]148
Jamaican Fruit Drink [2]149
Jerk Chicken [2]147
Plaintains [2]145
Rice and Peas [2]144
Jamaican Christmas Cake [2]148
Jamaican Fruit Drink [2]149
Jansson's Frestelse ("Jansson's Temptation") [4]14
Japan [2}153
Beef Sukijaki [2]157
Broiled Salmon [2]162
Chicken Teriyaki [2]157
Gohan [2]155
Miso Soup [2]156
Onigiri [2]156
Ozoni [2]159
Ramen [2]161

Sweet Peanut Mochi [2]159
Yaki-Soba [2]158
Yakitori [2]161
Jerk Chicken (Jamaica) [2]147
Jewish Americans (United States) [4]105
Apple and Carrot Tsimmes [4]111
Charoset [4]110
Chopped Chicken Liver [4]107
Herring Dip [4]113
Matzo Balls [4]111
Matzo Brie [4]112
Mother's Chicken Soup [4]106
New York Cheesecake [4]113
Noodle Kugel [4]107
Potato Latkes [4]110
Johnnycakes (Northeast Region, United States) [4]141
Jollof Rice (Liberia) [3]41
Jollof Rice (Nigeria) [3]79
Jota (Slovenia) [3]146
Julgröt (Swedish Christmas Porridge) [4]18

K

Ka Nom Jeen Sour Nam (Pineapple-Fish Noodles, Thailand) [4]42
Ka'ak Cookies (Lebanon) [3]34
Kamja Guk (Potato Soup, Korea) [3]20
Kapsa (Chicken and Rice, Saudi Arabia) [3]136
Kartoffelknödeln (Potato Dumplings, Germany) [2]4
Kartoplia Solimkoi (Deep-Fried Straw Potatoes, Ukraine) [4]60
Kategna (Ethiopia) [1]144
Kaymakli Kuru Kayisi (Cream-Stuffed Apricots, Turkey) [4]46
Kazakhstan [3]1
Basturma [3]2
Baursaki [3]4
Mutton Kespe [3]4
Plov [3]3
Rice Sorpa [3]7
Kebab Morgh (Grilled Skewered Chicken, Iran) [2]85
Kebabs (Iraq) [2]99
Kedjenou (Seasoned Meat and Vegetable Sauce, Côte d'Ivoire) [1]107
Kelapa Susu (Coconut Milk, Indonesia) [2]71
Kelewele (Ghana) [2]15
Kenkey (Ground Cornmeal, Ghana) [2]19

Kenya [3]9
Githeri [3]14
Irio [3]10
Matoke [3]14
Nyama Choma [3]14
Sukuma Wiki [3]12
Ugali [3]12
Western Kenya Cabbage and Egg [3]11
Yogurt Chutney [3]13
Kheer (Rice Pudding, India) [2]65
Kheer (Rice Pudding, Pakistan) [3]88
Khoshaf (Egypt) [1]138
Khubaz (Pita with Jelly, Iraq) [2]99
Kibbe Batata (Potato-Beef Casserole, Iraq) [2]100
Kielbasa and Cabbage (Poland) [3]119
Kimaje (Flat Bread, Saudi Arabia) [3]137
Kimchi (Korea) [3]20
Kitfo (Spiced Raw Beef, Ethiopia) [1]147
Klimp (Dumplings, Sweden) [4]15
Klobasa and Kisdo Zelje (Sausage and Sauerkraut, Slovenia) [3]146
Klyukva S Sakharom (Frosted Cranberries, Russia) [3]130
Knedlíky (Czech Dumplings) [1]125
Köfte (Turkish Meatballs) [4]50
Komkomer Sambal (South Africa) [3]156
Korea [3]17
Chap Ch'ae [3]22
Ch'o Kanjang [3]24
Kamja Guk [3]20
Korean Spinach [3]25
Mandu [3]23
Pulgogi [3]24
Soo Chunkwa (Ginger Drink) [3]18
Toasted Sesame Seeds [3]21
Korean Spinach [3]25
Kotlety Po-Kyivskomy (Chicken Kiev, Ukraine) [4]61
Köttbulla (Swedish Meatballs) [4]14
Kourabiethes (Butter Cookies, Greece) [2]27
Koushari (Lentils, Macaroni, Rice, and Chickpeas, Egypt) [1]133
Kure Na Paprice (Chicken Paprikas, Czech Republic) [1]126
Kutya (Sweet Porridge,Ukraine) [4]63
Kwanzaa Brownies (African Americans, United States) [4]83

L

La Galette des Rois (King's Cake, France) [1]157
Lab (Ethiopian Cheese) [1]146
Laban Drink (Yogurt Drink, Saudi Arabia) [3]138
Lahmacun (Turkish Pizza) [4]55
Lake T'ana [1]143
Lamb on Skewers (Greece) [2]24
Lamingtons (Austalia) [1]23
Land of Eternal Spring see Guatemala [2]31
Lassi (Yogurt Drink, Pakistan) [3]88
Latino Americans (United States) [4]115
Chili Corn Bread [4]121
Cuban Avocado and Pineapple Salad [4]121
Cuban Beans and Rice [4]117
Fried Plantains [4]117
Gazpacho [4]120
Guacamole [4]117
Mexican Fried Ice Cream [4]119
Puerto Rican Christmas Salad [4]120
Salsa Cruda [4]116
Tropical Fruit Salad [4]121
Lebanese Fresh Fruit Salad (Lebanon) [3]35
Lebanese Rice Pudding [3]28
Lebanon [3]27
Baked Kibbeh [3]31
Easy Lebanese Baklava [3]32
Hummus be Tahini [3]36
Ka'ak Cookies [3]34
Lebanese Fresh Fruit Salad [3]35
Lebanese Rice Pudding [3]28
Limoonada [3]35
Pita Bread [3]28
Sugared Almonds [3]34
Tabbouleh [3]30
Lebkuchen (Germany) [2]6
Leche Flan (Caramel Custard, Peru) [3]102
Lemon and Garlic Potato Salad (Egypt) [1]135
Lemon Curd (United Kingdom) [4]68
Lemon Grass Tea (Liberia) [3]42
Lemon Soda (Vietnam) [4]176
Lentil Soup, Red (Iraq) [2]96
Lentils (India) [2]62
Lentils with Lemon Juice (Iraq) [2]96
Lettuce Dipped in Honey and Vinegar Dressing (Iran) [2]88
Lettuce Salad (Egypt) [1]138

Liberia [3]39

Ginger Beer [3]42

Goat Soup [3]43

Jollof Rice [3]41

Lemon Grass Tea [3]42

Palava [3]40

Rice Bread [3]41

Sweet Potato Pone [3]41

Limoonada (Lemonade, Lebanon) [3]35

Little Meat Pies (Argentina) [1]13

Locum (Turkish Candy) [4]52

Lokma (Golden Fritters, Turkey) [4]53

Lussekatter (St. Lucia Saffron Buns, Sweden) [4]17

M

Ma'mounia (Wheat Pudding, Iraq) [2]98

Maast (Homemade Yogurt, Iran) [2]91

Macadamia and Fruit Snack (Aborigines and Bush Tucker, Australia) [1]33

Macadamia Nut Cookies (Aborigines and Bush Tucker, Australia) [1]33

Macaroni and Cheese (Great Lakes, United States) [4]99

Main dishes

Adobong Hiponsa Gata (Philippines) [3]107

Arni Souvlaki (Lamb on Skewers) [2]24

Aterkek Alecha (Ethiopia) [1]148

Australian Meat Pies (Australia) [1]21

Baguette Sandwich (France) [1]153

Baked Kibbeh (Lebanon) [3]31

Baked Macaroni and Cheese (African Americans, United States) [4]82

Basturma (Kazakstan) [3]2

Beef Sukiyaki (Japan) [2]157

Beef with Fruit (Iraq) [2]94

Bigos (Poland) [3]114

Birthday Noodles with Peanut Sauce [1]99

Bisteeya (Morocco) [3]59

Bliny (Russia) [3]125

Bobotie (South Africa) [3]157

Borscht (Russia) [3]129

Bratwurst [2]4

Brazilian Black Beans (Afro-Brazilian, Brazil) [1]49

Broiled Salmon (Japan) [2]162

Broiled Salmon Steaks (Western Region, United States) [4]164

Brown-Stewed Fish (Jamaica) [2]146

Buffalo Chicken Wings (Great Lakes, United States) [4]100

Buffalo Stew (Native Americans, United States) [4]135

Cabbage Pirozhki (Russia) [3]126

Calalou (Côte d'Ivoire) [1]109

Canadian Bacon with Maple Glaze (Canada) [1]63

Carbonada Criolla (Argentina) [1]12

Ceviche (Peru) [3]99

Chap Ch'ae (Korea) [3]22

Chicken and Sausage Gumbo (Southern Region, United States) [4]153

Chicken Karaii (Pakistan) [3]86

Chicken Satay (Thailand) [4]38

Chicken Tajine with Almonds and Prunes (Morocco) [3]56

Chicken Teriyaki (Japan) [2]157

Chuck Wagon Brisket (Western Region, United States) [4]161

Coconut-Chicken Soup (Thailand) [4]43

Collard Greens with Hamhocks (Southern Region, United States) [4]157

Corned Beef with Cabbage (Ireland) [2]106

Cornhusker's Casserole (Midwest Region, United States) [4]129

Cornish Pasties [4]69

Creole Seasoning (Southern Region, United States) [4]153

Crêpes de la Chandeleur (Canada) [1]74

Cuban Beans and Rice (Latino Americans, United States) [4]117

Curry Chicken (Jamaica) [2]150

Dal (India) [2]62

Dhal (Pakistan) [3]85

Dolma (Iran) [2]82

Dovi (Zimbabwe) [4]183

Dublin Coddle (Ireland) [2]110

Dutch Pancakes (Great Lakes, United States) [4]98

Easy Fufu (Cameroon) [1]55

Egg Fu Yung (China) [1]101

Empadas (Brazil) [1]50

Fazolovy Gulás S Hovemzim Masem (Czech Republic) [1]126

Feijoada (Brazil) [1]38

Felafel (Israel) [2]128

Fettucine Alfredo (Italy) [2]136

Fish Boil (Great Lakes, United States) [4]97

French Pea Soup (French Canadians, Canada)

Fried Rice (China) [1]97

Main dishes *(continued)*

Frijoles Negros Volteados (Guatemala) [2]33
Frittata (Italy) [2]140
Fufu (Ghana) [2]14
Ful Mudammas (Egypt) [1]132
Golabki (Poland) [3]116
Golaz (Slovenia) [3]144
Green Bean Salad (South Africa) [3]154
Groundnut Stew (Ghana) [2]18
Gulyás (Hungary) [2]51
Haggis (United Kingdom) [4]68
Harira (Morocco) [3]61
Holubtsi (Ukraine) [4]60
Houbova Polevka Myslivecka (Czech Republic) [1]124
Hungarian Cold Plate (Hungary) [2]56
Irio (Kenya) [3]10
Jerk Chicken (Jamaica) [2]147
Jollof Rice (Liberia) [3]41
Jollof Rice (Nigeria) [3]79
Jota (Slovenia) [3]146
Ka Nom Jeen Sour Nam (Thailand) [4]42
Kapsa (Saudi Arabia) [3]136
Kebab Morgh (Iran) [2]85
Kebabs (Iraq) [2]99
Kedjenou (Côte d'Ivoire) [1]107
Kibbe Batata (Iraq) [2]100
Kielbasa and Cabbage (Poland) [3]119
Kitfo (Ethiopia) [1]147
Klobasa and Kisdo Zelje (Slovenia) [3]146
Köfte (Turkey) [4]50
Kotlety Po-Kyivskomy (Ukraine) [4]61
Köttbulla (Swedish Meatballs, Sweden) [4]14
Koushari (Egypt) [1]133
Kure Na Paprice (Czech Republic) [1]126
Lahmacun (Turkey) [4]55
Macaroni and Cheese (Great Lakes, United States) [4]99
Mala Sousta Se Syre (Czech Republic) [1]129
Matata (Mozambique) [3]69
Matzo Balls (Jewish Americans, United States) [4]111
Midwestern Chili (Midwest Region, United States) [4]125
Midwestern Pork Chop Dinner (Midwest Region, United States) [4]130
Miso Soup (Japan) [2]156
Moors and Christians (Cuba) [1]114
Moqueca (Afro-Brazilians, Brazil) [1]47

Moqueca aos Ovos (Afro-Brazilians, Brazil) [1]47
Mother's Chicken Soup (Jewish Americans, United States) [4]106
Moussaka (Greece) [2]23
Mushroom Barley Soup (Poland) [3]119
Mutton Kespe (Kazakhstan) [3]4
Nasi Goreng (Indonesia) [2]71
Ndole (Cameroon) [1]56
New England Boiled Dinner (Northeast Region, United States) [4]144
Nigerian Stew [3]77
Nyama Choma (Kenya) [3]14
Ojibwa Wild Rice (Great Lakes, United States) [4]96
Old Fashioned Turnip Soup (Southern Region, United States) [4]151
Oto (Ghana) [2]17
Ozoni (Japan) [2]159
Pad Thai (Thailand) [4]42
Palava (Liberia) [3]40
Pansit Mami (Philippines) [3]110
Papas a la Huancaína (Peru) [3]97
Paprika Chicken (Hungary) [2]52
Papaya Chicken and Coconut Milk (Islands of the Pacific) [2]118
Pasta e Fagioli (Italy) [2]135
Pasta with Yogurt-Mint Sauce (Turkey) [4]47
Pastel de Choclo (Chile) [1]84
Pepper Soup (Ghaha) [2]19
Pierogi (Poland) [3]115
Pita Sandwiches (Israel) [2]131
Plättar (Sweden) [4]19
Poa Pee (Thailand) [4]39
Poisson Cru (Islands of the Pacific) [2]116
Pork Chops with Sauerkraut and Potatoes (Amish and Pennsylvania Dutch, United States) [4]89
Pork Cutlets with Potatoes [2]53
Pörkölt (Hungary) [2]51
Potato Latkes (Jewish Americans, United States) [4]110
Potato Lefse (Great Lakes, United States) [4]102
Puerto Rican Christmas Salad (Latino Americans, United States) [4]120
Pulgogi (Korea) [3]24
Putupap (South Africa) [3]158
Quesadillas (Mexico) [3]52
Quiche au Saumon et Crevettes (France) [1]155
Ragoût de Boulettes (Canada) [1]74
Ramen (Japan) [2]161

Main dishes (*continued*)

Red Beans and Rice (African Americans, United States) [4]80

Rice and Peas (Jamaica) [2]144

Rice Sorpa [3]7

Safou a la Sauce Tomate (Cameroon) [1]54

Salmon Kedgeree (United Kingdom) [4]66

Saltimbocca all Romana (Italy) [2]137

Shakshooka [2]126

Southern Fried Chicken (Southern Region, United States) [4]152

Spanish Tortilla (Guatemala) [2]33

Spiced Chicken (China) [1]99

Spicy Oven-Fried Chicken (Amish and Pennsylvania Dutch, United States) [4]91

Spring Rolls (Vietnam) [4]177

Stuffed Green Peppers (Hungary) [2]52

Succotash (Northeast Region, United States) [4]141

Sushi (Japan) [2]155

Swedish Meatballs (Great Lakes, United States) [4]102

Sweet and Sour Pork (China) [1]96

Tahu Goreng (Indonesia [2]75

Tandoori Chicken [2]63

Thai Beef Curry [4]37

Toad-in-the-Hole (United Kingdom) [4]70

Topinky S Vejci (Czech Republic) [1]128

Tortilla Española [4]3

Tourtière (Canada, French Canandian) [1]73

Traditional Irish Stew (Ireland) [2]105

Tuna in Sauce (Cuba) [1]117

Veal Meatballs with Dill [3]121

Vegetable Sandwich (India) [2]67

Weisse Bohnensuppe (Germany) [2]3

Welsh Rarebit (United Kingdom) [4]69

Western Kenya Cabbage and Egg [3]11

Yaki-Soba (Japan) [2]158

Yakitori (Japan) [2]161

Yalanchi (Iraq) [2]97

Yams (Ghana) [2]12

Maize Porridge (Mozambique) [3]68

Maja Blanco (Coconut Cake, Peru) [3]105

Makiwnyk (Poppy Seed Cake) [4]63

Makubi (Tanzania) [4]32

Mala Sousta Se Syre (Small Cheese Bites, Czech Republic) [1]129

Malasadas (Doughnuts, Mozambique) [3]69

Mandelbrot (Almond Cookies, Israel) [2]132

Mandu (Korean Dumplings, Korea) [3]23

Mango Juice (Haiti) [2]42

Mango Sherbet, Tropical (Cuba) [1]118

Mango-Orange Drink (Tanzania) [4]28

Man-O-Min (Aboriginals, Canada) [1]80

Mantequilla de ajo casera (Garlic Butter, Guatemala) [2]37

Maple Baked Beans (Native Americans, United Statess, United States) [4]134

Maple Butter (Northeast Region, United States) [4]142

Maple Sundae (Canada) [1]67

Maple Syrup Upside-Down Cake (Canada) [1]67

Mapopo (Papaya) Candy (Zimbabwe) [4]182

Mardi Gras King Cake (Southern Region, United States) [4]155

Marinated Artichokes (Western Region, United States) [4]163

Marzipan (Spain) [4]6

Matata (Seafood and Peanut Stew, Mozambique) [3]69

Maté (Brazil) [1]40

Mathis (Spicy Cookie, India) [2]67

Matoke (Kenya) [3]14

Matzo Balls (Jewish Americans, United States) [4]111

Matzo Brie (Jewish Americans, United States) [4]112

Mazapanes (Spain) [4]6

Mealie Soup (Corn Soup, South Africa) [3]153

Meat and Vegetable Stew (Côte d'Ivoire) [1]109

Meat Pie (French Canadians, Canada) [1]73

Meat, Grilled (Nyama Choma, Kenya) [3]14

Meatballs, Turkish (Turkey) [4]50

Melon Fingers with Lime (Côte d'Ivoire) [1]106

Melopitta (Honey Pie, Greece) [2]26

Mescouta (Date Cookies) [3]58

Mexican Fried Ice Cream (Latino Americans, United States) [4]119

Mexico [3]45

Arroz Blanco [3]53

Café de Olla [3]48

Chocolate Mexicana [3]53

Frijoles [3]47

Frijoles Refritos [3]47

Huevos Rancheros [3]50

Quesadillas [3]52

Rosca de Reyes [3]49

Mhalbi (Morocco) [3]63

Midwest Region (United States) [4]123

Bread Pudding [4]124

Caramel Corn (Midwest) [4]128

Corn on the Cob [4]127

Cornhusker's Casserole [4]129

Midwest Region *(continued)*
Deviled Eggs [4]126
Green Bean Casserole [4]127
Midwestern Chili [4]125
Midwestern Pork Chop Dinner [4]130
Reuben Sandwich [4]128
Midwestern Chili (Midwest Region, United States)
[4]125
Midwestern Pork Chop Dinner (Midwest Region,
United States) [4]130
Milk Jam (Argentina) [1]17
Milk with Chocolate Syrup (Argentina) [1]16
Mincemeat Pies, Individual (United Kingdom) [4]73
Miso Soup (Japan) [2]156
Mixed Vegetables with Cellophane Noodles (Korea)
[3]22
Molasses Water (African Americans, United States)
[4]79
Moors and Christians (Black Beans and Rice, Cuba)
[1]114
Moqueca (Spicy Fish and Coconut Milk Stew, Brazil)
[1]47
Moqueca aos Ovos (Spicy Egg Stew, Brazil) [1]47
Moravian Christmas Cookies (Czech Republic) [1]127
Moravske Vano ni Kukyse (Moravian Christmas Cook-
ies, Czech Republic) [1]127
Moroccan Mint Tea (Morocco) [3]58
Moroccan String of Doughnuts [3]63
Morocco [3]55
Bisteeya [3]59
Chicken Tajine with Almonds and Prunes [3]56
Chickpea, Feta, and Olive Salad [3]62
Fried Baby Carrots [3]61
Harira [3]61
Mescouta (Date Cookies) [3]58
Mhalbi [3]63
Moroccan Mint Tea [3]58
Moroccan String of Doughnuts [3]63
Sweet Grated Carrot Salad [3]63
Mother's Chicken Soup (Jewish Americans, United
States) [4]106
Moussaka (Lamb-Eggplant Casserole, Greece) [2]23
Mousse au Chocolat (Chocolate Mousse, France [1]155
Mozambique [3]68
Malasadas [3]69
Matata [3]69
Pãozinho [3]67
Piri-Piri Sauce [3]66
Salada Pera de Abacate [3]73
Sandes de Queijo [3]68
Sopa de Feijao Verde [3]72
Muhallabi (Rice Pudding, Turkey) [4]48
Mushroom Barley Soup (Poland) [3]119
Mushroom Tartlets (Spain) [4]8
Mutton Kespe (Kazakhstan) [3]4

N

Nachynka (Cornbread Stuffing, Ukaine) [4]61
Nam Pla Prig (Dipping Sauce, Thailand) [4]37
Nanaimo Bars (Canada) [1]65
Naneli Limonata (Lemonade with Mint, Turkey) [4]49
Nasi Goreng (Fried Rice, Indonesia) [2]71
Nasi Jagung (Corn Rice, Indonesia) [2]79
Nasi Kuning (Yellow Rice, Indonesia) [2]78
Native Americans (United States) [4]131
Buffalo Stew [4]135
Indian Fry Bread [4]137
Iroquois Strawberry Drink [4]137
Maple Baked Beans [4]134
Pinole [4]137
Popcorn [4]132
Popped Wild Rice [4]138
Pumpkin Bread [4]136
Pumpkin-Corn Sauce [4]135
Succotash [4]133
Ndizi Kaanga (Fried Bananas or Plantains, Tanzania)
[4]28
Ndole (Bitterleaf Soup, Cameroon) [1]56
New England Boiled Dinner (Northeast Region, United
States) [4]144
New England Clam Chowder (Northeast Region, United
States) [4]144
New Year's Honey Cake (Israel) [2]130
New Year's Soup (Japan) [2]159
New York Cheesecake (Jewish Americans, United
States) [4]113
Nigeria [3]75
Chinchin [3]81
Dodo [3]80
Efo [3]80
Isu [3]76
Iyan [3]79
Jollof Rice [3]79
Nigerian Stew [3]77
Nigerian Stew [3]77
Niter Kebbeh or Kibe (Spiced Butter, Ethiopia) [1]145

Noodle and Bean Soup (Italy) [2]135

Noodle Casserole (Jewish Americans, United States) [4]107

Noodles, Fried (Japan) [2]158

Noodle Kugel (Noodle Casserole, Jewish Americans, United States) [4]107

Noodle Soup (Japan) [2]161

Noodles with Poppy Seeds (Poland) [3]118

Northeast Region (United States) [4]139

    Boston Baked Beans [4]143

    Clam Chowder [4]144

    Coffee Milkshake [4]144

    Honey-Baked Appleas [4]146

    Hot Cranberry Punch [4]146

    Indian Pudding [4]140

    Johnnycakes [4]141

    Maple Butter [4]142

    New England Boiled Dinner [4]144

    New England Clam Chowder [4]144

    Succotash [4]141

Northwest United States see Western Region (United States)

Nuoc Cham (Vietnam) [4]171

Nyama Choma (Kenya) [3]14

O

Ojibwa Wild Rice (Aboriginals, Canada) [1]80

Ojibwa Wild Rice (Great Lakes, United States) [4]96

Okra, Sweet and Sour (Egypt) [1]137

Old-Fashioned Spicy Lemonade (Amish and Pennsylvania Dutch, United States) [4]93

Old Fashioned Turnip Soup (Southern Region, United States) [4]151

Olho de Sogra (Afro-Brazilians, Brazil) [1]51

Olive, Marinate (Cuba) [1]119

Onigiri (Rice Ball, Japan) [2]156

Onion Soup (France) [1]153

Orange Salad (Brazil) [1]39

Oto (Yams & Eggs, Ghana) [2]17

Oven-Fried Cheese (Egypt) [1]135

Ozoni (New Year's Soup, Japan) [2]159

P

Pacific Islands [2]113

    Badam Pistaz Barfi [2]118

    Baked Papaya Dessert [2]121

    Bananas and Sweet Potatoes [2]118

    Firifiri [2]121

    Fresh Grated Coconut [2]115

    Papaya Chicken and Coconut Milk [2]118

    Poisson Cru [2]116

    Roast Pork [2]117

    Tropical Fruit Dessert [2]121

    Tropical Fruit Shake [2]121

Pad Thai [4]42

Pain Haïtien (Haitian Bread) [2]46

Pakistan [3]83

    Aaloo Bukhary Ki Chutney [3]86

    Chicken Karaii [3]86

    Dhal [3]85

    Kheer [3]88

    Lassi [3]88

    Raitha [3]87

    Shahi Tukra [3]84

Palak Bhaji (Spicy Fried Spinach, India) [2]62

Palava (Liberia) [3]40

Palta Aji Sauce (Peru) [3]93

Pan de Banano (Banana Bread, Guatemala) [2]37

Pancakes, Apple (Germany) [2]5

Panettone (Italian Christmas Bread) [2]138

Pansit Mami (Noodles in Broth, Philippines) [3]110

Pãozinho (Portuguese Rolls, Mozambique) [3]67

Papas a la Huancaína (Potatoes with Cheese, Peru) [3]97

Papaya Candy (Zimbabwe) [4]182

Papaya Chicken and Coconut Milk (Islands of the Pacific) [2]118

Paprika Chicken (Hungary) [2]52

Parsley New Potatoes (Western Region, United States) [4]165

Pashka (Russia) [3]128

Pasta e Fagioli (Noodle and Bean Soup, Italy) [2]135

Pasta with Yogurt-Mint Sauce [4]47

Pastel de Choclo (Corn and Meat Pie, Chile) [1]84

Pavlova (Australia) [1]24

Pea Soup (Sweden) [4]20

Peachy Baked Apples (Amish and Pennsylvania Dutch, United States) [4]91

Peanut Butter and Molasses Spread (Amish and Pennsylvania Dutch, United States) [4]93

Peanut Butter Stew (Zimbabwe) [4]183

Pemmican Cakes (Canada) [1]78

Pennsylvania Dutch, Amish and (United States) [4]87

Pepinos Rellenos (Stuffed Cucumbers, Guatemala) [2]36

Pepparkakor (Ginger Cookies, Sweden) [4]16

Pepper Soup (Ghana) [2]19
Pepper-Scented Rice (Brazil) [1]41
Persia see Iran
Persian Fruit Salad (Iran) [2]91
Peru [3]91
    Arroz con Lech [3]99
    Baked Papas Skins [3]92
    Ceviche [3]99
    Choclo con Queso [3]95
    Flan [3]97
    Frozen Orange Delight [3]95
    Leche Flan [3]102
    Maja Blanco [3]105
    Palta Aji Sauce [3]93
    Papas a la Huancaína [3]97
    Picarones [3]93
Philippines [3]101
    Adobong Hiponsa Gata [3]107
    Pansit Mami [3]110
    Polvoron [3]110
    Singangag [3]108
    Tsokolate [3]108
Pho Bo (Vietnam) [4]172
Picado de Rabano (Radish Salad, Guatemala) [2]33
Picarones (Pumpkin Fritters) [3]93
Pico de Gallo (Mexican Salsa) [3]51
Pierogi (Dumplings, Poland) [3]115
Pineapple Nog (Haiti) [2]46
Pineapple Sherbet (Pineapple Smoothie, South Africa) [3]158
Pineapple-Orange Drink (Brazil) [1]43
Pinole (Cornmeal Drink, Native Americans, United States) [4]137
Piri-Piri Sauce (Mozambique) [3]66
Piroghi, Cabbage (Russia) [3]126
Pirozhki, Cabbage (Russia) [3]126
Pisang Goreng (Fried Banana Cakes, Indonesia) [2]77
Pita Bread (Lebanon) [3]28
Pita Sandwiches (Israel) [2]131
Pita with Jelly (Iraq) [2]99
Pizza, Turkish (Lahmacun) [4]55
Plantains (Jamaica) [2]145
Plantains and Cassava, Boiled (Côte d'Ivoire) [1]106
Plantains, Fried (Cuba) [1]115
Plantains, Fried (Ghana) [2]15
Plantains, Fried (Haiti) [2]43
Plantains, Fried (Nigeria) [3]80
Plantains, Fried (Tanzania) [4]28
Plantains, Mashed (Kenya) [3]14

Plättar (Swedish Pancakes, Sweden) [4]19
Plov (Rice Pilaf, Kazakhstan) [3]3
Poa Pee (Thai Egg Rolls, Thailand) [4]39
Poisson Cru (Islands of the Pacific) [2]116
Poland [3]113
    Bigos [3]114
    Cheesecake [3]117
    Dried Fruit Compote [3]118
    Golabki [3]116
    Kielbasa and Cabbage [3]119
    Mushroom Barley Soup [3]119
    Noodles with Poppy Seeds [3]118
    Pierogi [3]115
    Stuffed Eggs [3]121
    Veal Meatballs with Dill [3]121
Polenta (Italy) [2]136
Polenta, Brazil (Fried Corn Mush) [1]40
Polvoron (Powdered Milk Candy, Philippines) [3]110
Ponche (Berry Punch, Chile) [1]90
Poor Man's Pudidng (Canada) [1]72
Popcorn (Native Americans, United States) [4]132
Popped Wild Rice (Native Americans, United States) [4]138
Poppy Seed Cake (Ukraine) [4]63
Pork Chops with Sauerkraut and Potatoes (Amish and Pennsylvania Dutch, United States) [4]89
Pork Cutlets with Potatoes (Hungary) [2]53
Pörkölt (National Hungarian Stew) [2]51
Portuguese Rolls (Mozambique) [3]67
Potato Latkes (Potato Pancakes, Jewish Americans, United States) [4]110
Potato Lefse (Great Lakes, United States) [4]102
Potato Pancakes (Jewish Americans, United States) [4]110
Potato Salad (African Americans, United States) [4]81
Potato Salad, Lemon and Garlic (Egypt) [1]135
Potato Soup (Korea) [3]20
Potato Varenyky (Potato Dumplings) [4]58
Potato, Baked Skins (Peru) [3]92
Potato-Beef Casserole (Iraq) [2]100
Potatoes with Cheese (Peru) [3]97
Potatoes, Deep-Fried Straw (Ukraine) [4]60
Potica (Slovenia) [3]147
Poutine, Quebec (Canada) [1]75
Pralines (Southern Region, United States) [4]157
Pretzels, Soft (Germany) [2]9
Pudding au Chomeur (Poor Man's Pudding, Canada) [1]72

Pudding, Steamed Egg and Coconut Milk (Indonesia) [2]74

Pudim (Brazil) [1]42

Puerto Rican Christmas Salad (Latino Americans, United States) [4]120

Pulgogi (Korean Beef) [3]24

Pumpkin Bread (Native Americans, United States) [4]136

Pumpkin Fritters (Peru) [3]93

Pumpkin, Braised with Coconut Milk (Vietnam) [4]174

Pumpkin-Corn Sauce (Native Americans, United States) [4]135

Putupap (Cornmeal Porridge, South Africa) [3]158

Q

Qahwa [3]141

Qahwa (Arabic Coffee, Saudi Arabia) [3]141

Quebec Poutine (Canada) [1]75

Quejadinhas (Coconut and Cheese Snacks) [1]43

Quesadillas (Mexico) [3]52

Quiabo (Okra, Brazil) [1]46

Quiche au Saumon et Crevettes (Salmon and Shrimp Quiche, France) [1]155

Quick No-Cook Mini-Pavlova (Australia) [1]25

Quindins (Afro-Brazilians, Brazil) [1]48

R

Rågbröd (Swedish Rye Bread) [4]20

Ragoût de Boulettes (Spicy Meatballs, Canada) [1]74

Raitha (Yogurt and Vegetable Salad, Pakistan) [3]87

Ramen (Noodle Soup, Japan) [2]161

Ranch-Style Eggs (Mexico) [3]50

Red Beans and Rice (African Americans, United States) [4]80

Red Coleslaw (Germany) [2]9

Red Lentil Soup (Iraq) [2]96

Reuben Sandwich (Midwest Region, United States) [4]128

Rice Ball (Japan) [2]156

Rice Bread (Liberia) [3]41

Rice Cakes (Japan) [2]159

Rice Cakes, Iranian (Iran) [2]88

Rice in Coconut Milk (Tanzania) [4]28

Rice and Milk (Peru) [3]99

Rice and Peas (Jamaica) [2]144

Rice Pilaf (Kazakhstan) [3]3

Rice Pudding (Chile) [1]90

Rice Pudding (Cuba) [1]120

Rice Pudding (Iran) [2]88

Rice Pudding (Pakistan) [3]88

Rice Pudding, Lebanese [3]28

Rice and Red Beans (Haiti) [2]44

Rice Sorpa (Kazakhstan) [3]7

Rice, Basic (Brazil) [1]46

Rice, Boiled (Japan) [2]155

Rice, Corn (Indonesia) [2]79

Rice, Fancy (India) [2]65

Rice, Fried (Indonesia) [2]71

Rice, Garlic (Philippines) [3]108

Rice, Saudi Style (Saudi Arabia) [3]139

Rice, White (Mexico) [3]53

Rice, Yellow (Indonesia) [2]78

Rice, Yellow (South Africa) [3]156

Riz Djon-Djon (Rice and Haitian Mushrooms, Haiti) [2]44

Riz et Pois Rouges (Rice and Red Beans,Haiti) [2]44

Roast Pork (Islands of the Pacific) [2]117

Roasted Butternut Squash (Zimbabwe) [4]182

Rock Shandy (Zimbabwe) [4]186

Rosca de Reyes (Three Kings Sweet Bread, Mexico) [3]49

Rose Hip Soup (Sweden) [4]12

Rosh Hashanah
   New Year's Honey Cake (Israel) [2]130

Russia [3]123
   Bliny [3]125
   Bliny Filling [3]126
   Chai Po-Russki [3]131
   Klyukva S Sakharom [3]130
   Pashka [3]128
   Salat Olivier [3]124
   Semechki [3]131
   Sharlotka [3]130

Russian National Winter Beverage [3]128

Russian Pancakes [3]125

Russian Salad [3]124

Rye Bread (Germany) [2]5

Rye Bread, Swedish [4]20

S

Sadza (Zimbabwe) [4]183

Saffron and Raisin Couscous with Fresh Mint (Algeria) [1]2

Safou a la Sauce Tomate (Prunes in Tomato Sauce, Cameroon) [1]54

Sahlab (Algeria) [1]4

Saint Lucia Saffron Buns (Sweden) [4]17

Salads

Algerian Cooked Carrot Salad [1]7

Avocado with Groundnut Dressing (Côte d'Ivoire) [1]111

Banadura Salata B'Kizbara (Algeria) [1]5

Banana and Pineapple Salad (Cameroon) [1]58

Charoset (Jewish Americans, United States) [4]110

Chickpea, Feta, and Olive Salad (Morocco) [3]62

Chlada Fakya (Algeria) [1]8

Cuban Avocado and Pineapple Salad (Latino Americans, United States) [4]121

Cucumber Salad (Thailand) [4]39

Cucumber with Yogurt (Lebanon) [3]29

Dandelion Salad (Slovenia) [3]147

Desser Miveh (Iran) [2]91

Deviled Eggs (Midwest Region, United States) [4]126

Ensalada Chilena (Chile) [1]84

Ensalada Cubana (Cuba) [1]119

French-Style Lettuce Salad (Haiti) [2]40

Frouta Ke Yaourti (Greece) [2]29

Fruit Salad with Frozen Yogurt (Argentina) [1]15

Gado Gado (Indonesia) [2]78

German Potato Salad (Great Lakes, United States) [4]98

Grated Carrot, Apple, and Raisin Salad (Australia) [1]20

Greek Salad (Greece) [2]28

Green Bean Salad (South Africa) [3]154

Haitian Fruit Salad [2]44

Israeli Vegetable Salad (Israel) [2]129

Kimchi (Korea) [3]20

Lebanese Fresh Fruit Salad (Lebanon) [3]35

Lemon and Garlic Potato Salad (Egypt) [1]135

Lettuce Salad (Egypt) [1]138

Orange Salad (Brazil) [1]39

Picado de Rabano (Guatemala) [2]33

Potato Salad (African Americans, United States) [4]81

Puerto Rican Christmas Salad (Latino Americans, United States) [4]120

Raitha (Pakistan) [3]87

Red Coleslaw (Germany) [2]9

Salada Pera de Abacate (Mozambique) [3]73

Salat Olivier (Russia) [3]124

Shirazi (Iran) [2]85

Sweet Grated Carrot Salae (Morocco) [3]63

Tabbouleh (Lebanon) [3]30

Tabbouleh (Saudi Arabia) [3]139

Tomato, Cucumber, and Onion Salad (African Americans, United States) [4]84

Tropical Fruit Salad (Latino Americans, United States) [4]121

Salada Pera de Abacate (Tomato and Avocado Salad, Mozambique) [3]73

Salat Olivier (Russia) [3]124

Salmon and Shrimp Quiche (France) [1]155

Salmon Kedgeree (British-Indian Salmon) [4]66

Salsa Cruda (Latino Americans, United States) [4]116

Salsa, Mexican (Mexico) [3]51

Saltimbocca alla Romana (Veal Scallops with Sage and Prosciutto, Italy) [2]137

Sambal Kecap (Chili and Soy Sauce, Indonesia) [2]74

Sandes de Queijo (Baked Cheese Sandwich, Mozambique) [3]68

Sandwiches

Baguette Sandwich [1]153

Barros Jarpa (Chile) [1]89

Bocaditos (Argentina) [1]14

Cornish Pasty (Great Lakes, United States) [4]103

Croque-Monsieur (France) [1]154

Cucumber Sandwiches (United Kingdom) [4]71

Empanadas (Argentina) [1]13

Fried Bologna (African Americans, United States) [4]84

Khubaz (Iraq) [2]99

Peanut Butter and Molasses Spread (Amish and Pennsylvania Dutch, United States) [4]93

Pita Sandwiches (Israel) [2]131

Reuben Sandwich (Midwest Region, United States) [4]128

Sandes de Queijo (Mozambique) [3]68

Smörgås med ost och päron (Sweden) [4]22

Toast with Vegemite or Milo Spread (Australia) [1]27

Sang Ka Ya (Thai Coconut Custard, Thailand) [4]40

Sarikayo Telor (Steamed Egg and Coconut Milk Pudding, Indonesia) [2]74

Saskatoon Berry Snack (Aboriginals, Canada) [1]79

Saudi Arabia [3]133

Arabic Coffee [3]141

Fatir [3]134

Hawayij [3]134

Haysa Al-Tumreya [3]135

Saudi Arabia *(continued)*

Hummus [3]140

Kapsa [3]136

Kimaje [3]137

Laban Drink [3]138

Rice, Saudi Style [3]139

Tabbouleh [3]139

Sausage and Sauerkraut (Slovenia) [3]146

Sauteed Fiddleheads (Canada) [1]63

Sbiten (Russian National Winter Beverage) [3]128

Scones (Ireland) [2]110

Scones (United Kingdom) [4]71

Seafood and Peanut Stew (Mozambique) [3]69

Seafood, Marinated (Peru) [3]99

Seasoned Meat and Vegetable Sauce (Côte d'Ivoire) [1]107

Semechki (Toasted Sunflower Seeds, Russia) [3]131

Sesame Candy (Israel) [2]127

Sesame Seeds, Toasted (Korea) [3]21

Shahi Tukra (Pakistan) [3]84

Shai (Mint Tea, Egypt) [1]134

Shakshooka (Egg-and-Tomato Dish, Israel) [2]126

Sharlotka (Apple Cake, Russia) [3]130

Shigumch'i Namul (Korean Spinach) [3]25

Shirazi (Cucumber and Tomato Salad, Iran) [2]85

Shir-Berenj (Rice Pudding, Iran) [2]88

Shoofly Pie (Amish and Pennsylvania Dutch, United States) [4]89

Shrimp Adobo in Coconut Milk (Philippines) [3]107

Side dishes

Aaloo Bukhary Ki Chutney (Pakistan) [3]86

Acaçá (Afro-Brazilian, Brazil) [1]51

Aceitunas Alinadas (Cuba) [1]119

Adas Bil Hamod (Iraq) [2]96

Akara (Ghana) [2]19

Angu de Milho (Brazil) [1]49

Apple and Carrot Tsimmes (Jewish Americans, United States) [4]111

Apple Sauerkraut (Great Lakes, United States) [4]101

Arroz Guatemalteco [2]34

Baigan Bhartha (India) [2]60

Baked Macaroni and Cheese (African Americans, United States) [4]82

Baked Papas Skins (Peru) [3]92

Baked Yams (Côte d'Ivoire) [1]109

Bamia (Egypt) [1]137

Banana Frita (Brazil) [1]42

Bananas and Sweet Potatoes (Islands of the Pacific) [2]118

Boiled Cassava (Cameroon) [1]59

Boston Baked Beans (Northeast, United States) [4]143

Brazilian Black Beans [1]49

Bread Pudding (Midwest Region, United States) [4]124

Bulgur Pilavi [4]53

Canh Bi Ro Ham Dua (Vietnam) [4]174

Carrot Bredie (South Africa) [3]154

Champ (Ireland) [2]106

Charoset (Jewish Americans, United States) [4]110

Chili Corn Bread (Latino Americans, United States) [4]121

Choclo con Queso (Peru) [3]95

Clam Chowder (Northeast, United States) [4]144

Colcannon (Ireland) [2]107

Collard Greens (African Americans, United States) [4]78

Collard Greens with Hamhocks (Southern Region, United States) [4]157

Corn on the Cob (Midwest Region, United States) [4]127

Corn on the Cob (South Africa) [3]157

Cornbread (Southern Region, United States) [4]152

Cornish Pasty (Great Lakes, United States) [4]103

Cornmeal Porridge (Haiti) [2]47

Cream of Cabbage Soup (Amish and Pennsylvania Dutch, United States)) [4]89

Cuban Avocado and Pineapple Salad (Latino Americans, United States) [4]121

Cuban Beans and Rice (Latino Americans, United States) [4]117

Dal (India) [2]62

Damper European Style (Aborigines and Bush Tucker, Australia) [1]32

Dandelion Salad (Slovenia) [3]147

Deep Fried Potatoes (Slovenia) [3]145

Deviled Eggs (Midwest Region, United States) [4]126

Dhal (Pakistan) [3]85

Dodo (Nigeria) [3]80

Easy Fufu (Cameroon) [1]55

Efo (Nigeria) [3]80

Fancy Rice (India) [2]65

Fish Boil (Great Lakes, United States) [4]97

Fried Apples (African Americans, United States) [4]83

Fried Baby Carrots (Morocco) [3]61

Side dishes (*continued*)

Fried Bologna (African Americans, United States) [4]84

Fried Plantains (Cuba) [1]115

Fried Plantains (Latino Americans, United States) [4]117

Frijoles (Mexico) [3]47

Frijoles Refritos (Mexico) [3]47

Frittata (Italy) [2]140

Fruit Salad with Frozen Yogurt (Argentina) [1]15

Fufu (Côte d'Ivoire) [1]106

Fufu (Ghana) [2]14

Ful Mudammas (Egypt) [1]132

German Potato Salad (Great Lakes, United States) [4]98

Githeri (Kenya) [3]14

Gohan (Japan) [2]155

Grated Carrot, Apple, and Raisin Salad (Australia) [1]20

Green Bean Casserole (Midwest Region, United States) [4]127

Green Bean Salad (South Africa) [3]154

Hasselbackspotatis (Sweden) [4]21

Herring Dip (Jewish Americans, United States) [4]113

Hin Pap (Korea) [3]21

Honey-Baked Apples (Northeast, United States) [4]146

Hummus (Great Lakes, United States) [4]99

Hummus (Saudi Arabia) [3]140

Hummus be Tahini (Lebanon) [3]36

Hush Puppies (African Americans, United States) [4]78

Indian Fry-Bread (Native Americans, United States) [4]137

Indian Pudding (Northeast, United States) [4]140

Iranian Rice Cakes (Iran) [2]88

Irio (Kenya) [3]10

Isu (Nigeria) [3]76

Iyan (Nigeria) [3]79

Jansson's Frestelse ("Jansson's Temptation", Sweden) [4]14

Johnnycakes (Northeast, United States) [4]141

Jollof rice (Nigeria) [3]79

Karoplia Solimkoi (Ukraine) [4]60

Kartoffelknödeln (Germany) [2]4

Kenkey (Ghana) [2]19

Kimchi (Korea) [3]20

Klimp (Sweden) [4]15

Knedlíky (Czech Republic) [1]125

Komkomer Sambal (South Africa) [3]156

Lab (Ethiopia) [1]146

Macaroni and Cheese (Great Lakes, United States) [4]99

Maize Porridge (Mozambique) [3]68

Makubi (Tanzania) [4]32

Mandu (Korea) [3]23

Maple Baked Beans (Native Americans, United States) [4]134

Marinated Artichokes (Western Region, United States) [4]163

Matoke (Kenya) [3]14

Matzo Balls (Jewish Americans, United States) [4]111

Mealie Soup (South Africa) [3]153

Moors and Christians (Cuba) [1]114

Mother's Chicken Soup (Jewish Americans, United States) [4]106

Nachynka (Cornbread Stuffing, Ukraine) [4]61

Nasi Goreng (Indonesia) [2]71

Nasi Jagung (Indonesia) [2]79

Nasi Kuning (Indonesia) [2]78

Ndizi Kaanga (Tanzania) [4]28

New England Clam Chowder (Northeast, United States) [4]144

Noodle Kugel (Jewish Americans, United States) [4]107

Noodles with Poppy Seeds (Poland) [3]118

Ojibwa Wild Rice (Great Lakes, United States) [4]96

Old Fashioned Turnip Soup (Southern Region, United States) [4]151

Palak Bhaji [2]62

Pansit Mami (Philippines) [3]110

Parsley New Potatoes (Western Region, United States) [4]165

Peachy Baked Apples (Amish and Pennsylvania Dutch, United States)) [4]91

Pepper-Scented Rice (Brazil) [1]41

Pierogi (Poland) [3]115

Plov (Kazakhstan) [3]3

Polenta (Brazil) [1]40

Polenta (Italy) [2]136

Popped Wild Rice (Native Americans, United States) [4]138

Potato Latkes (Jewish Americans, United States) [4]110

Potato Lefse (Great Lakes, United States) [4]102

Side dishes (*continued*)

Potato Salad (African Americans, United States) [4]81

Potato Varenyky (Ukraine) [4]58

Puerto Rican Christmas Salad (Latino Americans, United States) [4]120

Putupap (South Africa) [3]158

Quebec Poutine (French Canadians, Canada) [1]75

Red Beans and Rice (African Americans, United States) [4]80

Red Coleslaw (Germany) [2]9

Rice, Basic (Brazil) [1]46

Rice and Peas (Jamaica) [2]144

Rice, Saudi Style (Saudi Arabia) [3]139

Riz Djon-Djon (Haiti) [2]44

Riz et Pois Rouges (Haiti) [2]44

Roasted Butternut Squash (Zimbabwe) [4]182

Sadza (Zimbabwe) [4]183

Saffron and Raisin Couscous with Fresh Mint (Algeria) [1]2

Sauteed Fiddleheads (Canada) [1]63

Shigumch'i Namul (Korea) [3]25

Sinangag (Philippines) [3]108

Small Dumplings (Hungary) [2]56

Spanish Tortilla (Guatemala) [2]33

Spinach with Garlic [1]139

Spring Rolls (Vietnam) [4]177

Stuffed Eggs (Poland) [3]121

Succotash (Native Americans, United States) [4]133

Succotash (Northeast, United States) [4]141

Sukuma Wiki (Kenya) [3]12

Sunday Lunch Cauliflower Cheese (United Kingdom) [4]74

Sweet Corn Pancakes (Canada) [1]64

Sweet Potato Pone (Liberia) [3]41

Tabbouleh (Saudi Arabia) [3]139

Tahu Goreng (Indonesia) [2]75

Tatties n' Neeps (United Kingdom) [4]72

Toast with Vegemite or Milo Spread (Australia) [1]27

Tomaticán (Chile) [1]86

Tomato, Cucumber, and Onion Salad (African Americans, United States) [4]84

Tropical Fruit Salad (Latino Americans, United States) [4]121

Ugali (Kenya) [3]12

Ugali (Tanzania) [4]27

Wali wa Nazi (Tanzania) [4]28

Yams (Ghana) [2]12

Yellow Rice (Geel Rys, South Africa) [3]156

Yucca (Cuba)

Zimbabwe Greens (Zimbabwe) [4]185

Simit (Sesame Rings. Turkey) [4]51

Sinangag (Garlic Rice, Philippines) [3]108

Slovenia [3]143

Dandelion Salad [3]147

Deep Fried Potatoes [3]145

Golaz [3]144

Jota [3]146

Klobasa and Kisdo Zelje [3]146

Potica [3]147

Slovenian Almond Bars [3]148

Slovenian Almond Bars (Slovenia) [3]148

Small Dumplings (Hungary) [2]56

Smörgås med ost och päron (Cheese and Pear Sandwich, Sweden) [4]22

Snacks

Aceitunas Alinadas (Cuba) [1]119

ANZAC Biscuits (Australia) [1]22

Bannana Peze [2]43

Bocaditos (Argentina) [1]14

Bruschetta (Italy) [2]141

Buffalo Chicken Wings (Great Lakes, United States) [4]100

Butter Tarts (Canada) [1]71

Caramel Corn (Midwest Region, United States) [4]128

Chancho en Piedra (Chile) [1]89

Chili Corn Bread (Latino Americans, United States) [4]121

Chimichurri (Argentina) [1]13

Chocolate Crackles (Australia) [1]27

Chopped Chicken Liver (Jewish Americans, United States) [4]107

Christmas Shortbread (Australia) [1]24

Churros (Spain) [4]7

Coconut Chips (Jamaica) [2]146

Coffee Milkshake (Northeast, United States) [4]144

Cornish Pasty (Great Lakes, United States) [4]103

Cucumber Sandwiches (United Kingdom) [4]71

Dabo Kolo (Ethiopia) [1]147

Damper (Aboriginal) [1]32

Damper European Style (Aborigines and Bush Tucker, Australia) [1]32

Dates (Iraq) [2]95

Deviled Eggs (Midwest Region, United States) [4]126

Empanadas (Argentina) [1]13

Empadas (Brazil) [1]50

Snacks *(continued)*

Fava Bean Spread (Israel) [2]126

Fortune Cookies (Western Region, United States) [4]163

Fresh Oranges (Israel) [2]124

Fresh Sweet Dates (Algeria) [1]3

Fried Apples (African Americans, United States) [4]83

Fried Bologna (African Americans, United States) [4]84

Fried Wonton (China) [1]101

Gebna Makleyah (Egypt) [1]135

Guacamole (Guatemala) [2]33

Guacamole (Latino Americans, United States) [4]117

Haysa Al-Tumreya (Saudi Arabia) [3]135

Herring Dip (Jewish Americans, United States) [4]113

Hummus (Great Lakes, United States) [4]99

Hummus (Saudi Arabia) [3]140

Indian Fry-Bread (Native Americans, United States) [4]137

Kategna (Ethiopia) [1]144

Kelewele (Ghana) [2]15

Khubaz (Iraq) [2]99

Lahmacun (Turkey) [4]55

Lamingtons (Australia) [1]23

Lemon Curd (United Kingdom) [4]68

Macadamia and Fruit Snack (Aborigines and Bush Tucker, Australia) [1]33

Macadamia Nut Cookies (Aborigines and Bush Tucker, Australia) [1]33

Mala Sousta Se Syre (Czech Republic) [1]129

Maple Butter (Northeast, United States) [4]142

Matzo Brie (Jewish Americans, United States) [4]112

Old-Fashioned Spicy Lemonade (Amish and Pennsylvania Dutch, United States)) [4]93

Onigiri (Japan) [2]156

Pan de Banano (Guatemala) [2]37

Peachy Baked Apples (Amish and Pennsylvania Dutch, United States) [4]91

Peanut Butter and Molasses Spread (Amish and Pennsylvania Dutch, United States) [4]93

Pepinos Rellenos (Guatemala) [2]36

Pineapple Sherbet (South Africa) [3]158

Pinole (Native Americans, United States) [4]137

Popcorn (Native Americans, United States) [4]132

Pumpkin Bread (Native Americans, United States) [4]136

Quejadinhas (Brazil) [1]43

Quick No-Cook Mini-Pavlova (Australia) [1]25

Reuben Sandwich (Midwest Region, United States) [4]128

Salsa Cruda (Latino Americans, United States) [4]116

Saskatoon Berry Snack (Aboriginal Canadians) [1]79

Snow Ice Cream (Amish and Pennsylvania Dutch, United States) [4]93

Soft Pretzels (Germany) [2]9

Southern Fried Chicken (Southern Region, United States) [4]152

Spicy Oven-Fried Chicken (Amish and Pennsylvania Dutch, United States) [4]91

Springerle (Great Lakes, United States) [4]101

Stuffed Dates and Walnuts (Algeria) [1]6

Sugar Cookies (Amish and Pennsylvania Dutch, United States) [4]92

Sushi (Japan) [2]155

Swedish Meatballs (Great Lakes, United States) [4]102

Toast with Vegemite or Milo Spread (Australia) [1]27

Traditional Biltong and Dried Fruit Snack (South Africa) [3]152

Wild Rice Cakes (Aboriginals, Canada) [1]81

Snow Ice Cream (Amish and Pennsylvania Dutch, United States) [4]93

Soda Bread, Irish (Ireland) [2]105

Soda Chanh (Vietnam) [4]176

Soft Pretzels (Germany) [2]9

Soo Chunkwa (Ginger Drink, Korea) [3]18

Sopa de Feijao Verde (String Bean Soup, Mozambique) [3]72

Soupe à l'Oignon Gratinée (Onion Soup, France) [1]153

Soups

Artsoppa (Sweden) [4]20

Avgolemono [2]22

Blandad Fruktsoppa (Sweden) [4]15

Borscht (Russia) [3]129

Chicken and Sausage Gumbo (Southern Region, United States) [4]153

Chilled Avocado Soup (Côte d'Ivoire) [1]109

Clam Chowder (Northeast, United States) [4]144

Coconut Bean Soup (Tanzania) [4]25

Coconut-Chicken Soup (Thailand) [4]43

Cream of Cabbage Soup (Amish and Pennsylvania Dutch, United States) [4]89

Cucumber and Yogurt Soup (Algeria) [1]8

Cucumber Soup (Guatemala) [2]34

Eggdrop Soup (China) [1]96

Soups *(continued)*

Fish Boil (Great Lakes, United States) [4]97

French Pea Soup (Canada) [1]70

Gazpacho (Latino Americans, United States) [4]120

Gazpacho (Spain) [4]3

Goat Soup (Liberia) [3]43

Houbova Polevka Myslivecka (Czech Republic) [1]124

Kamja Guk (Korea) [3]20

Matzo Balls (Jewish Americans, United States) [4]111

Mealie Soup (South Africa) [3]153

Miso Soup (Japan) [2]156

Mother's Chicken Soup (Jewish Americans, United States) [4]106

Mushroom Barley Soup (Poland) [3]119

Ndole (Cameroon) [1]56

New England Clam Chowder (Northeast, United States) [4]144

Old Fashioned Turnip Soup (Southern Region, United States) [4]151

Ozoni (Japan) [2]159

Paste e Fagioli (Italy) [2]135

Pepper Soup (Ghana) [2]19

Pho Bo (Vietnam) [4]172

Ramen (Japan) [2]161

Red Lentil Soup (Iraq) [2]96

Rose Hip Soup (Sweden) [4]12

Sopa de Feijao Verde (Mozambique) [3]72

Soupe à l'Oignon Gratinée (France) [1]153

Summer Cucumber Soup (Hungary) [2]57

Supu Ya Ndizi (Tanzania) [4]30

Three Sisters Soup (Canada, Aboriginals) [1]79

Weisse Bohnensuppe (Germany) [2]3

Wonton Soup (China) [1]95

South Africa [3]151

Bobotie [3]157

Carrot Bredie [3]154

Corn on the Cob [3]157

Cucumber Relish [3]156

Geel Rys (Yellow Rice) [3]156

Green Bean Salad [3]154

Mealie Soup [3]153

Pineapple Sherbet [3]158

Putupap [3]158

Traditional Biltong and Dried Fruit Snack [3]152

Southern Fried Chicken (Southern Region, United States) [4]152

Southern Region (United States) [4]149

Chicken and Sausage Gumbo [4]153

Collard Greens with Hamhocks [4]157

Cornbread [4]152

Creole Seasoning [4]153

Fruitcake Cookies [4]154

Mardi Gras King Cake [4]155

Old Fashioned Turnip Soup [4]151

Pralines [4]157

Southern Fried Chicken [4]152

Sweet Potato Pie [4]154

Sweet Tea [4]157

Spain [4]1

Aceitunas Alinadas (Marinated Olives) [4]9

Churros [4]7

Crema de Cabrales [4]8

Flan [4]4

Gazpacho [4]3

Mazapanes [4]6

Tapas [4]8

Tartaletas de Champiñón (Mushroom Tartlets) [4]8

Tortilla Española [4]3

Spanish Omelet (Spain) [4]3

Spanish Tortilla (Guatemala) [2]33

Spargelgemuse (Fresh Asparagus, Germany) [2]5

Sparkling Yogurt Drink (Iran) [2]86

Spice Blend (Saudi Arabia) [3]134

Spice Paste (Ethiopia) [1]144

Spiced Chicken (China) [1]99

Spiced Cocoa (Haiti) [2]41

Spicy Cookie (India) [2]67

Spicy Egg Stew (Brazil) [1]47

Spicy Fish and Coconut Milk Stew (Brazil) [1]47

Spicy Meatballs (Canada) [1]74

Spicy Oven-Fried Chicken (Amish and Pennsylvania Dutch, United States) [4]91

Spicy Port Pate (Canada) [1]71

Spinach, Spicy Fried (India) [2]62

Spinach with Garlic (Egypt) [1]139

Springerle (Great Lakes, United States) [4]101

Spring Rolls (Vietnam) [4]177

Stews

Bigos (Poland) [3]114

Bobotie (South Africa) [3]157

Buffalo Stew (Native Americans, United States) [4]135

Carbonada Criolla (Argentina) [1]12

Chicken and Sausage Gumbo (Southern Region, United States) [4]153

Stews *(continued)*
  Feijoada (Brazil) [1]38
  Fish Boil (Great Lakes, United States) [4]97
  Golaz (Slovenia) [3]144
  Jota (Slovenia) [3]146
  Maple Baked Beans (Native Americans, United States) [4]134
  Midwestern Chili (Midwest Region, United States) [4]125
  Moqueca (Brazil) [1]47
  Moqueca aos Ovos (Brazil) [1]47
  New England Boiled Dinner (Northeast, United States) [4]144
  Putupap (South Africa) [3]158
  Red Beans and Rice (African Americans, United States) [4]80
  Spicy Egg Stew (Brazil) [1]47
  Stew with Meat, Vegetables, and Fruit (Argentina) [1]12
  Succotash [4]133
Strawberry Jam (Amish and Pennsylvania Dutch, United States) [4]93
Stuffed Cabbage Rolls (Poland) [3]116
Stuffed Cabbage Rolls (Ukraine) [4]60
Stuffed Dates and Walnuts (Algeria) [1]6
Stuffed Eggs (Poland) [3]121
Stuffed Grape Leaves (Iran) [2]82
Stuffed Green Peppers (Hungary) [2]52
Submarino (Milk with Chocolate Syrup, Argentina) [1]16
Succotash (Northeast, United States) [4]141
Succotash (Traditional Corn and Bean Stew, Native Americans, United States) [4]133
Sugar Cookies (Amish and Pennsylvania Dutch, United States) [4]92
Sugared Almonds (Lebanon) [3]34
Sukijaki, Beef (Japan) [2]157
Sukuma Wiki (Kenya) [3]12
Summer Cucumber Soup (Hungary) [2]57
Sunday Lunch Cauliflower Cheese (United Kingdom) [4]74
Sunflower Seeds, Toasted (Russia) [3]131
Supu Ya Ndizi (Plantain Soup, Tanzania) [4]30
Sushi (Japan) [2]155
Svart Vinbärsglögg (Black Currant Glögg, Sweden) [4]18
Sweden[4]11
  Artsoppa [4]20
  Blandad Fruktsoppa (Fruit Soup) [4]15

Creamy Dipping Sauce [4]13
Glazed Carrots [4]13
Hasselbackspotatis [4]21
Jansson's Frestelse ("Jansson's Temptation") [4]14
Julgröt (Swedish Christmas Porridge) [4]18
Klimp [4]15
Köttbulla (Swedish Meatballs) [4]14
Lussekatter [4]17
Pepparkakor (Sweden) [4]16
Plättar [4]19
Rågbröd [4]20
Rose Hip Soup [4]12
Smörgås med ost och päron [4]22
Svart Vinbärsglögg [4]18
Swedish Meatballs (Great Lakes, United States) [4]102
Swedish Pancakes [4]19
Sweet and Sour Okra (Egypt) [1]137
Sweet and Sour Pork (China) [1]96
Sweet Corn Pancakes (Canada) [1]64
Sweet Couscous Dessert (Algeria) [1]5
Sweet Grated Carrot Salad (Morocco) [3]63
Sweet Peanut Mochi (Rice Cakes, Japan) [2]159
Sweet Potato Fritters (Indonesia) [2]73
Sweet Potato Pie (African Americans, United States) [4]80
Sweet Potato Pie (Southern Region, United States) [4]154
Sweet Potato Pone (Liberia) [3]41
Sweet Potato Pudding (Tanzania) [4]31
Sweet Tea (Southern Region, United States) [4]157

T

Tabbouleh (Lebanon) [3]30
Tabbouleh (Saudi Arabia) [3]139
Tahini Sauce (Israel) [2]128
Tahu Goreng (Fried Tofu, Indonesia) [2]75
Tandoori Chicken (India) [2]63
Tanzania [4]23
  Chai [4]24
  Chapatti [4]27
  Coconut Bean Soup [4]25
  Date Nut Bread [4]30
  Makubi [4]32
  Mango-Orange Drink [4]28
  Ndizi Kaanga (Tanzania) [4]28
  Supu Ya Ndizi [4]30
  Sweet Potato Pudding [4]31

Tanzania *(continued)*
  Ugali [4]27
  Wali wa Nazi [4]28
Tapas (Spain) [4]8, [4]9
Tartaletas de Champiñón (Mushroom Tartlets, Spain) [4]8
Tarte au Sucre (Sugar Pie, Canada) [1]72
Tatties n' Neeps (United Kingdom) [4]72
Té con Leche (Tea with Milk, Chile) [1]84
Tea (Chai), Tanzania [4]24
Tea with Milk (United Kingdom) [4]75
Tea, Moroccan Mint [3]58
Teh Halia (Hot Ginger Tea, Indonesia) [2]77
Thai Beef Curry [4]37
Thailand [4]35
  Banana with Coconut Milk [4]41
  Chicken Satay [4]38
  Coconut-Chicken Soup [4]43
  Cucumber Salad [4]39
  Ka Nom Jeen Sour Nam [4]42
  Nam Pla Prig [4]37
  Pad Thai [4]42
  Poa Pee [4]39
  Sang Ka Yal [4]40
  Thai Beef Curry [4]37
Three Kings Sweet Bread (Mexico) [3]49
Three Sisters Soup (Canada, Aboriginals) [1]79
Ti-Malice (Spicy Haitian Sauce) [2]47
Toad-in-the-Hole (United Kingdom) [4]70
Toasted Sunflower Seeds (Russia) [3]131
Toast with Vegemite or Milo Spread (Australia) [1]27
Tofu, Fried (Indonesia) [2]75
Tomaticán (Tomato and Corn Stew, Chile) [1]86
Tomato and Avocado Salad [3]73
Tomato, Cucumber, and Onion Salad (African Americans, United States) [4]84
Tomatoes Stuffed with Rice (Iraq) [2]97
Topinky S Vejci (Eggs on Toast, Czech Republic) [1]128
Torta de Cumpleaños (Birthday Cake, Chile) [1]87
Tortilla Española (Spanish Omelet, Spain) [4]3
Tourtière (French Canadians, Canada) [1]73
Traditional Biltong and Dried Fruit Snack (South Africa) [3]152
Traditional Corn and Bean Stew (Native Americans, United States) [4]133
Traditional Irish Stew (Ireland) [2]105
Tropical Fruit Dessert (Islands of the Pacific) [2]121
Tropical Fruit Salad (Latino Americans, United States) [4]121

Tropical Fruit Shake (Islands of the Pacific) [2]121
Tsokolate (Hot Chocolate, Philippines) [3]108
Tuna in Sauce (Cuba) [1]117
Turkey [4]45
  Bulgur Pilavi [4]53
  Halva [4]50
  Kaymakli Kuru Kayisi (Cream-Stuffed Apricots [4]46
  Köfte [4]50
  Lahmacun [4]55
  Lokma [4]53
  Muhallabi (Rice Pudding) [4]48
  Naneli Limonata [4]49
  Pasta with Yogurt-Mint Sauce [4]47
  Simit [4]51
Tzatziki (Cucumber-Yogurt Sauce, Greece) [2]28

U

Ugali (Kenya) [3]12
Ugali (Tanzania) [4]27
Ukraine [4]57
  Holubtsi (Stuffed Cabbage Rolls) [4]60
  Karoplia Solimkoi [4]60
  Kotlety Po-Kyivskomy [4]61
  Kutya (Sweet Porridge) [4]63
  Makiwnyk [4]63
  Nachynka [4]61
  Potato Varenyky [4]58
Uli Petataws (Sweet Potato Fritters, Indonesia) [2]73
United Kingdom [4]65
  Cornish Pasties [4]69
  Cucumber Sandwiches [4]71
  Haggis [4]68
  incemeat Pies, Individual [4]73
  Lemon Curd [4]68
  Salmon Kedgeree [4]66
  Scones [4]71
  Sunday Lunch Cauliflower Cheese [4]74
  Tatties n' Neeps [4]72
  Tea with Milk [4]75
  Toad-in-the-Hole [4]70
  Wassail [4]74
  Welsh Rarebit [4]69
United States
  African Americans [4]77
  Amish and Pennsylvania Dutch [4]87

United States *(continued)*

Apple and Carrot Tsimmes (Jewish Americans) [4]111

Apple Crisp (Western Region) [4]165

Apple Sauerkraut [4]101

Baked Macaroni and Cheese (African Americans)[4]82

Blueberry Muffins (Western Region) [4]165

Boston Baked Beans (Northeast Region) [4]143

Bread Pudding (Midwest Region) [4]124

Broiled Salmon Steaks (Western Region) [4]164

Buffalo Chicken Wings (Great Lakes Region) [4]100

Buffalo Stew (Native Americans) [4]135

Caramel Corn (Midwest Region) [4]128

Charoset (Jewish Americans) [4]110

Chicken and Sausage Gumbo (Southern Region) [4]153

Chili Corn Bread (Latino Americans) [4]121

Chinese Peanut Sauce (Western Region) [4]164

Chopped Chicken Liver (Jewish Americans) [4]107

Chuck Wagon Brisket [4]161

Clam Chowder (Northeast Region) [4]144

Coffee Milkshake (Northeast Region) [4]144

Collard Greens (African Americans) [4]78

Collard Greens with Hamhocks (Southern Region) [4]157

Corn on the Cob (Midwest Region) [4]127

Cornbread (Southern Region) [4]152

Cornhusker's Casserole (Midwest Region) [4]129

Cornish Pasty (Great Lakes Region) [4]103

Cranberry Salsa (Western Region) [4]162

Cream of Cabbage Soup (Amish and Pennsylvania Dutch) [4]89

Creole Seasoning (Southern Region) [4]153

Cuban Avocado and Pineapple Salad (Latino Americans) [4]121

Cuban Beans and Rice (Latino Americans) [4]117

Deviled Eggs (Midwest Region) [4]126

Dutch Pancakes (Amish and Pennsylvania Dutch) [4]98

Fish Boil (Great Lakes Region) [4]97

Fortune Cookies (Western Region) [4]163

Fried Apples (African Americans) [4]83

Fried Bologna (African Americans) [4]84

Fried Plantains (Latino Americans) [4]117

Fruitcake Cookies (Southern Region) [4]154

Gazpacho (Latino Americans) [4]120

German Potato Salad (Great Lakes Region) [4]98

Great Lakes Region [4]95

Green Bean Casserole (Midwest Region) [4]127

Guacamole (Latino Americans) [4]117

Herring Dip (Jewish Americans) [4]113

Honey-Baked Apples (Northeast Region) [4]146

Hot Cranberry Punch (Northeast Region) [4]146

Hummus (Great Lakes Region) [4]99

Hush Puppies (African Americans) [4]78

Indian Fry Bread (Native Americans) [4]137

Indian Pudding (Native Americans) [4]140

Iroquois Strawberry Drink (Native Americans) [4]137

Jewish Americans [4]105

Johnnycakes (Northeast Region) [4]141

Kwanzaa Brownies (African Americans) [4]83

Latino Americans [4]115

Macaroni and Cheese (Great Lakes Region) [4]99

Maple Baked Beans (Northeast Region) [4]134

Maple Butter (Northeast Region) [4]142

Mardi Gras King Cake (Southern Region) [4]155

Marinated Artichokes (Western Region) [4]163

Matzo Balls (Jewish Americans) [4]111

Matzo Brie (Jewish Americans) [4]112

Mexican Fried Ice Cream (Latino Americans) [4]119

Midwestern Chili (Midwest Region) [4]125

Midwestern Pork Chop Dinner (Midwest Region) [4]130

Midwest Region [4]123

Molasses Water (African Americans) [4]79

Mother's Chicken Soup (Jewish Americans) [4]106

Native Americans [4]131

New England Boiled Dinner (Northeast Region) [4]144

New England Clam Chowder (Northeast Region) [4]144

New York Cheesecake (Jewish Americans) [4]113

Noodle Kugel (Jewish Americans) [4]107

Northeast Region [4]139

Ojibwa Wild Rice (Native Americans) [4]96

Old Fashioned Turnip Soup (Southern Region) [4]151

Old-Fashioned Spicy Lemonade (African American) [4]93

Parsley New Potatoes (Western Region) [4]165

Peachy Baked Apples (Amish and Pennsylvania Dutch) [4]91

Peanut Butter and Molasses Spread (Amish and Pennsylvania Dutch) [4]93

Pinole (Native Americans) [4]137

Popcorn (Native Americans) [4]132

United States *(continued)*

Popped Wild Rice (Native Americans) [4]138

Pork Chops with Sauerkraut and Potatoes (Amish and Pennsylvania Dutch) [4]89

Potato Latkes (Jewish Americans) [4]110

Potato Lefse (Great Lakes Region) [4]102

Potato Salad (African Americans) [4]81

Pralines (Southern Region) [4]157

Puerto Rican Christmas Salad (Latino Americans) [4]120

Pumpkin Bread (Native Americans) [4]136

Pumpkin-Corn Sauce (Native Americans) [4]135

Red Beans and Rice (African Americans) [4]80

Reuben Sandwich (Midwest Region) [4]128

Salsa Cruda (Latino Americnas) [4]116

Shoofly Pie (Amish and Pennsylvania Dutch) [4]89

Snow Ice Cream (Amish and Pennsylvania Dutch) [4]93

Southern Fried Chicken (Southern Region) [4]152

Southern Region [4]149

Spicy Oven-Fried Chicken (Amish and Pennsylvania Dutch) [4]91

Springerle (Great Lakes Region) [4]101

Strawberry Jam (Amish and Pennsylvania Dutch) [4]93

Succotash (Native Americans [4]133

Succotash (Northeast Region) [4]141

Sugar Cookies (Amish and Pennsylvania Dutch) [4]92

Swedish Meatballs (Great Lakes Region) [4]102

Sweet Potato Pie (African Americans) [4]80

Sweet Potato Pie (Southern Region) [4]154

Sweet Tea (Southern Region) [4]157

Tomato, Cucumber, and Onion Salad (African Americans) [4]84

Tropical Fruit Salad (Latino Americans) [4]121

Western Region [4]159

V

Veal Meatballs with Dill (Poland) [3]121

Veal Scallops with Sage and Prosciutto (Italy) [2]137

Vegetables

Apple Sauerkraut (Great Lakes, United States) [4]101

Aterkek Alecha (Ethiopia) [1]148

Boston Baked Beans (Northeast Region, United States) [4]143

Carrot Bredie (South Africa) [3]154

Collard Greens (African Americans) [4]78

Corn on the Cob (Midwest Region, United States) [4]127

Corn on the Cob (South Africa) [3]157

Cuban Avocado and Pineapple Salad (Latino Americans, United States) [4]121

Deep Fried Potatoes (Slovenia) [3]145

Fried Baby Carrots (Morocco) [3]61

Fried Plantains (Latino Americans, United States) [4]117

German Potato Salad (Great Lakes, United States) [4]98

Glazed Carrots (Sweden) [4]13

Grated Carrot, Apple, and Raisin Salad (Australia) [1]20

Green Bean Casserole (Midwest Region, United States) [4]127

Green Bean Salad (South Africa) [3]154

Guacamole (Latino Americans, United States) [4]117

Komkomer Sambal (South Africa) [3]156

Makubi [4]32

Maple Baked Beans (Native Americans, United States) [4]134

Marinated Artichokes (Western Region, United States) [4]163

Old Fashioned Turnip Soup (Southern Region, United States) [4]151

Palak Bhaji [2]62

Parsley New Potatoes (Western Region, United States) [4]165

Potato Latkes (Jewish Americans, United States) [4]110

Potato Lefse (Great Lakes, United States) [4]102

Potato Salad (African Americans, United States) [4]81

Quiabo (Brazil) [1]46

Salsa Cruda (Latino Americans, United States) [4]116

Sauteed Fiddleheads (Canada) [1]63

Spargelgemuse (Germany) [2]5

Succotash (Native Americans, United States) [4]133

Succotash (Northeast, United States) [4]141

Tomato, Cucumber, and Onion Salad (African Americans, United States) [4]84

Vegetable Salad with Peanut Sauce (Indonesia) [2]78

Vegetable Sandwich (India) [2]67

Vegetable Salad with Peanut Sauce (Indonesia) [2]78

Vegetable Sandwich (India) [2]67

Vietnam [4]169
Banh Chuoi Nuong (Banana Cake) [4]175
Canh Bi Ro Ham Dua (Braised Pumpkin with Coconut Milk) [4]174
Caphe [4]176
Coconut Custard [4]174
Nuoc Cham (Dipping Sauce) [4]171
Pho Bo (Beef Noodle Soup) [4]172
Soda Chanh (Lemon Soda) [4]176
Spring Rolls [4]177
Vietnamese Coffee [4]176
Vietnamese Coffee [4]176
Vinegar Soy Sauce (Korea) [3]24

W

Wali wa Nazi (Rice in Coconut Milk, Tanzania) [4]28
Wassail (United Kingdom) [4]74
Weisse Bohnensuppe (White Bean Soup, Germany) [2]3
Welsh Rarebit (United Kingdom) [4]69
Western Kenya Cabbage and Egg (Kenya) [3]11
Western Region (United States) [4]159
Apple Crisp [4]165
Blueberry Muffins [4]165
Broiled Salmon Steaks [4]164
Chinese Peanut Sauce [4]164
Chuck Wagon Brisket [4]161
Cranberry Salsa [4]162
Fortune Cookies [4]163
Marinated Artichokes [4]163
Parsley New Potatoes (Western Region) [4]165
Wheat Pudding (Iraq) [2]98

Wild Rice Cakes (Aboriginals, Canada) [1]81
Wonton Soup (China) [1]95

Y

Yaki-Soba (Fried Noodles, Japan) [2]158
Yakitori (Grilled Chicken on Skewers, Japan) [2]161
Yalanchi (Tomatoes Stuffed with Rice, Iraq) [2]97
Yams (Ghana) [2]12
Yams, Spiced Boiled (Nigeria) [3]76
Yellow Rice (Indonesia) [2]78
Yellow Rice (South Africa) [3]156
Yogurt Chutney (Kenya) [3]13
Yogurt Drink (Saudi Arabia) [3]138
Yogurt Drink, Sparkling (Iran) [2]86
Yogurt, Homemade (Iran) [2]91
Yogurt and Mint Sauce (Iran) [2]83
Yucca (Cuba) [1]117

Z

Zanzibar see Tanzania
Zimbabwe [4]181
Cornmeal Cake [4]184
Dovi [4]183
Greens, Zimbabwe [4]185
Mapopo [4]182
Roasted Butternut Squash [4]182
Sadza [4]183
Zimbabwe Greens [4]185